POLITICAL MIRAGES:

RUSSIA AT THE CROSSROADS

POLITICAL MIRAGES:

RUSSIA AT THE CROSSROADS

Leonid M. Batkin

Translated by L.A. Ermolaev

Nova Science Publishers, Inc.
New York

Art Director: Maria Ester Hawrys
Assistant Director: Elenor Kallberg
Graphics: Denise Dieterich, Kerri Pfister,
        Erika Cassutti and Barbara Minerd
Manuscript Coordinator: Roseann Pena
Book Production: Tammy Sauter, Benjamin Fung
Circulation: Irene Kwartiroff and Annette Hellinger

Library of Congress Cataloging-in-Publication Data

Batkin, Leonid M. (Leonid Mikhailovich)
    Political mirages : Russia at the crossroads / Leonid M. Batkin.
        p.   cm.
    Includes bibliographical references and index.
    ISBN 1-56072-265-7 : $59
    1. Russia (Federation) -- Politics and government -- 1991-
    I. Title.
JN6692.B38   1995
320.947'09'045 -- dc20   95-39043
                                                                   CIP

Printed in the United States of America

Contents

PREFACE TO THE
AMERICAN EDITION

Experienced people have forewarned me to heed the tastes and interests of the American public when selecting materials and preparing a book of political publicism.

I have no doubts whatsoever that it is true.

But, first of all, I have never lived in nor have I even visited the United States. I can read but have never even tried to utter a phrase in English. Hence, my ideas in respect of those tastes and interest either taken from books or based on spoken words can hardly be used for any practical purpose. Second, even in case an American journalist gives me friendly advice, i.e. which extracts are better to be cut and which need explanations or corrections, I would nevertheless have no desire to avail myself of these advises.

And here is the reason why.,

Certain details, names, allusions to concrete circumstances. literary reminiscences or plays on words will require watchfulness and sometimes footnotes from a translator, but this is quite natural. Readers will definitely find some places boring, which is true, frankly speaking. you see, these are but articles from newspapers and magazines written between February 1990 and April 1992 each time under the impression of concrete events and circumstances of public life in Russia. These events have passed deep-rooted historic problems and tendencies which I have intended to catch, have by no means vanished; on the contrary, they are assuming new appearances (otherwise what benefit can one hope to derive at all from such collected articles in general?)

By and large, it was a dramatic and unforgettable experience. However, the book often deals with facts quickly erased form public memory even here in Russia. Persons already quitting the stage, topics of yester-day and the day before, grimaces and forgeries of the Soviet and post-Soviet political machinations. In short, it was indispensable to revert to the litter of history which, nevertheless helps to take it for real life.

Essentially it covers the first uneven steps of the Russian democracy, failure of the communist "perestroika", the election of Yeltsin, the fiasco of Gorbachev, August 1991, the collapse of the USSR, and the hopes and new disappointments that followed, It also contains meditations about Sakharov, with whom I had the honour to collaborate, polemics with Solzhenitsin and finally the Russian national problem about which we have debated as far back as 1980. I had the occasion to participate in these debates.

If you choose not to read the book from beginning to end in chrono-logical order, do it as you like. Generally speaking, who on earth reads page by page, the more so if a book is a collection?

Nonetheless, if you are interested in what has been recently happen-ing in Russian and how it has been taken by a participant and a witness; if you wish somehow to touch or feel political, social and psychological real-ity unknown and foreign to you formed, as is always the case, and de-rived form serious and long-lasting processes, a kaleidoscope of casual circumstances, vivid trifles of life, vague changes - then the mixed charac-ter of subjects of this book might seem to you not devoid of a certain logic, unity of historical colouring.

To a certain extent I am familiar with the style of Western journalism and pay a high tribute to it. I am placing at the disposal of readers infor-mation condensed and interpreted as required to catch the most essential and provide an opportunity for everyone to form his or her own option of what is going on.

However , I am no journalist. I do not obtain information, but receive it, like all others (to put aside certain personal ties and direct observa-tions). i.e. by reading newspapers and watching TV. Besides I had the oc-casion in the past - for instance as Chairman of the Board of the Political Club of Intellectuals "The Moscow Tribune" or as a member of the man-agement of the "Democratic Russia" movement - to a very modest degree, to try to influence myself certain events, say, to organize the USSR's first rally on May 21, 1989, in Luzhniki attended by two hundred thousand people. It is clear that I have my own view of what is going on, not as an observer and an expert, abut as one of a great many participants.

So I started to write for newspapers in order to do what seems to happen in the West more seldom than here (especially among those writ-ing themselves and not resorting to the services of speech-writers)./ I expressed not only my personal estimates but also emotions. I not only discussed, but gave vent to wrath and disgust, wrote ironically, shared my doubts and anxieties, tried to call to persons holding the same views and to convince those who were hesitating. To make a long story short, the articles, especially those contained in the second section of the book, are plunged into our boiling pot of the struggle of people and ides. The same is characteristic of present-day Russian for those who appear in the mass media; not only reflection and analysis of the political clashes but also grains of them.

Hence it appeared necessary to mull over my reasons for the general public; to look for graphic examples, to repeat and to repeat again certain ideological motives which have not yet become habitual and intelligible in our country. This explains arguments ad hominen, literary or even rhetorical devices. This has resulted in unavoidable almost arguments in each case. So, neither information nor simple analysis neither estimation, nor prognostication are on the foreground but disputes and disputes again... often and inevitably heated.

It is so because it matters not which candidate from which party will win the elections or to what extent social programs are to be financed, or how to get the better of the next economic depression, and not even how to do away with such terrible disasters as drug trafficking, outbreaks of mass violence, etc. A stable comparatively successful, but at the same time living and changing society, may face any amount of serious and painful problems. However, in Russia the problem is whether such a society itself will be formed after the disintegration of what Reagan had the full right to call "The Empire of Evil". Or we shall run into new lies and a new lack of freedom, suffering ourselves and terrifying the world,

This is the most general reason (besides weaknesses to be attributed to the author) why lately the public statements in Russia, like those collected here, contain so many works, perhaps more than I wished, more than should be used in a less tricky critical historical situation.

Or, perhaps, this may be explained, to a certain extent, by the fact that we kept silent our whole lives.

Hamlet said with a sneer and not without bitterness: "Words, word, words". It is true but who else in the Shakespearean play utters more words than Hamlet himself? It can be understood in his tragic and unclear situation, but the Russian choice today is not a bit simpler.

That is why any attempt to adapt a book like this to the tastes of the American reader in my opinion will be not only impossible but also lacking in a practical sense. Why should a Russian specialist in Italian Renaissance suddenly find himself involved in political passions (which is typical among our intellectuals) playing political scientist as it is understood in the West? You know, in this case it is a *different reality*, though difficult or even irritating, may present an interest. In case you desire to comprehend another country form the inside, to try to grasp the essence of foreign disputes, problems, life circumstances, it is most reasonable of all to avail yourself of any opportunity to observe everything as it stands, wrapped up in itself, not at all meant for your understanding.

I dare say that perhaps this is the case. In other words I hope that my book will happen to be sufficiently alien in order to attract the attention of the American reader - of course only those not indifferent to the present-day Russian political, moral, and cultural collisions.

INTRODUCTION

This book is a collection of articles written between February 1990 and April 1992 or newspapers and magazines.

Generally speaking, from a chronological point of view, selection happened to be accidental: my earlier political writings in which I started to be involved since 1987, were included in my previous book "Renewal of History" (Moscow, 1991) and the last date simply marks the moment when a New York publishing house made me an offer to compile this new book.

Nevertheless, it is quite easy to find in the time period under consideration the particular and quite objective contents with which the insignificant personal casual circumstances mentioned above seem to coincide. It is not only the case that the stunningly rapid downfall of the communist regime and the disintegration of the USSR turned out to be the great and pivotal event of these two years. But, perhaps, it is the events that occurred approximately between the spring of 1990 and the spring of 1992 that make up a real historic intrigue, forming a kind of an arch. They started and ended (rather, started *anew*) as two very different, but having much in common, *eves*; two poignant knots, two symmetric questions for the future, and August 1991 is the axis of this symmetry.

The Gorbachev "perestroika", i.e. finally openly revealed all-around the deepest crisis of the party machinery regime: semi-instinctive, convulsive attempts to preserve its "socialist" economic an political bases by modernizing them and relaxing that blind oppression unwillingly, step by step, giving up "the cold war" and world expansion, granting certain freedoms, creating a semblance of parliamentarism and allowing wretched elements of a state-controlled market - "perestroika" getting the West to make a sigh of understandable relief and giving birth to sincere but ignorant "Gorbomania" as an expression of gratitude, exhausted its resources and came to a deadlock already by the fall of 1989.

At that time in October I remembered, declaring at the conference of *Espresso* magazine in Rome that "perestroika" was over and though I spoke practical banality, the Western audience took it as a political maximalism of a ply of wit. As you know, Gorbachev continued to succeed in his relations with the West: nuclear disarmament went on and some new reassuring speeches were still heard form this mysterious Russia.

Few people concluded then from the fact that, at plenary sessions of the Central Committee in 1989 and in the reports of the General Secretary, an intention was demonstrated to maintain kolkhoz-sovkhoz agrarian decay, imperial power of the "center", the "leading" role of the CPUs, etc. That *nothing was decided* at the 1st Congress shook us so much with an unusual sense of relief. And that *after* this Congress in the summer and fall *not a single* realistic step was taken towards reforms. And that the party reformers (beginning with Gorbachev) were stuck not only with the opposition of the party machinery, the military industry or the KGB but also by their own narrow-mindedness both social and personal.

In each of these, "progressivists", bigwigs nursed by the regime there sat at least with his own Ligachev or Pugo at this side and nothing could be done about it. There was no really new, *quite* normal and free person "on the top:. No one capable of comprehending what was going on. (Everything else would be supernatural though.)

So "perestroika" ran short. Gorbachev, in his domestic policy, more and more vividly tried to put the brakes on the avalanches caused by it. He tried his best to consolidate his own power through artificial and unlawful "presidency". He delivered more and more empty, long, and semiliterate speeches, and instead of a profound and providentially bold *policy*, was occupied with administrative maneuvers as usual. Though it was not so much his own fault as, of course, that of the horrible system headed by him, principally incapable of a certain great metamorphosis, a real transformation, a repudiation of his own ego.

By the Second Congress of the "people deputies" this became utterly evident. After many months of hesitation, the "inter-regional group" at last declared that they were joining the opposition and made a statement, the text of which I, though not a deputy, had the occasion to write for this group, among whom there were a few of my friends. Before the December Congress in 1989 A.D. Sakharov, for the first time, called for a symbolic political protest strike and it was he, who having worked out his constitutional draft, pointed the transition towards a more dramatic and mature state of political struggle, one with particular force and clarity, especially in his last speech, delivered only a few hours before his death. The opposition of the democratically-minded section of society and the Gorbachev "perestroika" was now incapable of developing further.

The departure of Andrei Dmitryyevich marked this boundary with a mournful line.

And as far back as in February 1990, an immense and newly politically colored rally was held in Moscow - the first step towards the "Democratic Russia" movement which would take shape in the fall of the same year. Another still more crowded gathering took place in late March, as far as I remember on March 28. A frightened Gorbachev invited tanks to Moscow and the final act of the play staged in 1917 began.

The tension of the finale became crucial at first in October 1990, when Gorbachev at the very lst moment suddenly betrayed Yavlinksy's program of economic reforms (previously supported by him) and broke his agreements with Yeltsin in this respect. At that moment it became utterly evident that, having failed to dare to become closer to Yeltsin (and relatively democratic ally "left Center") and being unable and unwilling to change his orientation in an alien and unfamiliar movement, Gorbachev had to take his *last chance*. Gorbachev, more definitely - but not more sincerely, (since this man being a born and even great administrator is simply unable to be sincere and frank) - was getting closer to the powerful reactionary high officials of the CPSU, military industrial complex and the KGB, like Kryuchov, Baklavov, Pavlov. Thus following the logic of history, the general secretary singed his own verdict, as from that time on Gorbachev, like the entire system, no longer had a future.

(The whole of 1990 I spent in hospitals. In the fall good people mad an attempt to drag me out be sending me to German physicians. Having learned in Koln about the failure of the "500 Days" program at Gorbachev's hand, I wrote a report in "Bundesinstiture" entitled "The Epoch of Gorbachev is coming to It's End". This time again the majority of the audience took this so trivial thesis as an exaggeration as the newly fledged "Nobel Prize Winner" seemed to be still at the height of world recognition and his power.)

Meanwhile in January 1991, the dying "perestroika" drew blood, this time in the Baltic republics. We realized who and what stood behind it. You know, there exists logic of a political course. Gorbachev was thinking over a state of emergency with hesitation while his team was rehearsing for August.

There is no doubt that Gorbachev's merits were great, with all their ambiguity and unexpectedness. This man opened a Pandora's box not even suspecting that a giant would fly up form inside. He, a party pragmatist, did understand (Oh, not since April 1985 when but a new thaw set in, i.e. when Khrushchev's bottle was again taken from the ice-house, but since the January plenum of 1987 and two subsequent years) that he had to open the box, at least show mercy on the dissidents, to stop the lost war, to give permission to private cooperators, "non-formals", to have elections with several candidates, to strongly liberalize censorship ("glasnost"!), etc.

At that time all people - above all in the West - were very much concerned with the strategic plans of Mikhail Sergeyevich and whether they included the break-away of Eastern Europe and the reunification of Germany, as if facts and documents were lacking for an analysis. (As if there might exist any secrets!) Answering such questions, I used to tell my German listeners a joke from the days of my youth. After the earthquake in Ashkhavad, a rescue team found an old Jew miraculously still alive in a toilet. When he was brought to his senses he was asked "how had it happened". He replied: "I never thought that such a disaster might happen if you pull this thing."

And enough of this.

In the second place the tension of the finale grew stronger by far when in February - March 1991 a political strike began to expand, threatening to turn into a general strike. For the first time after 1921. the population en masse openly and spontaneously expressed their unwillingness to tolerate this regime. Precisely this was the crucial moment: Gorbachev was forced once more to look for certain secret deals with Yeltsin and others. The world now heard a mysterious toponym: "Novo-Ogaryovo", but the ruling gang, headed by the general secretary, preferred a tougher method. The outcome was felt quicker and in a more fantastic way than it might have been with another more characteristically Gorbachev in slow reaction style.

However, now that I am writing these phrases, eight months after the intoxicating atmosphere of the last week in August 1991, it is necessary to say the following. *The August revolution* (the events resulting in the downfall of the CPSU and a little later in the disintegration of the USSR, you must agree that, nevertheless, there were reasons to call it so!) turns out to be strange illusory, sort of semi-revolution, like many other things which have happened before and after it. The "putsch" also had little resemblance to a putsch and still is veiled with mist, as is the president's semi-arrest. None seems to be in a hurry to clear it out (recently a very big democrat made an appeal to be generous and give up the idea of a trial of the criminals which is evidently *not needed* by successors and colleagues of

Kryuchkov or Baklanov[1]). Then, perhaps the revolution itself was...a little bit unreal?

The events were developing in certain streets and squares of the capital. Even in Moscow indifference prevailed in the minds of the majority of the population. Then they started to snatch away important posts, administrative buildings, funds, cars, apartments and so on. The victors happened to be the official political clique of the RSFSR (as well as other republics) rather than some opposition parties and movements (if we do not consider - almost symbolically - a small group of functionaries of the "Democratic Russia"[2] without any political independence, lounging about the new power and getting up their high horse. The included patriarchs, officials, generals, and KGB officers constituting the major part of the Supreme Soviet and the Congress of Deputies of Russia as well as the bulk of the executive power. The changes started after August were carried out, like in the "perestroika" time, from this top management instead of from the low circles, for partially renewed in its composition to not at all in this respect. (not to say about functions, methods and mechanisms of management), recoloured, disguised nomenclature. Though there appeared new, educated, honest figures, certain ministers and deputies as well - but so few in number. Yeltsin's "governor-generals" in the provinces. Like the local heads in general, are, for the most part, dead bodies. In mayoral offices and executive committees, the "experienced workers" were joined by still more impudent, complacent, rapacious and numerous officials than those previous communist ones. There remained (under new titles or "commercialised", MIC, KGB, army political bodies, the same generals, state farms and kolkhozes, privileges...and whatever you like. Qualitatively, only the rates of bribes have changed which you must five everywhere and for everything.

Neither property relations, nor the character of power, nor social and psychological climate in the main have become different after August.

That is why and not only due to the inevitable hardships of the administrative and financial reforms of Gaidar who, with his assistants, is doing (though with big mistakes) what is possible and necessary under the conditions of the total disorganization, *but within the framework of the*

---

[1] The heads of the KGB and the Military-Industrial Complex presently awaiting court hearings in the "Matrosskaya Tishina" prision, members of the Emergency State Committee (ESC) during the putsch.

[2] A political movement formed in the fall of 1990. The aughor of this bok left its leadership as a protest against its policy of trailing along at the back of Yeltsin's regime.

remaining Soviet socialist system - that is whey the main result of the post-August experiment is expressed in a single word - *disappointment*.

Recently this was written about by Yu G. Burtin with remarkable acuity)"Nezavisimaya Gazeta" newspaper, dated April 21, 1992) and I am prepared to put my own signature under his each and every word. His article is a part of a more extensive work which he could not publish as a complete version in Russia...The title of this work is worth much: "Gorbachev Continues".

Above all society feels it ever stronger: "look, the system is still the same!"

The heads are more or less familiar even when they are new. We may assume that the heads are really new but their policy and tricks (if we ignore minor and affected things) are essentially the same. In other words, they do not depend on the population for whom they act as protectors and benefactors - because of their generosity or because they are forced to - not forgetting their own interests; as a matter of fact they used to inveigh against privileges when striving for power - but now it would be tactless; more and more seldom they recall "civil society" or "free elections" or "human rights" or democratic law as guarantees in the first instance against state omnipotence, against priority of an official over a citizen. But, on the other hand, they indulge in an aggressive, absolutely illegal *armed* "Cossacks" becoming more and more dangerous. But they now love to suggest the necessity and beneficial character of *authoritarianism* under those "peculiar" Russian conditions of ours. They wish neither elections, nor legislative power, nor legal power, which by the way is almost nonexistent and still cannot be expected. In other words, they are making a transparent stake at a "progressive" (i.e. their own) dictatorship. It is also called a "president republic". They, the highest authorities, are demonstrating muscles in front of the neighbors (above all, the Ukraine) calling it "national state interests". More and more openly they attempt to place a new propagandistic foundation under themselves ("to fill an ideological vacuum") in the shape of *great-power chauvinism*. Of course, in spoken words, it is denied but by far not by all of the ruling persons...while some of them can hardly be distinguished from national-patriots.

Besides, in April 1992, the line of Yeltsin's authorities began to show, aimed at concessions to the "directors", i.e. the management of "Oboronka" (defenses).[3]

---

[3] A colloquial word for the Military Industrial Complex (MIC).

A peaceful social revolution has not yet started. And it will never be-gin until the society is stirred to a deep movement and takes the matter into their own hands. That is not yet the case, but it will come. Without this, radical structural reforms will not begin; they will be delayed and get bogged down and without them we shall not pull thorough.

That is why, in my opinion, if we witnessed a crisis, a deadlock, an exhaustion of "perestroika" between 1989-1990, then in the spring of 1992 we see a crisis, a deadlock and exhaustion of that, "post-August" of "post-perestroika" social, economic and political situation embodied in post-communist nomenclature. These are the direct results of the downfall of the party-soviet regime, and not what Gaidar's government is doing (as a whole deserving support) but what they *are not doing*, and, are perhaps, simply unable to do until the "democrats" remain at the helm, the same masters of life as before, a neoburaucratic layer absorbed with self-preservation and settling their own personal affairs.

After August journalists loved to write that Gorbachev "had returned to another country". Well, now he seems to live in his native place again.

Could it be otherwise?

The present-day transitional regime relates to the previous one as a positive photograph to the negative and will, however, exhaust its re-sources rapidly as well - regardless of the desires and qualities of even its best leaders and supporters due to its structural and objective character. Having forced an overcoming of the obstacles which seemed to be insur-mountable, we found ourselves on a small found swept with fire on the opposite bank of the same turbid river.

The first wave of the democratic offensive proved an unforgettable historic mission and yielded nothing.

When and how will the SECOND WAVE rise with the same internal necessity?

I consider Yeltsin's promises that already, by the end of 1992, all-round stabilization (i.e. the *real* perestroika, from the foundation) will take shape, and that life will gradually but appreciably become easier, unfea-sible.

Therefore the president has tow routes: either to make maneuvers be-tween the ruling circles (especially MIC, the Congress, the army, regional authorities) and populism in many ways repeating the tactics and destiny of Gorbachev.

Or - *to favor* the arrival of the second wave...The president is hardly prepared for this, and almost certainly - unprepared, and that is a pity.

All political contours have been and remain unsteady in this transi-tional, troubled time. All everyday terms and slogans lead astray. Politicians, national "capitalists" or, say, "Cossacks", "parties", "trade-unions", "Parliament", "Privatization", etc., constitute an enormous round dance of makers. Of course, there are exceptions but very few. "Democrats" are not democrats and even "communists" willingly uniting with "anti-Communists" reveal the imaginary characters of both terms. There is so much absurdity and so many persons almost gorgeous in this respect that sometimes I wish to pinch myself. for example, is Khasbulatov realistic?

Total imagination: It is not an amusing (or horrible) outer sing of the pre-August or post-August periods significantly tying them up - but something relating to the deepest essence of the present-day friable, shapeless society being born anew in pangs.

This has prompted the title of this book.

I repeat that though this is a separate collected work compositionally (within reasonable limits) well turned but continuing the previous one ("The Renewal of History"). In its own way, it is the next chapter of a political diary. In a diary it is important to pay attention to *the dates of writing* in order to treat each entry in the right way; to understand a discord, a mixed character and references. Something becomes antiquated in a month or in a year maintaining, perhaps, a certain significance of a modest historical evidence. On the other hand, something else becomes more interesting just at a distance thanks to and instructive lapse of time.

Interesting for whom? For myself? I have neither time nor desire to reread old newspapers. Or for certain readers? This is the publisher's concern. Though, of course, I would wish to know it beforehand without slyness.

And what an author would not wish it? That's it.

PART I
TWO PROJECTS

How Not to Do Harm
to the Arrangement
of Russia

1. You may argue with whomsoever you like from Chaadayev to Sakharov, not starting with awkward reservations and fearing that it will be considered a blasphemy.

You may do it with anyone you like but not with Alexander Isayevich Solzhenitsin.

Job made an attempt to retort to the Lord but everybody remembers how this ended. "I put my hand over my mouth". We can understand Job. The Lord spoke to him 'out of the storm": "Therefore I despise myself and repent in dust and ashes". That is, having risen against the Lord he ultimately behaved the same way as others, lover than he, had behaved: "When I went to the gate of the city and took my seat in the public square, the young men saw me and stepped aside and the old men rose to their feet". But the main is - "After I had spoken, they spoke no more..."

Solzhenitsin possibly has deserved that we rise to our feet at his appearance.

But - so much necessarily we have to reason further.

The subheading" Feasible Considerations" and the unpretentious character of the final chapter "Let Us Search" ("My task was only to offer certain separate considerations pretending to no kind of definitiveness and so on) is a tribute to the etiquette's rhetorical rules. The intonation to the text is sure to conform to it in no way. Alexander Isayevich writes in an apodictic way, i.e., by pointing out instead of proving, and with a conscious belief in his unique right to speak to nations rather than separate interlocutors. This is the genre of urbi et orbi, a real *encyclic* of Solzhenitsin! The Vermont hermit is lecturing, demanding, thundering out of the storm.

The very tone and genre of the appeal of Alexander Isayevich cannot be accepted. Not as such: Solzhenitsin must write the way he likes and is accustomed to. But, because of ourselves, due to our own long-standing habit to prostrate ourselves before the Highest Authorities: if we wish to become a modern country we should get rid of such habits.

Today we are just starting to rise from our knees.

We are just beginning to familiarize ourselves with the dignity of individual opinions.

It would be horrible if we have bent, not before logic and facts, but simply because of the understandable esteem for the legendary author of the "Archipelago GULAG" fearing to swim against the tide of *today's* public-opinion. On the contrary, it is no more difficult (and even easier). have we lived up to this indeed? - to reject the lies of the CPSU or to dispute its general secretary. Well, and to reject the ideas of Solzhenitsin himself? and not only (which is incomparably much easier) glazunovs and kunyayevs?

Alas, certain Russians including well-known politicians, democrats and men of letters, no matter what they think about Solzhenitsin's recent pamphlet, have hurried to publicly emphasize its sincere pain and moral grandeur; as a matter of fact not taking the trouble to read it. To enter into politics with Alexander Isayevich Solzhenitsin's concrete admonitions seems inconvenient, though they are not going to follow them. A certain ritual consent seems to be in this case precisely what is required...

However, let us try to proceed from the fact that many, though not all, people entering the discussion and meditating over the destiny of Russia with all their hearts and souls like Solzhenitsin, are grieving over and caring about it. Now, only after Alexander Isayevich, defying the horrible regime, has become almost the most recognized and frequently published author in his country. Can we argue with him without the slightest hesitations and without repeating everywhere that we do remember his tremendous service to the Motherland: as long as this is clear enough without it.

I think that A.I. Solzhenitsin's message can palpably damage the interest of Russia's renewal. As usual it contains many correct and wrathful remarks about the evil of the agonizing party "socialism" but they unwillingly are sounding but echoes of what is generally known and the author does realize it. It also has certain exact thoughts and proposals. They are also not a few in number for example, about the connection between "an independent citizen" and private property or, especially, about the impossibility of a democratic system without a highly developed local self-government. But, on the other hand, all correct ideas are inserted in a retrograde frame. Rather evident attempts to counterbalance something with reservations, to smooth something a little bit, to avoid, these do not compensate for the dreams to catch the world history napping but only add certain languor to the text, as was pointed out by sympathetic readers as well.

The harm of Solzhenitsin's pamphlet, perhaps, will be extenuated by the remarkable fact that his outlook has not been hidden from the public, but immediately published with a circulation of 25 million copies. Everyone who can will read the text to the end and think it over without haste. As long as little consideration of the present-day political reality is taken by the author, his message will be moved aside with the course of the developing events, noise around it having been over. Nevertheless people are sure to be found - (and indeed have been already found) thinking not without grounds that Solzhenitsin's positions are essentially close to their nationalistic ones, and wishing to use his truly profound conviction and influence which they themselves are lacking.

No matter how distressing it is, one cannot pass it in silence. because Solzhenitsin's ideas have ground in certain historic and not yet outdated peculiarities of the Russian and Soviet public life and consciousness.

2. It is with a strange feeling in which, perhaps, bitterness is mixed with a readiness to accept the inevitable order of things and almost satisfaction, that the author writes: "a man is made in such a way" that he is ready to put up with any lawlessness, misery and perdition, however, "if one offends our *nation*", then we...seize stones, canes, spears, guns and attack our neighbours to set their houses on fire and to kill".

However, nobody in Canada or Belgium seems to seize "spears" and to rush to kill neighbours. Neither in the Baltic countries... We shall not try to find out from Solzhenitsin whether it is really true that international animosity is not determined by certain political and economic conditions and circumstances and that inhuman atrocities in Sumgait, Fergana and Osha should not be explained by concrete local Soviet-Asian ground but that "a man is such" from his origin, everywhere and at all times. But how, in any case, a man of culture, a modern man with the XX century experience in this respect has to regard any, even harmless and peaceful, "only" ideological loyalty sentimental nationalism? Every preponderance of a collective (including national) feeling over independence of a personality? In particular, how should we consider the narrow "arrangement" of people from the point of view of Christian personalism? In brief, what is the principal viewpoint of Alexander Isayevich?

WE shall come to this a little bit later. And now, having put aside for later a citation from Vladimir Solovyev: "Love all other people as your own"., Alexander Isayevich states: "the national origin hides from us all the rest in our life" therefore "today a few people are free in our country" - i.e. a few people with democratic consciousness or simply people of good sense? An arguable point! For the majority of the USSR population and above all for Russians, from miners of Vorkuta and Kuzbass to Moscow and St. Petersburg it is fortunately sill unfair. Without an analysis and refection of the national obsession (particularly dangerous for the one hundred forty million people) the author hurries to "the immediate future" saying: "we (who are "we"?) are forced to start not with gnawing sores...but with an answer:...within what geographic borders shall we undergo a cure or die?"

However, if we start directly with the problem of Russia's *borders*, it will never come to pass. This is a mortally dangerous accentuation.

Solzhenitsin opens a discussion with a demand - a long as "the USSR" will *"all the same"* collapse (and here he is right) - "it must be declared without delay loudly and clearly" : ELEVEN republics *"will be separated without fail and irrevocably"*.

How do you like it? Not have the right to set up on their own, but are obliged to, will be forced to. As if "some of them hesitate whether to separate", we shall be "compelled to declare them about *our* separation from them with the same firmness and 'certainty' - we shall not carry our mutual burden!" In brief: go away, otherwise we shall leave. Those who have thought that V. Rasputin made a poor joke now see: it is no laughing matter.

So why do "we" (that is, Russians who will agree with Rasputin and Solzhenitsin) wish a forced break off? Because "we' must now make a tough choice: between saving the Empire, but ruining ourselves above all, and saving the Russian people. Well, but maybe another choice exists between the Empire and non-Empire. Perhaps a confederation or any other convenient form of close cooperation of truly sovereign and democratic countries instead of the USSR is possible.

Three reasons known to all - 1). economic ties; a potential common market beyond which *nobody* is yet able to go; 2). a demographic strip of land holding (60 million people - above all Russians - are beyond the Republic's frontiers); finally, 3). human personal ties, mixed marriages and the Russian language acting in this part of the Earth as an international means of intercourse like English, seem to prevent the countries of the

USSR from "simple" separation. IT is in the interests of all that we should look for a mutually acceptable way to liquidate the Empire while preserving the common economic, cultural and geopolitical space. Only further artificial hold-up of the "USSR" intensifies centrifugal tendencies. With a victory of the republican democracies, I think, we shall become witnesses (in a radically transformed way) to these centripetal tendencies. Of course we will see great differences and variations in statuses of the Soviet countries including a status of partially associated members, and this would be a vast improvement.

But Solzhenitsin, finding strong words against the claims of certain Russophiles to "extensive-sovereign" power, against imperial arrogance, demands refusal from the former tsarist and Stalin's territorial acquisitions for the sake of material and spiritual strengthening of Russia, though in more modest geographic limits For - "what for is this various motley alloy? - in order that Russians will lose their original face?" - the more so as "all the same" we have no force for the outskirts", "*we have no force for an Empire*: and we do not need it and let it fall off our shoulders..."

What a practical and kind attitude to the "outskirts". And if we *had* force?

So, Solzhenitsin proclaiming allegedly on behalf of "the Russians themselves" sees only such a choice:" to hold the great Empire" or to throw off the ballast of the "outskirts". Which is more beneficial for Russia? According to the long cherished idea of Alexander Isayevich it is more beneficial to create "a settling tank of the Russian nation". However, even after all of the separations, our state will inevitably remain multinational though we are not striving for it." How nice this "our" is sounding for others, "even big" nations in the RSFSR? - as if "we" (i.e. Russians) are not striving for "it". It means non-Russians are not included in the semantic meaning of the great-power "we". They are not striven for!" That's good if we have to live together "inevitably". As for the "small outskirts peoples" of the Northern Caucasus, etc., 'we' do not need their adherence, 'they' need it more. So welcome, if they want to stay with us." That's that.

Throughout the entire message - "we", "our" - and 'they", though hundreds of years living with us but not ours: "not to hold", to separate ones by force; - 'no choice" for others as Russia is spread around, the thirds who "before the Revolution were demonstrating their loyalty to the Russian throne, will probably think it hard if there is sense to be separated'; as they wish, though we feel no great need, - they are welcome.

Such anti-imperial thinking: as a continuation of the same imperial one but inside out.

Why only *eleven* republics in the first instance? Because Alexander Isayevich is ready to allow a sovereignty to "swelled Kazakhstan" only within the limits of the Southern arch of regions" where Kazakhs constitute the indigenous majority. Referring to the fact that the frontiers of the Kazakh SSR were established in the Stalin time, Solzhenitsin does not agree to give up the major part of its vast lands. As in the case of the separation of the Ukraine, he orders referendums in Donbass and other regions where the Russian population is so large.

In the civilized world, which gave shelter to exiled Solzhenitsin to question state frontiers established after 1945 and the present ones is prohibited in general. Otherwise you won't avoid troubles. In certain regions of certain countries all the world over, national minorities prevail, from Spain to Rumania, from India to, I think, Finland with its Swedes. All over the world they get accustomed to not attaching excessive importance to frontiers. But Alexander Isayevich does not wish to give up the ploughed Golodnaya Steppes, and look - a manifestation in already boiling in Alma-Ata against the demands of...Vermont. That is all we needed! Calm down please citizens Kazakhs. Neither the Russian people, nor their present government, certainly, will not follow the instructions of Alexander Isayevich; why do we need invented troubles if we have plenty of real ones.

Having spread a map on the floor Solzhenitsin is deciding where to put state frontiers, and like a child is casting burning matches. He pushes Moldavians to Rumania because in his opinion they are "more attached" there. He declares to the Ukraine and Byelorussia that their peoples are branches of the same stem as Russians, in fact varieties of the same Russians: Malo-Russians, Carpathorussians, Byelorussians, so they must separate by no means. Perhaps, in case the Ukrainian people "would really wish it"; of course, "nobody can dare to hold them by force." That sounds good...But if it is desirable to hold by kindness - it would be better not to expose Ukrainian nationalists even if they are wrong from a historical viewpoint, counting out from IX century (there were no Ukrainians at that time...however, and no Russians), it would be better not to call Galicia "Carpathorussia" and not to consider its tongue "a distorted unnational language" and in addition not to insult members of the Uniat Church with "catholicizing" and not to insist again on changing the frontiers in case of separation.

Oh, God!

Why can't Russians live in an independent (but most likely Union, however without the imperial Moscow) Ukraine? In independent (but most likely Union) Kazakhstan, Georgia, etc.? In the independent and growing rich states of Baltia? But... "Millions of people will face a difficult problem: to stay where they are living or to leave?...And not only for Russians from the *outskirts* (underlined by me; let's keep the expression in mind - L.B.0 but also the outskirts living now in Russia."

And this particular hasty prophesy is quite horrible. A total migration of people rushing in opposite directions (from Pogroms?) would be the concluding catastrophe. Now refugees would render impossible any "arrangement" of Russia and all the countries of the former USSR, for decades to come. We must avoid it *at all costs*.

However, Solzhenitsin, though writing that the national question "has rubbed sore our necks so much that it has distorted all feelings and the entire reality" - but he sees and suggests no alternative for the gigantic exodus unheard of in history. "With all this - shall we prepare migration for our compatriots losing residence? yes, inevitably!". He is enumerating (discussed at length in newspapers and even partially included in governmental republican programs) various reasonable means to cut expenses and "to collect means" (I don't know why, not distributing resulting savings among all the republics, but allotting profits only to Russia) and is proposing to immediately spend all these means for the migration of refugees.

Putting aside the moral and political aspects - how strange is Solzhenitsin's political economy! Not only will everything be spent for refugees but, in fact, having gained a "wooden" rouble for modernization of economy, our Russia would be unable to help refugees as well. Neither "500 days" nor 5,000 days would stand it, of course.

What else does Alexander Isayevich have in relation to "the national question"?

And what is more, he declares "the present hierarchy" of the republics, autonomies, regions and districts "to be just". Though seven autonomies have already opposed such a hierarchy and declared themselves Union ones.

And what is more, he explains using Stalin's well-known argument, that there cannot be sovereign states without outer frontiers in Russia. The fact that Kazan and Ufa took the peremptory instruction from Vermont? Thank God for this.

And what is more, he casually repeats the favourite thesis of our nationalists that "Russia haws given its vital juices tot he republics in these decades" (making a wise reservation "if" this "is true").

And what is more, having given kind advice regarding "the smallest nationalities" - he somehow forgets one and a half million Jews, two million Germans escaping from their native land in which their ancestors have rested in peace for 200-400 years. We seem "not to seek" to save their brains and hands for Russia? Is it not a national tragedy besides Germans and Jews, precisely for Russians themselves? Alexander Isayevich remembers and reasons everything ranging from lessening the load of school teachers to the opening of Academy's faculties in the lines of ministries, Stolypin like. It is hard to remember everything.

But in return, among all devastating instructions and inexorable demands, there is a citation from Vladimir Solovyov: "Love all other nations as your own". It is a good quotation, like a boletus amidst a trampled down glade.

Having acted as an arbiter of all the republic's destinies, having improved frontiers even where they do not yet exist, having moved all Russians back to Russia from "the outskirts" (i.e. taking the Ukraine, Georgia or Central Asia from the viewpoint of a man from the imperial center, *the Russian metroply*! - "this Russia has been so much worn, out everyone is cursing it untimely and out of place") - Solzhenitsin suggests to rest on the seventh day of political creation." And it is here, from this threshold - we can and must reveal to all our great wisdom and kindness, *only from this moment* can and must we use all efforts of reason and heartiness" (underlined by me - L.B.). And *before* this moment? *Before* this threshold?

Can't we really be hearty? And don't we need reason?

It is sad.

3. "To rob out", "unliftingly heavy", "neglectness", "peacier and openlier", "to wheel around", "not for long ago", "damnedness", "fastanding", "disordedness". "by outrobbing", "decoyful", "breathless-lying", "underwaterness", "revivening", "topcrowning", "choosener", "diffinterpretadedness", "twothirding", "mangorging", "to hopeless", "combineful"... and so on. Such is a language the author of the "knots" of the "Red Whells" has chosen to speak with his compatriots how to turn Russia into a prosperous modern country.

Or...not modern? But in a country where (in XVIII century? or - better - in XVII century?) things passed from great-grandfathers to their great-grandsons without wearing out; prices remained unchanged in the lives of three generations ("for ages"); women stayed at home and brought up children; young people "did not frolic from satiety" with heavy metal rock and break dancing, but with moderate means, perhaps, "knocked the nonsense out of their heads" with fisticuffs wall against wall, with village chastooshkas and at worst with a town quadrille; there were no telecasts at daytime or even a whole day a week like in Iceland, and was no TV at all; there was no "liquid manure" of mass culture, "most vulgar fashions", publicity, "plump newspapers". Though there was placid feudalism, quiet serfdom or, this is still acceptable, the very early capitalism. There lived tsarine Elizabeth, Pyotr Ivanovich Shuvalov with this marvelous though, of course, unrealised "Project of Saving People" (oh, it means that even then they had to think about their saving?). Here is Russia! - Shuvalov, Stolypin, consultative duma representing new "estates", Zemstvo which brought so many benefits some time ago - and, of course, all the good from the present century, many things from Western arrangements, however, without their problems and defects, only good things. Such is an arranged Russia Alexander Isayevich is dreaming of.

Perhaps it is a beautiful daydream, a colour dream where one can fly.

It is very likely that it was not accidental that Solzhenitsin sees precisely forty cultural and economic "life and light centers" in this unusual Russia; "Forty Cities" heading Russian regions - immediately "forty times forty Moscow churches" come to mind; a folklore, fantastic number. Oh, how wonderful it would be.

However, Alexander Isayevich wakes up at the close of XX century and notices - everything is wrong. Everything must be different.

So Alexander Isayevich puts his seat on a square and the truly great prisoner, a fearless exposer of the communist totalitaris, thunders out of the cloud, however, almost all get it hot.

The mighty and of Solzhenitsin strikes at, not to mention "XX century materialism beheading humanity" and Western democracy as "a substitute of faith for an intellectual deprived of religion" nameless, of course.

Givriil Popov for a "pleasant caution" of a notion of "administrative commanding system' introduced by him and for his "insensitiveness to the Motherland feeding the capital city" (this already refers to the Moscow Soviet for trade against presenting passports);

Yury Afanasyev or, I do not remember, somebody else spoke a slightly premature phrase about "a new February revolution" at the rally of February 4; the very February revolution of 1917 with its "buffoonery attires".

Mikhail Gorbachev for "inner central-committee transpositions" (a really apt wording novelty!) and his pitiful "perestroika";

Andrei Sakharov for his searches for "a most convenient form of the state system" as who else but Sakharov - who "hastefully wrote a remarkable constitution, paragraph one, paragraph forty-five", the first version of Sakharov's constitution containing exactly 45 clauses and Andrei Dmitriyevich was indeed in a great hurry until the last day of his (Solzhenitsin himself had not very consistently dedicated a half of his pamphlet to inventing a Russian state system and even to describing it in the smallest detail);

Polozkov for the disgraceful RCP - and young sympathetic Moscow "anarchosyndicalists";

the vegetating UNO" - a simple clip on the back of its head, just in passing;

with reservations at human-right defenders by criticism of "fashionable" but non-existent "human rights";

professional politicians receiving salaries for their work and the preponderance of lawyers and advocates in parliaments, "jurocracy";

the new administration of Russia, B. Yeltsin with this hopes for free economic zones and foreign investments ("not to attract Western capital" - oh, God, how really to attract it? - as "only come and rule us...and we shall be turned into a colony", a most dangerous idea" - whose? Where has Alexander Isayevich read it?

Now then we happen to hear these fears about the Western capitalist Dragon Gorynych from ignorant "patriots", not knowing how the economy of any open and civilized country is functioning).

He strikes at new parties: why are parties being formed if there is no reason for that? Parties have outlived themselves and so if we had not enough suffering form the CPSU alone (also familiar reasoning);

and at the "Memorial" and representative parliamentarism, and Trotsky, and people's fronts - why shall we need people's fronts?

and at somebody else.

Such a universal thrashing!

While Solzhenitsyn invites, as allies, citations from rather different authors, often without layers of his own reasonings, simply one after another like in a calendar. IV. Ilyin, S. Krzhizhanovsky, Titus Livius, D. Shipov, V. Solovyov, O. Spengler, P. Novgorodtsev, Aristotle, M. Dragomanov, F. Dostoyevsky, Ronald Reagan, John Paul II, K. Popper, G. Fedotov, M. Katkov, L. Tikhomirov, Montesquieu, P. Milyukov, V. Maklakov, J. Mill, S. Frank, B. Chicherin, H. Staub, V.l Rozanov, Tocqueville, S. Levitsky the Old Testament...Alexander Isayevich is lavish in larding his pamphlet with citations he liked so much, sometimes not coordinated with each other, borrowed from cosmically alien or even mutually hostile spiritual contexts but at least proving the author's rightness each time. To tell the truth, this intellectual rigging makes a fantastic impression on those readers who prefer analytic work with another's thoughts to a prayer or admonition book.

However, *authoritative evidence* selected for this or another place perfectly fit the genre and language of an instruction chosen by the author; they are organic in their way.

I do not have V. Dal's dictionary at hand, that compost with which Alexander Isayevich cultivated his amazing style in order to check which of the above-mentioned wonderful words were in use 100-150 years ago and which he has invented himself, stylizing them after Russian antiquity and common parlance, the more so in respect of this pamphlet. There is no need to start profound linguistic and aesthetic considerations; in fact we have before our eyes a strictly urgent political document.

An erudite commentator of the "liberty", B. Paramonov has expressed approximately the following opinion: we have a writer and not a politician, and his deliberately provincial, heavily archaized language is an instrument required for creation of a special artistic world - the inimitable "myth of Solzhenitsin". Of course, the writer should not have to apply himself to other people's work, says Paramonov; the result was no good, but it is untimely to object, as the root of the author's blunders and retrograde stand is deeply aesthetic and as such, everything assumes an original, already imprescriptible sense, remarkable in its way. What a graceful turn of though, but nothing will come of it except tactless insults for both Solzhenitsin and the readers taking his ideas seriously.

The author himself will not agree with such a turn of thought, will not give up his civil, teaching mission as he understands it. As for the artistic and literary level of Solzhenitsin's archaisation, a direct ideological pathos of his latest novels in particular, is a subject of a special discussion.

And, on the other hand, now few people can be found in Russia sharing or not sharing Solzhenitsin's views who would both wish and be able to interpret the Vermont message in such a refined way, i.e. as "playful". But they do not start games when a house is on fire; in fact Alexander Isayevich started no aesthetic games, thinking of nothing else but how to extinguish a fire, to build a new edifice on a ground burnt by fire, to cure Russia.

I repeat, the rules of analysis have been set by the purpose of the pamphlet. Regardless of its unusual coloring, this is a message divulged to dozens of millions of countrymen, suffering, embittered, indigent, frightened and wishing a comparatively safe way out an easing of general and each personal destiny. An answer can be found only in the same political and practical key, which has been so insistently proposed by Solzhenitsin. A cultural dessert to it we shall taste sometime later - when having a feast dedicated to a Russian housewarming.

That is why Solzhenitsin's language in this case is not a mere expression of a writer's lexical freedom, a measure of his taste and cultural tact: something else is important here. If Alexander Isayevich strives to speak to all Russians and all for whom the Russian language is native (or at least understandable), we must say that his readers either intellectuals or semi-literate, express themselves differently. The country speaks another language, not Solzhenitsin's. Consequently for the author it turns out to be much more important than a simple intelligibility. His intention was to gain a foot-hold beyond modern reality, to find a *proper*, indeed, the only worthy counting point over realities; in short to propose an ideal structure on all the levels of the text from conceptual to stylistic to his contemporaries for meeting their urgent needs. Therefore "neglectedness", "by outrobbing", "combineful", "to hopeless" are flying like banners, like gonfalons!

4. A genre of political reasoning is bad because if, in a novel, something will seem defiant to the facts, it is called a flight of imagination, an aesthetic myth and so on; and if such a thing is found in "a word to nations" - we ought to call it differently. And if a writer contradicts himself in a novel, it is called an artistic or even highly artistic device; while in reasoning it is already an alogism (to put it more simply - nonsense).
Here are a few examples:

a). Solzhenitsin maintains that before October 1917 in Russia "a tranquil co-existence" and even "a slumbering indistinguishability of nations was almost reached" - though 'with a regrettable exception". But the author mentions "the ill-considered conquest of Alexander II" and the pressing (till now?) weight of the Central Asian underbelly". (Is Central Asia a *Russian* underbelly?), "disgraceful edicts" of the same tsar against the Ukrainian language and "indivisiblers" of 1914. But the author also sympathetically cites S. Kryzhanovsky who "at the beginning of the century" warned that "the native Russia" is short of forces "for assimilation of all the outskirts"! So, that's how it is amidst slumbering, the tsarist administration was seeking assimilation as a condition of :"indistinguishability"? It means that the Soviet "indistinguishability" is not so new? Perhaps Stolypin's 1910 bans of the Ukrainian culture not mentioned by the author, the notion of "non-Russians", the black hundred and "slumbering" pogroms of Jews and the Beilis court hearing are just deplorable exceptions unworthy of mentioning, as well as the persistent scattering of people from "the one and indivisible" from 1917-1921.

b) If both Imperial and communist Russia failed to be the metropoly, the bearer of a heavy state system suppressed and deprived with it in a peculiar manner. The Russian people were destined by "the Part" to become the back-bone and at the same time, the victims of the lack of freedom, the monster of the "USSR" - why then does Alexander Isayevich call 12 republics "outskirts" and write "that we have no forces for an Empire", and when we throw off the "outskirts" it will result "only in a saving of physical forces"?

I fail to understand anything in all this.

c) If there has been, not since the IX century, of course, but since XIII-XIV centuries, a "special Ukrainian nation with a special non-Russian language", - then why, when accepting its right to its culture and even the rift "to separate themselves" - only an autonomy inside the indivisible "Russian Union" is destined for it? "Unmixibly and indivisibly". If "unmixibly" than in what sense "indivisibly"? Either "indivisibly" or a complete break off? - is there no third choice, i.e. a confederation or a common market and currency for the Ukraine or Byelorussia?

d) If we "achieve nothing worthy before the communist Lenin's party...fully withdraw from any influencing of economic and state life" before "the nomenclature bureaucracy", a political police, etc. disappear how can our future legal state" "inevitably be smoothly successive"? (That is, following the inevitable logic and practice, successive of the party authoritarism, of the same nomenclature, etc.) And if it is not so, if a democratic break-through has long ripened, then immediate privatization of property, free elections, liberation from the power of the CPSU and from any non-democratic, extra-governmental power and influence mechanism of the army, militia, courts, office of the public prosecutor are needed. If replacement of the existing artificial pseudo-parliamentary structures is needed, then from where is this opposition to a gradualness that is quite consistent with the official position? Something in the present state system has to be accepted for the time being simply because it is already existing". Well, in general, it is indisputable. But what has to be accepted in particular, and mainly, what does "for the time being" mean? It goes without saying that all cannot be changed at once. But we are appreciably plunging into an economic and national-state chaos, while "the existing state system" seems to reveal an inability to effect further rapid evolution. How is it possible without a radical turn, without a bloodless revolution, like in the February so fiercely hated by Solzhenitsin, like in Poland or Czechoslovakia?

e) If it is "not only a state system that matters" (of course, not only this, but, as it is provided by the most recent experience of the economic reform and the new Union treaty, it is almost the key matter), if we do not have to speed up political changes because of urgent economic troubles - then who will handle this economic dislocation? And how will they do so? The events of the very day when the country was offered the chance to read Alexander Isayevich's enthusiastic Zemstvo projects, proved that under the existing All-Union power structure the RSFSR is almost power-less; the quarter-democratic Supreme Soviet of the USSR can take no economic steps forward. Extraordinary Presidential decrees resemble the famous Chinese "serious warnings" to America. Nothing else is left but to play solitaire from three economists, but it shows a public place on the Staraya square and on unclear long road. At the very last moment, the excited President, as usual, mixes his cards.

So, for all that, if "it is impossible for us to immediately attempt to settle the matter of a state system simultaneously with land...property, finances, the army" and what other system, (perhaps the present one) can reform the army, finances, property and land relations?

f) If it is our responsibility to "prevent troubles" and "a split only that which is really inevitable", why then is Alexander Isayevich so tough and hostile in bringing disasters without waiting for people's will, discarding ones, cleaving others, touching the third, ignoring the mass exodus of the fourth and not noticing solemn declarations of the fifth? As a matter of fact, there is no doubt that he wishes Russians only good and no evil to others as well. But where is an elementary tact and caution in "preventing troubles"?

5. In this feverish mess, their exist logic and inner ideological grounds. Four such unbreakable grounds may be pointed to.

a) *Solzhenitsin's Antidemocratism*

By word of mouth the author grudgingly agrees to democracy for Russia. What else can be done: - "you cannot say that we have a wide choice: judging by the entire current of events we shall undoubtedly choose democracy". Either democracy or totalitarian tyranny. The author has to accept this. What a sigh of relief was uttered by certain liberals, with what joy did they take it! "You see? Though someone told that Solzhenitsin's devotion to authoritarianism with a touch of patriarchal character covered his longing for father tsar. Not all all". Alexander Isayevich orders the establishment of democracy after all, but not a monarchy.

First of all, and this is the main point, democracy must be without a *direct* suffrage, and without an *equal* one - with a settlement qualification not only for local elections (which is normal) but due to the four-stage election of each higher "Zemstvo" by a lower one right up to the "All-Zemstvo Assembly", - this qualification would echo up to the state top. Besides, it would be better to debar young people from "a decision of the people's destiny". Let them start voting at the age of 20 or older (that is, let students stay at home and soldiers in barracks); and be elected at 30 years of age. Or, Alexander Isayevich is thoughtfully hesitating, at 28 years? As our young people are poorly brought up, superficially educated and 'sometimes susceptible to the most irresponsible influence" (which cannot be said, we must assume, about those who are older and pensioners). No, in general, we must not allow "the insipid quantity" overweigh 'the substantial Quality". When voting we must discover the "People's Will" rather than the simple interests of the entire population consisting of "scattered individuals". Otherwise we shall fail to select the most moral, wise and most experienced people to the Duma: it would be best of all to abstain from "a general voting" and to resort to "a poll of the opinion of the wisest" as was "with mountaineers in the Caucasus" in the past. "However, there is no unquestionable method of selection as such people 'at the present time, All-Union level, so to say, Russian aksakals. Nevertheless "a certain substitute" could be found in "the highest moral instance with a deliberative vote" representing "professions and spheres of labour application", an Areopagus of the "competent", the top of the new "estates". (All this was said without a shadow of a smile). We shall not get the necessary strong power of the Head of State with universal voting. So, no, we in Russia shall not "slip down" to the "absurd" universal suffrage as Britain did since 1918".

A monarchy above and self-government similar to a village community, Zemstvo, a Cossack gathering, veche assembly, the council of the wise, etc. below? No, impossible. Another combination of authoritarianism and an ancient community system is needed, not the system which existed before the February revolution. But only "an addition of an aristocratic or even monarchical element is inevitable in a government". (See, Aristotle and landman Appenzel in Swiderland). Not a monarchy but "an addition of its element": "A mixed system".

A secret ballot is not required, "it is also not a decoration". There is no need to fear pressure and intimidation of the voters, "to relieve indirectness of a soul": vote openly fearlessly raise your hand! "There are places now on earth where they vote openly". The USSR, was such a place, where voters did not enter booths watched by KGB agents, but went directly to a ballot-box with an openness of the heart? As for a step-by-step voting system from the lowest to highest bodies, this system too was well tested in the CPSU. In local party organizations they elected delegates to a district party duma; in district ones - to a city committee and so on up to the duma plenum and political bureau of the wisest and most competent, "with an addition of an aristocratic or even monarchial element".

So, democracy, yes! - but without direct and equal suffrage and with a secret ballot. Without a rotten parliamentarism, and without parties and party electoral rolls. We shall manage it! We shall save "the county's foundations" with its tsarist and bolshevik history. Let us go back to what French people destroyed "in the revolution of 1848" and the British in the years of bolshevism's victory here. Oh, how wonderful it was before 1848!

Second, a democracy must be *without division of powers*. As it is necessary to conform to the "people's tradition", "the given people". And the *given* people do not want power, Solzhenitsin thinks, not without reason (but perhaps, using somewhat out-dated information) but do want ORDER". Strong power is required to establish order, preferably one which "does not depend on the assembly of legislators and reports back to them only after a sufficient period of time" (See G. Fedotov). "Perhaps, this is too much", Alexander Isayevich sighs in brackets.

Third, there must be not only a direct democracy *up the top*, though by no means a representative one; but, consequently, professional politicians are not needed, the very "jurocracy".

Solzhenitsin is right in reminding that a democracy is not an ideal state system, that with it problems and contradictions constantly occur. The author thoroughly selects all known arguments against the Western democracy ranging from Tocqueville's observations in the last century to the Soviet propaganda thesis that "with universal legal equality actual inequality of rich and poor remains", "the power of money bags". Here is no opportunity to enter a long and dull dispute. Yes, "injustice takes place under democracy too and swindlers can escape responsibility". There is no denying this. But only under democracy with magnificent *formal* rights (one of the best inventions of the Western society) swindlers succeed with greater difficulties and more seldom. I do not wish to repeat Churchill's citation. It is better to ask Alexander Isayevich: why could he not find a single argument against his authoritative-estate, 'combined" system vertically organized? An intellectually responsible author is obliged to point to possible weaknesses and dangers of *his own* structure as well.

Besides its (obvious even for puzzled admirers of Solzhneitsin's ideology) armchair inverted character let us notice only one thing: people, a citizen transfers his right to decide to a complicated "zemstvo" pyramid;

he cannot see who will elect whom above and in the All-Union Duma there will be persons whom he never elected, does not know and has no power to influence. Without "equalisation', without "electoral publicity", without "pluralism of ideas" but with their "absoluteness". This we have already known quite well.

So: a tradition, amicability, even "an opinion without voting", "Russian village committees through ages", and "a Cossack Assembly" and a new Zemstvo with strictly limited suffrage, without judicial formalism, without the "absurd" inventions of XIX and XX century democracy - that is what Solzhenitsin's "FURTHER AHEAD" means. "Further ahead"? Or further behind?

Basing on traditions of the imperial, prior to the reforms - and by the way, Soviet too, in essential aspects, Russia, this way or another, would be falling out of the modern world and towards a Utopian, retrograde and happily unfeasible ideal.

b) *Solzhenitsin's Isolationism*

Regarding this point Alexander Isayevich is much more cautious that in his publicistic works, speeches and interviews of the first years of his exile. The author neither exposes nor teaches Western society. To put aside democracy, which allegedly is primarily "filled with a sense of Christian responsibility" and now "is pressed by the dictatorship of banality, fashion and group interests". And "it knows how to deprive protests of common people of their force, to refuse their sounding outlest". And with it "money secures a real power", so that a formal right covers a preponderance of "the monetary aristocracy" as we have already heard. "We are entering democracy not at its best time" (i.e. it was more developed and attractive in the last century, but still better - in ancient Athens). Additionally, parliamentary intrigues, lobbyism, "the rule of mediocracy", a fruitless struggle of parties, "liquid manure" of pop music, everything which is "foreingly attractive" for our young people, etc. Certain points in all this are right, of course, though strikingly banal; we could even add something to his: nowhere else such a passionate criticism of painful aspects and problems of Western life is heard so strongly as in the West; because the West has been living through crisis already for four centuries; crisis is a permanent and normal form of historical development and uninterrupted self-formation for it. Besides, others of Solzhenitsin's superficial remarks are wrong. And, perhaps, we are entering democracy, if we are, just at the time of its maturity and amazing achievements.

Solzhenitsin, however, utters words of approval about Germany, not the late "GDR", of course, but Western Germany. It 'was filled with a could of repentance" which was followed by "an economic prosperity". Likewise about a hard-working moral of the Japanese, and eve about useful details of the American state system. He reminds us of incomparably high standards of life. He thinks that "from the above-mentioned critical remarks it by no means appears that democracy is not needed by the future Russian Union, "*needed*". And the author is simply thrilled with the Swiss municipal government because, as we already know, he cherishes a direct democracy, "a democracy of small space", above all.

So, there is none of the anathematizing of the Western civilisation, in many cases traditional for Russian village writers since the last century. Though we cannot avoid *which* "democracy" to be "needed badly" by Alexander Isayevich and suitable for Russia in his opinion without "competitive publicity", an egg without a yolk.

There is the problem of modernization of our economy. Solzhenitsin demands "a moderate private property" above all for peasantry, as well as "a healthy, clever, honest trade"; a support for small enterprises; anti-monopoly laws which would make "unrestrained concentration of capital" impossible. But no modern country can be a country of only small owners (plus a large-scale state property) of which Solzhenitsin seems to be dreaming also in old time haze; - or as "Muravia", the main character in Tvardovsky's poem. Alexander Isayevich is prepared. Let banks also operate but without credit rates of interest ("usurious surpluses"). Let firms exist, but without ever throwing new kinds of goods, improved models on the market, without "a direct lechery" of competition, struggle for consumers' preferences. Let there be a private trade - but without "the pressure of mercenariness!". And let there be private property, but "we must not allow property pressure". So, in the opinion of Alexander Isayevich, Russia will be able to achieve "a qualitative balance with the developed countries" not only without *their* democracy but without their *capitalism*, - something morally unattractive.

An important element of this patriarchal Utopia is not to allow "a foreign capital" to acquire from us real estate, lands, mines, oil-wells, "especially forests". Though, in this case, forests would not be exterminated, timber would be processed three times more effectively. Gas torches would not be burning, oil would not be extracted predatorily without complete exploitation of oil-wells, etc.

And millions of wasted and cluttered up acres of land would provide food to Russia. It goes without saying that there is no need to object against "a strict channel of laws which would regulate the activity of foreign capital which not a single Western country refuses; but it would be ridiculous to expect "an economic enlivening introduced by it" simultaneously having deprived it of "high profits".

Solzhenitsin would like to make omelets without breaking eggs.

Some day reality would be so, that we shall become one of the "Western" countries, like Japan or at least Brazil. We would prefer to our present-day troubles, new problems without which no society can exist. And a balance of "taking away profits" (why at the same time shouldn't we promote reinvestment in our own economy?) and much more effective use of "our natural environments". That is a balance of benefits not at a minimum level (without any profits for them and without a real "enlivening" for us) but at a dynamic and maximum level (so that both "they" and we fatten).

How it is done is known neither in Seoul, nor Bangkok, nor the States themselves, whose economy is unthinkable without foreign investments. It might happen that our grandchildren start to buy mines in South America, or forests in Canada, or land in Vermont. It is a normal business.

Here, from arguing about democracy and property, about a state system and faultless morals which we would like to show off in front of the rest of mankind, we are passing to a traditional approach: a unique road for Russia. And in many aspects it is also similar as well. And if unique then how can we measure and achieve this uniquality?

How can we object to Gorbachev who says: "not to adopt others' experience mechanically?" How can we object to Solzhenitsin as well saying "but to adopt a foreign type of economy developed there through centuries and in stages with a thoughtless imitation is also destructive"?

Similar formulas contain inner tautologies; they themselves extinguish their sense. Who would ever say that it must be done "mechanically" with a "thoughtless imitation"? An answer to such general, rhetorical words would inevitably be no more substantial...Well, *not* thoughtlessly, but wisely, *not* mechanically, but cautiously

Here an exclusively practical, specific approach is needed.

Two simple and understandable considerations are sufficient. First, the modern economy has developed such international methods, infrastructures (financial, organizational, and technological) which, operating on the world market but not on a close- provincial, autarkic one, can vary (and rather flexibly) from one country to another, from one local condition to other, remaining basically common possessions of humanity. This universality and, from the viewpoint of the technological, financial, and economic leveling role played by capital, was noticed by Marx and Engels in their "Manifesto" (they were not after all such narrow-minded and savage people as it is in fashion to try to prove nowadays, but profound observers and critics of the civilization of their time).

Second, Solzhenitsin seems to wish to build up a new Russia, including its economy and policy. But the economy is not built-up, it *shapes itself*, and a policy too in many aspects. It is sufficient for the democrats to secure a social space, openness, "formal" (neutral) in respect of all kinds of property, any honest enterprise, statutes. And then and economy will continue to develop. And such and such will be ahead in stimuli of optimal effectiveness and interests. We have already spent enough time and effort "to build up". No version of an authoritarian upbuilding after a certain *social project*, including a restoration, is realistic.

Alexander Isayevich persistently builds up his dream in all directions: economic, political, moral-aesthetic; and this is a dream of "a unique road" for Russia. However, any unique road will save us only if it is the speediest modernization which means our return to the main road of the world civilization. There is only one universal civilization in the world though: that from the depth of which we have heard Solzhenitsin's nostalgic appeals. Either together with "the West" (which is now on all the continents) or...there is no 'or" except that which we have been fed up with.

Nevertheless hasn't Russia unique conditions? And won't they prompt a unique road, its own road to a free economy and a liberal-legal state? Its own road to the West? There is no doubt that it will be so. Russia will become "Western" somehow in a different way than any other country; not like Armenia or Uzbekistan in due time. Moreover, though Siberia will do it rather differently than, say, St. Petersburg and North-West, it will be *settled* through competition of different economic forms and undertakings and through the self-development of society

Any culture is known to be the triumph of the unique, but it does not seek to be unique: this just *happens*. It is not "proud" of its originality; it does not care about such nationalistic tricks and foolishness. As a man does not need to speak and think to be a man, so the Russian culture has always been and will remain original Russian; the Georgian one - Georgian, etc.

c) *Solzhenitsin's Collectivism*

Solzhenitsin's position in this respect is a compromise. On one hand, the author often starts to speak about "a healthy private initiative": private property, "not suppressing others" but providing "a stabilization of a personality", about the necessity to have "private paid schools going ahead of the general rise of the entire school system". He welcomes "all the good in the West: civil unrestriction, self-esteem, variety of personal activity".

"Fashionable" human rights sound good, but "we ourselves should watch our rights not broadened at the expense of others". It has been known for two hundred years that individual freedom has limits in nothing but itself, i.e. in the freedom of another. To watch *ourselves* is realistic only in a social sense when it is watched also be a legal state and serves precisely this cause. It is evidently too early in our country to speak about human rights except with irony and certain disdain. However, Solzhenitsin is worried beforehand that "human rights" may mean "a freedom to seize and feed themselves", and will bring us to the level of animals.

Solzhenitsin and human rights defenders seem to spread different languages. Why to mention "a freedom to seize"? Why "all the ruling classes and groups of history", as if not every man is concerned, but only "the ruling classes". It smells of the criticism of capitalism (legal equality hand in hand with inevitable poverty inequality) traditional for people from Slavophiles to leninists. And side by side with "an esteem for a personality we find in Solzhenitsin's work attacks against "the capital city's intellectuals" for whom freedom of speech, press and emigration are dear but who would allegedly be ready to prohibit "rights" as they are "understood by common people" and to maintain "passport registration". As if it is not in a single package and rights defenders did not demand a freedom of transportation both *beyond* the country's frontiers and *inside* the country. But Solzhenitsin (like the majority of the Congress of People's Deputies) is suspicious of "the Moscow influential public" who having been depraved with a special supply of the capital city, "for decades did not express real pains of the country". Well, are they expressing it now?

"However human rights must not be raised so high not to push society rights into the background".

We have heard it for seventy years and seen that "society rights" in *contrast* to individualism is a deceit, and that somebody inevitably takes the liberty to speak on behalf of "society", "people" or the "nation", thus suppressing a personality under this resounding pretext. That id danger, either ecological or war would occur, it is nothing the case when everyone's interests must coincide. When they say "a society" they mean the state, i.e. interests of the rulers. If it is truly a society, then why is A.I. Solzhenitsin opposed to the "equalizing" of civil individuals, against universal and equal suffrage; and if it is truly society as a whole, then how does one explain (with the dislike of the "intellectual pseudo-elite") corporativism, "an addition of monarchical and aristocratic elements", divided into the wise and worthy and "common People", perhaps?

Alexander Isayevich is hesitating. A. Stolypin well-to-do peasant free also from "the community" is before his mental eye. But the village "community" was splendid too. A personality, yes, but also an assembly and an order. In addition to this: responsibilities must have priority over rights, a strong state, self-restriction, singularity of ideas and deeds, submission of a personality to society are needed as well as 'an absolute character of the notions of the Good and the Evil".

No, no it is not a bolshevik submission of the right to proletarian justice, not an absolute character of Lenin's only true teaching for a personality where there is Good and where there is Evil: not the party assembly of the best, not the priority of responsibilities cultivated in children's minds since kindergarten age, not 'a self-discipline" demanded from a communist ("a conscious discipline"). not a distrust of the partocratic mob towards intellectuals, in a word, *not this* "collectivism" that Solzhenitsin desires, except for God. He is mortally hating it and has served its approaching destruction.

But he would wish *quite another* collectivism, Christian, patriarchal, traditional, and peacefully hierarchic.

That old, ages-long Russian tradition which was broken but served to a considerable extent as a historic ground for *this*...

d) *Solzhenitsin's Moral Didactism*

"Such is a man" in the predominance of the national self-esteem over other human interests - Alexander Isayevich is both grieving and not opposing; well, shall we in fact oppose the nature of a man? It is local. "A man is nationalistic. Caius is human, consequently he is nationalistic", how they have been writing in manuals since the time of Aristotle.

And in addition: "to purse his interests is always human". That is absolutely true. But this time Solzhenitsin does not wish to submit. A man is such, O.K., but he nevertheless must become different.

How? Self-improvement is the whole thing. "If there is no justice and no honesty in people themselves, then it will come out in each system. But it would seem that from this, another irrefutable consideration, it does not follow that a good man is good under totalitarianism and a bad man is bad even under Western democracy with the reservation that in "capitalist enterprises" there are no "thieves" and under socialism "thieves' are not bad people, as the entire nation is "a thief").

It would seem that every man should be left with his conscience and we should discuss in which political system and which social-legal and economic relations a man is prevented less from self-improvement, with which Solzhenitsin's booklet is dealing, after all.

But all of a sudden "a state system is more secondary than the very air of human relations". "With people's generosity any honest system is permissible, with people's animosity and self-seeking even the most resounding democracy is unbearable".

Is it a slip of the tongue/ Didn't Alexander Isayevich want to say "any dishonest system is permissible"? Yes, really, and if *dis*honest? Otherwise logic turns out to be not Aristotle's but as in a joke: "It's better to be rich and healthy than poor *but* ill".

Solzhenitsin writes another similar idea: "Purity of social relations is more important than a level of abundance". "A stable society can be reached not with an equality of resistance (i.e. not with a system of power division and constitutional counterbalance), but with a conscious self-restriction with fact that we must always yield to moral justice".

These are moral, well-meant considerations. However, each person may have his own "justice" as he understands it (in contrast to a system and a law), or what will be decided by a Zemstvo assembly? but how can a new man be born in Russia and the moral code of Zemstvo's upbuilding be observed?

A.I. Solzhenitsin's understanding is this: justice is just a minimum of morality, its lowest grade or level". A moral aspect must stand above a legal one. Justice a correspondence first with a moral right and later with "a legal one". It is amazing! Consequently I may ignore observance of the law if it does not correspond with my inner sense of justice. "Self-consciousness" whether revolutionary or splendour is above the law.

Such was the custom in Russia since ancient times where there was one law for the rich, another for the poor, always foreign, hostile, forced, hard to understand, where a slave was dodging in order to feed his little children. You cannot sell without cheating, but, at least, it was understandable that it (to cheat when selling) was unfair, against one's conscience. But to unscrew a nut from a railway track for a plummet - in a famous Chekhov's story - what is unfair in it? It never occurred to the man.

The same was in the Soviet Russia - ones pressed for the sake of a class justice, others dodged as they could against "the Law" foreign to them, for the sake of *their* justice.

Here is a very "Russian" (i.e. forced on Russians by history), arrangement of Solzhenitsin's consciousness! But how many of us have a different on?

Suppose, we are honest, suppose, we are noble, accustomed and know: in reply to "passport registration" there comes a fake marriage, and it is fair, after all! IN reply to "sanitary norms of living space" or the impossibility of parents leaving a flat to their children, a fake registration; in reply to the prohibition of "jobs combining" we got "unauthorized work, foolish plans sent down from the top" resulted in upward distortions in reports. And so on, and so forth. There was no legal *freedom* in Russia on people were escaping to join Cossacks, to Siberia, to robber gangs. There were always lots of superiors per capita - well, to deceive someone of them was a nice job. And we never used rights but talked about them. And all this is quite perfectly fair, really and truly, the only saving!

I reread Solzhenitsin's booklet thinking: why there are consistency and whole-heartedness in utter alogisms" Why are platitudes expressed with enthusiasm? Why does a weak, generally speaking, text bear a reflection of something strong?

Because it is a reflection of a sufficiently large mass consciousness. All of us are a little bit Solzhenitsins, though without his talent.

Consider Alexander Solzhenitsin a mirror of the Russian evolution, or be more precise: tsarist and Soviet ones.

I can only repeat that all four bases of Solzhenitsin's ideology are reliably interwoven. What is characteristic of Solzhenitsin is that he does not distinguish among a moral - a law, justice, and morality - putting them instead in the same semantic rank: he is either making them synonymous or having them oppose each other in the same rank.

However: *law,* regulating the outer world of human relations is not the lowest, minimum "justice"; it is simply a different notion. Law is senseless if it is not formal; and it, of course is "unjust" in its essence using the same yard stick to knowingly different people;

Justice may be understood as an inner measure of morality; this measure is felt by public opinion or an individual, and in most cases this is justice from the viewpoint of a certain social group or a system of values.

A *moral* is a generally accepted (often also within a given group, nationality, etc., always historically concrete) rule of behavior in more of less standard situations; or in extreme situations when a necessity of prohibition is evident; this is a system of prohibitions, above all;

and finally *morality* is a notion which it would be wise to leave for the depths of inner and individual world of a personality facing a complicated, sometimes painful choice.

We can and must work out and fix by parliamentary procedures a law defending the freedoms of a man limited by the same freedoms and needs of another; we can mutually work out and apply to certain cases a sense of justice' we can read morals, a part of which is evidently justice. It is impossible, however, to establish morality from the outside; the entire sense and value of which is that it is wholly a matter of this personality, his heart, his free will for which he is fully accountable to himself. (For a believer, it is a conversation with God).

6. Coming back from abstract matters to the topic of the day, we can only be surprises with what a keen insight and, what is most important, in what a timely fashion Solzhenitsin's ideas were made public.

He just said that Tatars, or course, had to be allowed to return to the Crimea but "the hundred-thousand-strong (?) Tatar people could not demand possession" of the Crimea (as if they demand the whole Crimea for themselves), and immediately authorities were forced to send militia to Yalta and other places where Tatars were being beaten. And the phrase of A.I. Solzhenitsin cannot seem to be innocent.

As soon as he spoke in favour of Presidential elections at the Congress (that is to say, all the All-Zemstvo Assembly) granting him "strong powers", maybe "independent of the Council of Legislators - and the Supreme Soviet, though with already diminished authorities[1], obediently gave the President "additional" power to interfere with economy. Again the feasible idea of Alexander Isayevich does not look harmless and abstract.

As soon as he made a disdainful remark about the "uselessness" of the UNO, this remarkable organization manifested its unprecedented effectiveness by giving a rebuff to the "Arab Hitler", a cunningly crazy Saddam Husein.

As soon as he declared that foreigners must be by no means permitted to buy real estate, Czechoslovakia (seeming to have much more land) canceled the previous socialist limitations in this respect making us think hard.

As soon as he appealed to Ukrainians to purse that, together with Russians and Byelorussians, they are a part of a single people and they had to stay in the Russian Union - the Ukraine stirred with demands of a sovereignty in October.

As soon as he rejected the formation of parties as *not our* invention, "screening the national interest" and "distorting people's will". Moreover, "with its own existence rejecting the unity of a nation and the very notion of Motherland" (one feels terrified for the whole world except North Korea, Iraq, Iran and other countries where Motherland is still out of danger. Alexander Isayevich writes that "a society is alive precisely with its dif-

---

[1] In accordance with the USSR Constituion the USSR Supreme Soviet is to be annually renewed by 1/5 of its number (a rotation principle). The present body was elected 16 *months* agao but there was no rotation. It means that the USSR Supreme Soviet is incompetent since June 1990.

ferentiation", "an organization in social groups", though strictly in professional "estates"). Immediately constituent congresses of Russian parties started and it became painfully evident just how much Russia is short of precise "movements" or "a front" which would unite democrats and would have enough force to challenge district and regional committees of the CPSU and RCP in the entire country.

It is of no use to speak about instigating declarations in respect of Kazakhstan and Moldavia with any good intentions of Alexander Isayevich.

However, isn't it funny to take seriously and practically, considerations modestly submitted for preliminary discussion by no more than a writer, a private person, an exile and not by the government of the CPSU Central Committee? It is not at all funny if this writer is Solzhenitsin whose voice here now has greater authority and influence upon human minds than that of the government (who on earth is listening to the government and is interested in the plenums of the Central Committee), and if the public weight of this private person is heavier than that of Tolstoy, Dostoyevsky and Nekrasov together in their time, and if his considerations are published in newspapers in such a volume which has been previously provided only for reports and resolutions of the Central Committee itself.

The publication in major part enthusiastically received in the USSR by both "the right wing" and "the left wing" is an ideological event which must be treated practically and seriously.

In the course of five years, the Vermont hermit kept a mysteriously significant silence, letting his supporters and opponents argue about what his real views are on what is going on in Russia. At last he has spoken, and arguments exploded with a new force.

Some people are moved by the fact that Alexander "Isayevich did not forget Russia, that he is still suffering for it and still considering himself to be one of "us", being a Russian writer. This is insulting to Solzhenitsin: as every political emigree or exile, for anyone thinking and writing in Russian, it is absurd and insulting.

Others find a pretext for satisfaction that Solzhenitsin made new attacks on the KBG or, say, the kolkhoz-state-farm system or treated the Polozkov's party with disgust. Here even the ideas repeated by Solzhenitsin will not give more credence to what is undeniable; in this instance statements against the KGB and certain of its officers, and certain chairmen of kolkhozes against kolkhozes are more significant and interesting.

Still others are glad that Solzhenitsin (an admirer of Stolypin, in fact!) called to restore the private property of peasants; that he considers monarch unnecessary for Russia, that he delves into the past while referring to the present, that he accepts usefulness of the law and democracy, while suggesting the most essential limitations and introducing them into a particular non-democratic overly legal context. They take out "good", liberal, fitting phrases, and with hesitation, call phrases nonliberal, categorical and sharp to be lame and distressing deviations of Solzhenitsin from the correct positions. However, wouldn't it be better to take the text as a whole, and to consider it systematically?

It will not be of help that Solzhenitsin himself tried to smooth over certain corners - to make the text more familiar to liberal intellectuals, to display *a tactical caution*. Whatever it may be, we face a very Solzhenitsin-like text, a single one in coloring; a bold, emotional document.

It is sad to argue with the person whose figure, after the death of Andrei Dmitiyevich Sakharov, is beyond comparison in the Soviet dissident movement, in the Russian public opinion.

Furious Solzhenitsin has always been in the alienation of all that is hatefully Soviet; the author of "The Archipelago" has been great in his repudiation. It was with eagerness and sympathy that we have been harking to speeches, the temperament and style of which have recalled the correspondence of Prince Kurbsky with Ivan the terrible.

However, the retrograde character of Solzhenitsin's positive views did distress us even then. Today when a direct road has been opened from words to deeds this, combined with Solzhenitsin's authority makes his pamphlet in its general concept, ideas, important details - rather harmful for the cause of Russian liberty. We are now on the bottom of a deep ditch - like Joseph the Beautiful. For what purpose must Joseph use his strength, having found himself there and facing extreme danger? I think that only tow purposes do exist for it.

Either to think about lofty things, to work for the intransient, and for people of culture, to attend to their direct purpose. Because Russian culture has existed and will continue to exist in the future, and Russia with it. It is sufficient to care for the creation of new values, a s people of culture did in 1918 and the years that followed. But then - in order that a text will live in the future as well - it must be polysemantic; difficult to exhaust in its sense, rich with tints of thinking, keenly comprehending the fathomlessness of the moment we are living in. It is an appropriate occupation for Joseph. Think about how to get out from the ditch, call to a caravan of merchants passing by.

In our present wretched situation, in an agony of the system we need culture because it is always needed. We need politics, the most practical one seeking no slogans, general reasoning, nor bold protests, we had them enough, but a technology of a new power, a new economy. We need honest and competent figures, manager, financial people, politicians, we need philosophers, we need poets.

Here are two necessary poles; cultural and social pragmatism, lofty thinking and day's work. But a situation is different when one is sitting in a ditch having neither time, nor force, nor right. And, generally speaking, with what fills a space between these two poles producing a magnetic field? It is filled with ideology, and it is an excessive luxury and expenditure of our last intellectual forces and will power. Which ideology? In my opinion - any one: Communist, nationalist, antiquated, newly invented - any ideology, any though most with sincere rhetoric and reverie. I would not wish one illusion to be replaced with opposite ones, our country turning around in one place with everything repeating as in a bad dream. But I think - *all the same* nothing will come of it, nothing will come true.

And if something does come true? How can we allow otherwise? How can history stop? How can it not be? Then a unique Russia will appear which will differ from others: no more, but not at all less than the USA from Japan, Italy from Sweden, Canada from Singapore.

ON THE CONSTITUTION PROJECT OF ANDREI SAKHAROV

At first reading, the project gives rise to astonishment by the very fact of its existence. Not as certain theses and remarks on the text of the future document, but precisely in the form of such a text: forty-six articles of the draft Constitution. And all was done by a single man in such a way understanding his duties as a member of a large commission elected by the First Congress of People's Deputies of the USSR to work out a new Soviet Constitution. As for ourselves we have even forgotten that such a commission exist.

In fact, what could be done by such a commission, perhaps the most important of all committees and commissions created by the Congress? For half a year it was never summoned. Only after this unheard of scandal was revealed at one of the latest sittings of the second session of the Supreme Soviet of the USSR, the Constitution commission was nevertheless convened in haste and it adopted an original and useful decision: at last it would start the work it was destined for.

Still at the First congress, A.D. Sakharov insisted that construction of a house cannot be started from the roof. It is inconceivable to indulge oneself in law-making at random, moving with small steps from one law or enactment to another and repeatedly running across its unclarified legal and social coordination, independency without preliminary determination of their *system*. It is like conducting experiments and insisting on the significance of the results without any general theory. A physicist whom Sakharov had brought into politics, his experience of pragmatic correlation of theory and practice, considered it necessary *to proceed* from a new constitution; from a fundamental transformation of principles and norms concerning the essence of our social system. Possessing a certain master plan, the principle basis would be to strive for legal details, corroboration, realisation of the *basis* which we would agree to use as a foundation of the future Soviet life. Therefore Sakharov's very first motion in the parliament was the "Decree On Power". In his opinion, the main proposition to be adopted in the first instance, would be not a bit groundless or artificial. This main point was sufficiently well proved by the world and (though in a negative sense) by our national history: the entire painful, disgraceful past and present was confirmed by the tremendous upsurge following March 1989, by the total crisis of the "real Socialism" and developing revolutionary situation.

On the contrary, Sakharov's official opponents considered that as long as life is impossible to change "in a single night" (with which A.D. Sakharov agreed, of course), they must proceed, not to a still unimaginable new Constitution, but it should be reached with extreme gradualness and caution. Laws must be changed in part, bit by bit, so that by using a series of limited stabilizing innovations to crawl out of the economic ditch and to prepare the population (but mostly, of course, it is the impenitent leadership of the ruling party who should be treated with utmost caution) for the future constitutional choice. And which particular choice, whether really radical and to what an extent, time will tell. First let the situation improve, the CPSU modernize and M.S. Gorbachev consolidate his power. It is no wonder that with the chosen political line (indeterminate reformism of the right-wing kind) there was no time for meetings of the Constitution commission.

The Supreme Soviet could see with their own eyes that adoption of any law legally impedes the contents of subsequent laws, to say nothing of the fact that any important and desirable law differs with a worthless constitution from the beginning to the end. Deputies found themselves in alogical and political impasse.

It so happened that the Brezhnev Constitution can be referred to if there is need: they say we should not start by violating not yet abrogated constitutional provisions when beginning to build up a "legal state". It is possible, also id it pays, to spit upon the Constitution, even upon its freshest amendments. For example, the Supreme Soviet now has the right to adopt and immediately put into action an unconstitutional laws without waiting for the nearest Congress where it would require a two thirds vote. And what will happen if the Congress disagrees with the Supreme Soviet as was the case in the past? Will people trust fundamental laws adopted and enacted but not yet approved and remaining undecided? The situation is dubious both from legal and political points of view.

Recently, the Extraordinary Congress made a regular amendment to the Constitution about the President and the order of this election by the people, and at the same time considered it possible to ignore this order in the first instance; i.e. proclamation of a constitutional norm is accompanied by its legislative cancellation. This, if I am not mistaken, has no precedent in the world, and is remarkable in its way. Of course, it is possible to interpret this as a step forward towards a "legal state" in this way.

At the time of setting up the Committee of the Constitution Supervision, solemn assertions were heard from the rostrum that the said Committee would try by no means to protest but would, in every possible way, favor reforming of the acting Fundamental Law. Consequently do they intend to wink at its transformational infringements? Or they will nevertheless be forced to protect the dead, false letter till its abrogation? Or will they start acting...depending on the circumstances? As was put by one esteemed deputy, simply high merits and progressiveness of the members of the Constitution Supervision will finally serve as a guarantee of the right actions of the Committee. There is no denying, it is a remarkable guarantee but, alas, the only one and not legal due to the lack, in addition to a personal sense of justice, of anything else to lean on. I think that in the entire history of humanity, including the post-revolutionary destinies of 1918, there was no legal body more mysterious than this Committee bound to supervise the inviolability of a practically nonexistent Constitution.

It goes without saying, however, that the historic events of the recent months have exerted far more considerable influence than the formal, legal absurdity of the attempts to change property relations, a political system and so on, while keeping intact the Brezhnev-Suslov Fundamental Law: the break-up of the "socialist camp", communist parties and regimes in Eastern Europe happened with overwhelming rapidity, indignation in the USSR with Clause 6 of the Constitution, nation-wide demands of parliamentary mulitparty system, the necessity of saving the Soviet economy. And, at last, openly revealed disorganization of the national state system forced M.S. Gorbachev to declare in Lithuania that "we have not yet lived in a federation". This means that the very name of the "USSR" is a misnomer; there is neither a "union of republics" nor republics as 'sovereign socialist states".

To make a long story short, everything has confirmed an absolute need to begin perestroika anew five years after: with the roots of the system, with liquidation of the patriarchy, with the separation of the state from the economy. To begin this time with the foundation instead of the roof, i.e. again from the Constitution in political and legal aspects.

That is why they had to specify and promise that the country would get the new Constitution in 1990. A.D. Sakharov, once more forestalling the event in May-June 1989, was right again! He was right from the viewpoint of the most realistic policy.

Sakharov's conception of the inseparable connection of human rights and peace on earth, the survival of humanity and the openness of each separate society was considered to be at best starry-eyed, naive reasoning having little in common with political reality. Today it has been declared here a state course and called a "new thinking". Sakharov's demands to stop the Soviet aggression in Afghanistan, or, say, to restore statehood of the Crimean Tatars, or to secure a free exit of citizens and their return into the USSR, and so on, were regarded by even sympathizing liberally minded people as difficult to realize or unrealizable at all still three or four years ago. Nowadays these and other similar demands have come true or seem to be close to realization, or in any case are what is called "put on the agenda by the life itself". They are discussed by the government, are appearing in newspapers and sound commonplace.

So, perhaps, Sakharov's constitutional ideas as well are a basic working document rather than abstract fantasies, good intentions, more than a simple "inspiring banner"?

Having studied it critically and later having the honour to spend a few hours with Andrei Dimitryevich discussing clause after clause, I came to the conclusion that is precisely so. Sakharov's draft is full of responsibility, it is constructive and most important it is practical.

Of course, it has not been completed. Perhaps we can find in it roughness in sense or style, it also lacks certain sections: for example, on the order of elections, ways to settle possible conflicts between two legislative chambers, on a more concrete mechanism and term for placing and overriding the President's veto (Clause 36), on the character of a Congressional control over the Central bank and the degree of independence of the latter, excluding the emission of money (Clause 31). When and how are the Congresses to be convened? Can the President, and if so, under what circumstances, dissolve the Congress and fix the day for new elections? Do the two chambers have permanent speakers (chairmen)? What are the composition, number and manner of work of the Presidium of the Congress, if any is needed at all? (Clause 32). Is it necessary to provide in a constitutional way, terms and conditions for declaring an emergency state and the status of presidential governing in districts of calamities or conflicts? Why is the qualifying majority for removal of the President's veto exactly 55%? (Clause 36).

Sections on the army are insufficient. There is nothing about local self-government, too little about a judicial system and nothing about local self-government, too little about a judicial system and nothing about legal proceedings (Clauses 9, 23, 34). Complete independence of the judicial power has not been legalized, and the status and powers of the Constitutional Court have not been developed.

Perhaps, other sides and wording of the Sakharov draft will cause questions, proposals, requirements to work out details. And others will arouse principal objections and disputes; this is natural and unavoidable.

Andrei Dmitiyevich continued his work on the text of the Constitution literally until the last hour of his life. However, the unfinished state of the Sakharov draft is relative and affects, in my opinion, only minor details of procedure and protocol (however even "minor" things are impor tant in the Constitution). AT the same time A.D. Sakharov in the main succeed to finish the draft and left us his views on the optimal future of the country.

I would like to:

1). Express certain observations on the paradoxical character of the very task of writing the Constitution for a not yet existing society so much unlike the present one. From this viewpoint certain expressive features of Sakharov text are interesting in which urgent, near and infinitely remote, potential historic plans seem to be coexisting. There are two realities: the present and the future.

2) Accordingly as to how the draft constitution of A.D. Sakharov is connected with an absolutely concrete situation in the Soviet and East-European societies in the fall of 1989, and not to a lesser degree adjusted to the large-scale results of the XXth century as a whole; an alloy of the specifically local political with that of the world-history.

3) In brief to record the structure and ideas of Sakharov's Constitution.

4) As was already mentioned, the draft was published in two versions (with minor variations). I have to substantiate why one of them should be considered more mature and what are the motives for the changes made by A.D. Sakharov in the initial version.

After midnight of November 21 - 22, 1989, at a quarter to 1 a.m. I was roused from bed by a phone call of Andrei Dmitrivevich. I must say that it was the first time that Andrei Dmitriyevich had called so late. As usual, without empty introductory "polite" words, he began: "how do you consider the situation in the Interregional group? The situation in the country before the Congress? In general, what in your opinion, is going on?" His voice was very fresh, quick, perhaps, even unusually elated.

I was taken aback. My sleep flew away in the blink of an eye. I was speaking for several minutes. Then A.D. Sakharov said: "I have prepared a draft Constitution. Could you read it and make your remarks?" So, this was the real cause of the midnight call! "Of course, Andrei Dmitiyevich, but how urgent is it? I am going on a mission in three days and my report is not yet ready". He answered firmly: "Tomorrow morning I shall send you the text with my driver. And we shall meet the day after tomorrow". It became clear that A.D. Sakharov attached particularly great importance to the speedy completion of the draft. Therefore the above mentioned conversation seems worthy of mentioning.

The text received by me I the morning (11 typewritten pages, 45 clauses) was (absolutely word for word) the same which would appear on December 22 in the "Novoye Vryemya" magazine (No. 52) printed from a manuscript after his death. So, having retyped this initial text, A.D. Sakharov began to share it with a certain circle of people ant to make amendments and revisions. On November 23 I arrived at this home at 3 p.m. sharp saying there until 7:30 p.m. The major part of this conversation was dedicated to the analysis of the draft Constitution.

I remember only two distractions. In one instance Andrei Dmitriyevich spoke with great vivacity about the precise meaning of the term "exploitation" used by Marx in the "Capital" in connection with surplus value. To what extent does the rational meaning of this notion increase, if it exists in general, with regard to the Soviet state-owned economic production. On the second occasion I asked him to explain in what way and under what conditions (from both organizational and technical points of view) belying intercontinental rockets can be destroyed with a central signal. (By the way, the word in "The Commander-in-Chief has the right to cancel a nuclear attack started in error" definitely contains a slip of the pen; it should read: "The Commander-in-Chief must cancel...etc."; Andrei Dmitriyevich agreed with this but the initial wording nevertheless remained in the final version by an oversight.

Andrei Dmitriyevich, lying on an ottoman in his favorite posture on his side, leaning on his left arm, was taking notes with his right hand. He changed certain things at once without hesitation or commentaries. Certain proposals were reflected with the same determination but usually without discussion, thinking to himself and clearly disagreeing (I shall mention below a few such moments). At last, certain themes which, in his mind, were not sufficiently convincing and clear left for further thought. There seemed to remain quite a number of such difficult themes.

The only publication of the draft made when he was alive and consequently the only authorized one (the "Komsomolyskaya pravda" newspaper, Vilnius, December 12, 1989) contains all the changes and alterations made by A.D. Sakharov on November 23. I remember well the motives and considerations on which new wordings were based. In the draft's essence these changes and alterations affected nothing.

Changes of 23 out of 45 clauses of the initial text were included in the new version; two more clauses were merged an another one was divided in two; an additional clause was introduced. If I am not mistaken, there are twenty-six versions in all. They are aimed at a growing sovereignty of republics, making the political system more stable and efficient and the economic system more versatile and flexible.

Why Andrei Dmitriyevich was in such a hurry at that time at the end of November to polish the text of the document became clear to me only recently from the worlds of Yelena Georgiyevna. November 27 had been chosen for that first meeting of the Constitution Commission under the chairmanship of M.S. Gorbachev, though with a delay of almost half a year. In any case, at least one of the Commission's members prepared himself. On November 27, 1989, Andrei Dmitriyevich submitted his draft of the future Conception of the Soviet Union to M. Gorbachev.

A new country must bear a new name. A.D. Sakharov successfully availed himself of he well-known formula of Lenin who wrote abut the Union of Republics of Europe and Asia. But the meaning of the formula has been strikingly changed. After the victory in the Civil War Lenin expected the development of the world revolution ranging from Europe to India and China. The Soviet Union seemed to him, like to all the bolsheviks, as a matter of act, to be the first form the :bourgeoisie" springboard of such a revolution to which new countries would join later. Russia, which had set the world on fire, would ultimately become a rather modest part of a gigantic commonwealth which would include both the most numerous nations of the Orient and Western countries far more advanced than Russia.

Instead of the revolutionist pathos of the old Lenin formula, the conception of the "European-Asian Union" implies the synthesis of "moral and cultural traditions of Europe and Asia" in addition to the evident geopolitical fact. A.D. Sakharov also says: "...the entire humanity, all races and peoples" (Clause 3). Clause 2 proclaims "prosperity, peace and security for all people on earth (this and below has been underlined by the author) to be the aim of the people of the "Union of Soviet Republics of Europe and Asia". Clause 12 particularly emphasizes that the "union has no aims of expansion, aggression and Messianism".

Thus, our county will never attain aspire to play the role of saviour and benefactor of the rest of the world. A political Messianism of any kind (bolshevik, Orthodox-chauvinistic, Islam-fundamentalist, etc.) is prohibited by the Constitution. Consequently, nobody would fear that the Soviet state will impose its ideology or way of life again.

The "Earth" with a capital letter and the "Earth as a whole" are mentioned in A.D. Sakharov's draft also for the second time in Clause 4 which reads: "The global aims of survival of humanity have the priority before any regional, state, national, class, party, group and personal aims". Never before was this idea written in the constitution of any country of the world. Of course, now that it has enjoyed the widest international acclaim, it sounds almost trivial but hardly anybody else but Sakharov contributed so much for this. The "priority" of values common for all mankind was interpreted by Andrei Dmitriyevich in a positive way: as a necessity in the name of survival the "harmonizing of economic, social and political development in the whole world". And "harmonization" could mean but one thing, what A.D. Sakharov called "convergence" twenty years before, the idea which he considered the most important to himself.

I suggested that Andrei Dmitriyevich should exclude the word "convergence" put in brackets in the text of Clause 4 because, first, its meaning is described in detail in the whole phrase ("mutual pluralistic rapprochement of the socialist and capitalist systems"). Second, a foreign term sounds strange and unintelligible for the majority of Soviet citizens; third, too many ideological misinterpretations surround it. Finally, the Constitution seems to have no reason to mention the "capitalist and socialist systems". Different people may understand differently what "capitalism": and "socialism" are; the latter in particular sounds hardly comforting for the majority of people given the last 72 years. It is rather a cabalistic sign. The Constitution may and must fix only what can be fixed legally: civil, state judicial and other forms (institutions, procedures) which have a normative character for the population of a country regardless of a "social system" i.e. mobile and concrete filling of these forms which depends already on circumstances, traditions, historic struggle within the framework of the Constitution. A law is not restricted tot he "reflection" of group interest but it defends the interests of each group from one other; in short, it creates a formalized, neutral field of community where eternally colliding living interests of people are balanced, brought to a compromise, and wisely limited with. The Constitution must only secure for the people an opportunity to make a "system" to arrange social relations to their taste, as a case may be, without violation of the law.

However, Andrei Dmitriyevich, listening with much attention, remained adhered to is own opinion. Evidently he believed that "mutual pluralistic rapprochement" did not sufficiently express the most complex process of paradoxical transformation. A.D. Sakharov was convinced that having started with the most modest cooperation ("rapprochement") eventually one effective and secure "system" - with all local diversity - will appear on Earth somewhere, and it will be difficult to consider it "capitalist" of "socialist". The world "convergence" polysemantically determined this entire process, both long and urgent, including momentary small political steps and the future of all humanity. For A.D. Sakharov "convergence" contained Alpha and Omega, micro- and macrolevels of "survival".

As for the terms "socialist", etc., A.D. Sakharov paid little attention to their theoretical meaning. I should emphasize it time and again that A.D. Sakharov was a realist and a pragmatist. Two entirely different social systems and military-political blocs do exist, and it is evident that their extreme difference will leave its imprint on the world community for many years to come.

I must add that Sakharov's "convergence" also opposes the Khrushchev-Brezhnev "competition of the two systems" though "peaceful". That means two identical, impervious and fighting "camps" (true, wisely "cooperating" but following the same economics, ideology and propaganda, save, perhaps that of military struggle). A.D. Sakharov's Constitution radically rejects and, more than that, prohibits this habitual, stupid confrontation with the "capitalist system" as threatening to humanity and our own survival.

And until this constitutional and moral norm does not come to pass; until both "systems" fear each other and keep nuclear weapons in readiness, A.D. Sakharov thinks it obligatory for the first time to introduce in the Constitution not only the principle of the "defensive sufficiency" (Clause 12) but also an extensive Clause 13 describing principles and rules minimizing the threat to use nuclear weapon.

So, Clauses 2, 3, 4, two final phrases of Clause 5 as well as Clause 12, 13 and the final phrase of Clause 14 form the basis of the Constitution of the Soviet Union and establish it as a member of a peaceful world Community. This is the first, initial idea of the project.

The second initial ideal of the Constitution necessarily process from A.D. Sakharov's globalist, all-humanity principle. To be more exact the idea is two in one. The rights of an individual man come first and above all in Sakharov's neo-European hierarchy of values (of course, not intended by him but wholly perceived by his mind and heart) with all the other rights ensuing: national (as inalienable from an individual), social group rights, collective in gnarl, up to "the interests of the society in whole" (as belonging to an individual and consequently to individual's associations of different character as well). Any collective right is, on the one side, one of the rights of an individual as a member of this collective; on the other, a collective right limits the rights of an individual with the same rights of another member of this group; and finally, it coordinates the rights of individuals belonging to different groups. All the groups (nationalities, social groups, religions, etc.) are equal, as all the individuals belonging to them are born equal. And any national group affiliation is apart of an individual, one suitably or freely chose by him.

Sakharov's Constitution fully dedicates Clauses 5 - 11, 41 and indirectly also Clauses 2, 14, 37-40, 42 to human rights. With all this, Andrei Dmitriyevich gives a scrupulous list of personal freedoms noted in the Western world, socio-economic rights of an individual usually emphasized in our country, rights connected with the disposing of his labor, ("physical and intellectual working abilities") and finally property rights and rights of succession. Reference to the "UNO General Declaration of Human Rights", Human Rights Pacts" and other international treaties signed by the USSR is essential as "having in the territory of the Soviet Union a direct effect and priority over the laws of the Union and republics" (Clause 5).

The third ideas that carries through the draft of A.D. Sakharov is the constitutional security of a multi-party parliamentary democracy. This idea was never clearly defined, There is, however Clause 7: The "political, cultural and ideological lives of society are based on the principles of pluralism and tolerance". "Freedom of speech and information exchange" were stipulated as well as "Freedom of associations, rallies and manifestations" (Clause 6). The activity of secret political police is prohibited in any form (Clause 14).

Also prohibited are substitution of the state power ("the entire absolute power" which is bested in the democratically elected government), interference in execution of this "higher power in the country" by the "authorities of any party" (Clause 28). In other words, the Constitution prohibits authoritative decrees or orders by the Political Bureau, Central Committee of the CPSU, a congress of this or any other party. The over-party character of the functions of the President is proclaimed. Finally, universal and direct elections to both chambers of the Congress and same elections of the President is proclaimed. Finally, universal and direct elections of the President on an alternating basis (Clauses 29, 35) as well as the entire system of prerogatives and balance of the legislative, executive and judicial powers; all this (Clauses 28-36) undoubtedly corresponds to the principles of consistent democracy, with a strong parliament and a strong president. Sakharov willingly took into consideration the world, especially the North-American experience.

At the same time, however, Andrei Dmitriyevich did not overestimate the scientific significance of precedents, fully understanding to what extent present-day conditions differ from everything that was and is in the countries of the world. This unique character of the USSR demands, when working out a Constitution, knowledge of the national notions, political imagination, and the uninhibited and intellectual ingenuity. (They are "simply clever people" as SD Sakharov used to say).

Before passing of this most extensive (Clauses 15-26, also partially Clauses 27, 29, 31, 33, 40, 43) as well as the most unusual, complex and evidently most arguable part of A.D. Sakharov's draft constitution, I shall touch upon an episode revealing how personal was the attitude of Andrei Dmitriyevich to the draft he was working on. As far as I could notice in this sole instance of direct citing from the American "Declaration of Independence" of 1776, Andrei

Dmitriyevich was unaware of this. These words wee engraved on his memory and he used them unintentionally. "We hold these truths to be self-evident, that all men are created equal, that they are endowed by their Creator with certain inalienable right, that among these being the rights to life, liberty and the pursuit of happiness..." And A.D. Sakharov's draft reads: "All people have the right to life, liberty and happiness". Andrei Dmitriyevich said that as one of the readers of his draft objected, the expression "right to happiness" lacks legal sense, as each man interprets "happiness" in his own way. In fact without regard for the religious rhetoric of the great American Declaration basing all the rights on the "laws of nature and its Creator", "with a firm reliance on the protection of divine Providence", the same worlds regarding "the right to happiness" in the quite different style of Sakharov's draft stood out in a strange way, in contrast to the Declaration where they were absolutely amalgamated with stylistic flow. I myself did not think about a likeness at that time; in a different historic and cultural context a real likeness did not occur to such an extent that the words also seemed to be quite different.

And at that time in our conversation, I agreed with the absence of legal sense and even proposed the following reading of the beginning of Clause 5, having changed the order of the two last phrases: "All the people have the right to life, liberty and happiness as they understand it. Execution of the rights of an individual must not contradict to the rights of other people. The purpose and obligation of the state...", etc. Thus "the right to happiness" would mean the right of each man to love his own way without interfering with others, i.e. it would express the principle of individual self-realization.

Andrei Dmitriyevich heard it in silence. I started to interpret once again the formula "as they understand it" (or "as everyone understands it") referring to Wilhelm von Humboldt and others. Andrei Dmitriyevich smiled in confusion and gave a simpler explanation: "I would wish to use some lofty worlds..."

Thus we came to this conclusion. Andrei Dmitriyevich left Clause 5 without changes. "The legally empty" notion of happiness was used in the draft even twice. The draft even begins with it.

Clause 2: "The aim of the people of the union of Soviet Republics of Europe and Asia is a happy, full sense of life"...A.D. Sakharov needed "lofty words" in this text not because of sentimental motives. A political Constitution must have an over-political, all-mankind, humanistic aim. If "happiness" is "a life full of sense" then complete sense for each individual existence is nothing but culture.

The conception of the national-state system (a new Union treaty based on the Constitution) was worked out by A.D. Sakharov long ago and first laid out (in collaboration with G.V. Starovoitova) I the program documents of the Inter-regional Group of the USSR People's Deputies). Now this has assumed a concrete legislative form.

What is the fourth idea of the draft?

First, "Initially structural components of the Union of Soviet Republics of Europe an Asia are National and Autonomous republics, National Autonomous regions and National Areas of the former Union of Soviet Socialist Republics" (Clause 25). Stalin's division of all the national-state formations in the USSR into four categories subordinated in vertical order, this inequality is destroyed. The new Union Treaty is to be signed by all the former parts of the USSR as equal republics regardless of their size, existence of a border, or population. In particular, for the first time there will be a Republic of Russia separate from other republics.

There is no "center" over and above the republics. But the strong (i.e. sovereign) republics voluntarily, in conformity with the Union treaty, pass a precisely agreed upon minimum of authorization of the Central Government formed by them (Clause 23). The entire constitutional process of transformations is accompanied from the bottom to the top. It is not the center who "broadens the rights of the republics"; on the contrary, they entrust them to the center. They transfer to the center of those affecting the interest of all the republics, i.e. foreign relations; organization of a joint defense (army) and defense industry; an inter-republican (All-Union) monetary unit and the common part of the budget, allotted by the republics from their budgets; transportation and communication of the All-Union significance, the tow-chamber Congress, President, Council of Minister, and the High Court.

Second, (and perhaps here is the gist of the proposed structure. In addition to the obligatory minimum of authorizations which the republics vest to the Central Government elected and controlled by them, each republic has also the right at its will and discretion to pass other economic, administrative and other management functions. A republic may sign a Special Protocol to the Union Treaty.

In accordance with an additional agreement, rights of a republic may be narrowed and broadened as we.. For example, a republic may possess its own national military (under joint command) and its own monetary unit or it may not. An additional protocol is signed by each republic with the Central Government and is to be ratified by the Congress; in essence it is signed with all other members of the Union. That is to say, consent is required for additional terms and conditions of both a joining republic and the Union.

And this means that a degree of integration of this or that republic in the Union (or, if you like, a volume of its *real* sovereignty) will inevitably happen to be *extremely diverse*, specific. And will connections of certain republics with the Union as a whole will be reduced to a minimum, the ties of the other members of the Union with the Center will, in fact, differ little from the existing ones. However, the territorial, ecological, economic, cultural, or language interests of each republic will be reliably secured by the Treaty and the Special Protocol exactly *to the extent* with which a republic itself will consider t necessary and feasible.

As is known, state sovereignty is not only a right, but also a heavy burden of self-provision including financial expenditures, "own" bureaucracy, well-trained personnel and so on.

In this respect A.D. Sakharov's Constitution provides a tremendous (individual!) degree of *flexibility and diversity* of the forms of inclusion of each republic in the Union - and this constitutes the strongest aspect of the draft. The rights of nationalities without their own territories are also provided. Four dozen of the present autonomies will be satisfied as well as those who intend to form them (Germans, Crimean Tatars and others).

Either we speak about a federal state, a "real" federation (contrasted to the alleged one existing nowadays) or the Union as it has been described in A.D. Sakharov's Constitution; it is a confederation ain't it? On the one hand, the future Soviet Union can be nothing but a confederation, otherwise it will break itself into pieces. Many republics will not wish to enter such a commonwealth of nations which will hurt their state sovereignty, will submit them to the center, will turn them into but a part of a democratized state. A sovereign republic will be desired by peoples not only form the Baltic region, the Transcaucasus, the Ukraine of Moldavia, Tataria or Korelia but also, of course, Russians themselves. With all that the Republic of Russia will determine itself whether autonomous regions would be formed within it unbounded space: say, - North-West, Central Russia, the Volga region, the Urals, Western Siberia, Eastern Siberia, and the Far East.

On the other hand, historically established common economic; rally existing unofficial of nationalities' communication; 60-million-strong migration among the republics; plenty of mixed marriages, a mixture of languages and dialects (especially in Byleorussian and the Ukraine); life habits no matter which but still in a single country, without internal visas, customs, etc.; lack of their own real statehood (in any case for a period of the lst one and a half, three or even five and more centuries); a small number of certain ethnic groups not needing their ministry of foreign affairs or their own monetary unit but simply the preservation of their national-cultural autonomy, their traditional mode of life, their land or water tenure, clear ecological recesses ad so on and so forth - all this will inevitably give any features of a real federation to the future Soviet Union. Even for major sovereign republics in the Union a "confederation" may become tighter (more organic, more beneficial) than this political term usually means.

A hybrid of a federation and a confederation! An unprecedented state association having no parallel in the world, too mixed in development levels, historic and cultural roots and ...too common for such a diversity...it rather depends from what point it can be looked at.

It is not a good occasion to detail the appropriate facets of A.D. Sakharov's draft as well as his Constitution as a whole. I shall omit many aspects worthy of being mentioned and commented upon: from the clause on *the exclusion* from the Union t quotas advantageous for minor peoples at the elections the Chamber of Nationalities: from a proposal to carefully freeze further changes of border within the Union for 10 years (in general, by doing so to introduce and idea of a transitional period at the time of forming the Union) in the Constitution - to inevitable disputable or unclear issues. (For example, in discussions with Andrei Dmitriyevich I objected to the provision that "both chambers meet in joint sessions but for a number of issues determined by the regulations of the Congress they vote separately" (Clause 29). This is how it is interpreted presently, and I think it lacks sense, The *two* chambers in all democracies of the world, as a rule, meet separately; they have several different functions and in particular one is the upper and the other the lower chamber; if the chambers differ not only in norms and order of election but to some extent in functions and rights, then it becomes unclear why it is necessary to have *two* of them. It is also beyond my comprehension why, if emission of special republican currency is possible, its issue ad cancellation are in the exclusive power of the Central Bank of the Soviet Union. However, analysis of A.D. Sakharov's draft is still forthcoming.

I cannot let it pass in silence that the present-day violence and conflicts, especially in the Transcaucasus, makes the implementation of A.D. Sakharov's draft, intended for a sort of civilized and rational revolution, hardly realizable, I had many talks with Andrey Dmitriyevich about what would come out of an attempt to enact such a constitution just now, whether we speak of the Nagorny Karabakh, Abkhazia, South Ossetia, etc....Andrei Dmitriyevich indulged in a hard thought, spoke of a deadlock situation when there was no convincing, practically invulnerable decision and cannot yet be in general.

However, it was in such "hopeless" situations, having convinced himself that any proposals and plans conflict with the political reality, that wise compromises do not work, that Andrei Dmitiyevich did find it (just because of this) *most practical* to adhere to *the principle*. Principles are fruits of a whole epoch (in this case, the epoch of the fall of colonial empires and the rapid growth of the number of independent states in the world of the XXth century); fruits of often bitter, prolonged, bloody but *true experience*, Therefore when no way out is seen, it is wiser and more practical t rely on a principle. That is why it makes the beginning of the statement of the foundations of the national-state transformation of the "former USSR" in the Constitution. This is Clause 15. "The right to self-determination is the basic and priority right of each nation and republic".

A.D. Sakharov's draft would be faultless on the condition of autonomy on all levels in a decentralized country. Each municipality, district, etc. would be to a considerable degree removed, dissolved in the process of such total, all-penetrating autonomization: self-governing of any human communities in solving he matters concerning them and nobody else. But until now it has not been provided even in A.D. Sakharov's draft.

As for the clauses of the Constitution regulating property relations, they provide for free "pluralistic" competition of all kinds and forms of economic activity without limitation. Such is the fifth idea of A.D. Sakharov's project. "Enterprises with any form of property exist in equal economic, social and legal conditions" (Clause 44), "the principles of market and competition" constitute the foundation of economic regulation in the Soviet Union" (Clause 46). With all this, the state actively interferes with and regulates the development of the economy through taxation, crediting and investment policies, restricts the sale, transference and maximum sizes of property, as well as prevents speculation and mismanagement in agriculture. The state remains the highest (titled) owner and distributor of mineral wealth and water resources; it redistributes national income for the purpose of social justice, and the defense of those unable to feed themselves, guaranteeing a subsistence minimum for all members of society.

Our economy is entirely based on hired labor. With wages for the labor force being extremely low and the choice of where or how to apply this labor is negligible, also due to extreme monopolisation of production. And wherever you go to offer your ands - the terms are similar.

And they keep telling us with serious faces about the "incompatibility of socialism with exploitation of man by man"...In other words only the state can be the total master-exploiter? And about what *the equality* of a "private trader", "Private property" with other forms of property? About what market "competition" can we speak if a future farmer, owner of a bakery, a butcher's shop, a bootmaking shop or a dry cleaning shop or even an imaginary plant producing cement, ceramics or transistors is unable to hire workers?

A.D. Sakharov's draft rejects this ideological hypocrisy. The state is to regulate the market of goods, services, capitals and labour, and to watch the fulfillment of honest rules of competition.

Evidently those forms will prevail which in an honest, regulated competition will turn out to be more productive, and more effective. People do not need ideological "-isms"; not capitalism or socialism, but an abundance of goods at acceptable prices, prosperity for working people, modern high living standards, self-realization of each individual in the performance of his work, a sense of social protection and dignity, and charity for old, ill and weak people. Regardless of what "-ism" will be invented to lead our society to success on the eve of the third millennium.

Let society take care of the equality of individual starting opportunities (political, educational, etc.). Private property of any kind, but desirably modern share-holding, cooperative, of a collective-private nature. Hired labour, having become liberated, will exclude the "exploitation of man by man" as well as exploitation of man by the state. Everyone will be protected by democratic laws, independent trade unions, associated fellow-citizens, guaranteed conditions of work and payment, a social security system.

Again Andrei Dmitriyevich was compelled to make a lonely step, and once more this step was well-thought over, dictated and vividly marked with the efficiency so characteristic of him.

In the mournful days you could hear from all sides frequently, with repentance and sincerity, the words about A.D. Sakharov's "self-devotion", "conscientiousness", :moral purity", martyrdom, quite often subdued religious overtones. Well, all these worlds were deserved, though A.D. Sakharov was an atheist. For the last several centuries in Europe and from XIXth century Russia as well, there were plenty of atheists of the highest moral and cultural standard.

The first words of Yelena Georgiyevna pronounced from the TV screen on the eve of the funeral were "Sakharov was a happy man". And another insistent phrase: "he was happy". Further on the woman to whom Andrei Dmitriyevich was obliged for a great part of this happiness declared: "I would not like Andrei to be treated as a saint". He was neither a "saint", nor an oddity, nor a "God's fool", nor "a big unprotected child", etc., but a wise, sober, tough nonconformist public figure.

I had the chance to become acquainted with Andrey Dmitriyevich from 1969 - 1979 and to closely collaborate with him from 1988 -1989. In public life A.D. Sakharov was a rationalist and an intellectual of the "Western" type. Perhaps, not so rare in the post-Peter, particularly post-Decembrist, the more so - the post-reform[1] Russia, but nevertheless by no means a popular human type. In our country these qualities of mind and willpower are usually ascribed to strangers, a certain Schtolz, as if Russia failed to give birth to dense shoots of businessmen with European education or great scientists. A.D. Sakharov was a Russian European though his appearance and behavior were both shy and awkward. At the same time his independent manners could arouse in an accidental observer who had read a lot of Dostoyevsky, superficial associations with Prince Myshkin or Alyosha Karamazov. But A.D. Sakharov was a restrained man, above all

---

[1] Refomrs of 1860's/L.E.?

thinking clearly and independently, relying on facts and logic, weighing possible results.

In the 1970's Andrei Dmitriyevich used to repeat that "he is not a politician", though it did not prevent him from writing several very accurate and prophetic political and social texts. They say that he lacked political experience, but he participated in conferences of nuclear scientist chaired by Beria, he knew Khrushchev, he watched many statesmen, KGB officials, dissidents, journalists, diplomats; and later M.S. Gorbachev, A.N. Yakovlev, numerous other dignitaries, people's deputies, "nonformals", workers, prime ministers and presidents. For the last year and a half before his departure, his ability to study people and circumstances and to make important practical decisions based on these observations received extraordinary development.

In fact, far from being a politician in his psychological mold, Andrei Dmitriyevich very early doomed himself to play a political role, He fulfilled it "unprofessionally" in his own way; but it was exactly the new, democratic, people's, intelligent way to be a politician which, by the end of XX century, (and perhaps here in particular) turned into a new political professionalism.

Among dissidents there were people not all inferior to Andrei Dmitriyevich in their greatness of spirituality, their self-sacrifice, and their intrepid civic honesty. A great many experienced more persecution and suffering than did A.D. Sakharov. However, in my opinion not a single Russian dissident became a political figure in the new ("Gorbachev") situation, the more so, a political figure of such a democratic accuracy, consistency, scope as A.D. Sakharov. To his ability to be uncompromising in principles, and to go against the tide were added the skill of tactical compromise ad diplomatic tact. No former dissidents could join with such an energy the "non-dissident" legal stage of political activity appealing to the entire country. It is simply because nobody else possessed such authority and the possibility of winning the Nobel Peace Prize. The answer is in A.D. Sakharov himself, how exactly did he understood his new civic tasks, and *what and how* was he doing for their implementation.

It is important to remember that A.D. Sakharov created his draft Constitution in the fall of 1989, and this was an absolutely crucial moment. An historic political background of his meditations was an exhaustion (not simply a break-up) of the official policy, slogans and forms of perestroika. On the eve of the Second Congress of the People's Deputies, it became evident that no really deep problems would be solved or even put up for discussion. Within a few weeks, communist regimes in Eastern Europe broke up and our country immediately found itself at the tail-end of this historic process.

The notion of the official "perestroika" was compromised in the eyes of millions: after the growing threat of economic catastrophe in 1989; due to the plan of gradual unpatching proposed by the government and doomed to failure; as the result of bloodshed in the Transcaucasus and Central Asia; after several reactionary plenums of the party's Central Committee demonstrating the utter inability of the stagnant and dull majority in the Central Committee and the Political Bureau to realise just how deep and irreversible were the processes that were developing the in the country: in connection with the activization of the "new right wing"; at the sight of a panic growth of emigration of the paralysis of the railways; at the failures of remarkable attempts by miners to change at least particulars without waiting for changes of the foundations of the political and economic systems of the country as a whole; facing the actual collapse of the CPSU, and the spontaneous "overthrow" of regional and city party committees ranging from Tyumen to Volgograd, and a great man other events the majority of which Andrei Dmitriyevich had no time to see and feel deeply.

The last program document signed by him four days before his death (the Declaration of 94 People's Deputies form the Inter-Regional Group" on Perestroika Today and Invisible Future") contains sufficiently extensive analysis of the dramatic crisis of perestroika. The appeal of A.D. Sakharov for a two-hour warning strike on the eve of the Congress was an act of desperation. There was (and still is) no powerful mass organization capable of taking up and implementing this initiative. However, in that situation Sakharov considered such and improvised appeal justified, realizing that there was neither time nor political means to really carry out a mass general strike. The call was simply put on the air, into the boundless Russian space. Sakharov thought that even the symbolic importance of an appeal by the five deputies would be great; it would contribute to polarizations of the country. When Andrei Dmitriyevich phoned asking my opinion, I was among whose who, without hesitation, supported the political and psychological justification of this gesture. I think that the unprecedented half-million-strong manifestation on February 4, 1990, in Moscow was but the first echo of Sakharov's appeal for the unification of all democratic forces, for the beginning of mighty actions out of the parliament and for a distinct formation of the parliament's opposition at the Congress.

In his last interview A.D. Sakharov spoke about confirming his readiness to support Gorbachev but on definite political conditions; to support him on behalf to he independent, liberal and radical opposition for the sake of changing the very foundations of the regime. In this last speech (December 14 at the meeting of the Inter-Regional Group), exceptional for its brevity, force, logic and brilliance, A.D. Sakharov persuaded his colleagues that why they would not fulfill their duties if they did not openly oppose the present policy of the CPSU leadership, the government, and the routine majority at the Congress.

Approximately three hours after this speech in the Kremlin, A.D. Sakharov passed away.

Nowadays we hear again that the Constitution would not be speeded up, that it is a complicated matter and we must not determine any term of its drawing up and adoption..."We should not be in a hurry, should we"? But "to hurry" is not a matter of time, but of the quality of thinking. One may think slowly but badly. It is possible to think with maximum speed when circumstances dictate urgency and correctness. Therefore let us ask ourselves about A.D. Sakharov's draft, whether it is correct. If so, then we must hurry up its polishing.

While "presidium" of the Congress and the very name of the parliament were transferred into the draft after being almost automatically extrapolated from the present structure, it was not mechanically that Andrei Dmitriyevich included into the Constitution the "freedom against arbitrary arrests and psychological hospitalization not prompted by medical necessity" (Clause 6). The next phrase leaves no doubt that A.D. Sakharov had in mind political "lunatic asylums" in which many of his compatriots and friends suffered. Clause 8 is also related hers "No one may be put to the tortures and exposed to cruel treatment". A.D. Sakharov knew from his own experience as well what "a cruel treatment" meant. In Clause 14 he sums up the seventy-year-long Soviet experience, adding a rather simple condition without which Clause 6 or 8 as well as many others would remain false declarations; "In the Union actions of any secret services for protection of public and state order are not permitted". I hope that after the recent events in Prague or Berlin the number of aseptic smiles addressed t A.D. Sakharov's "quixoticsm" will be somehow reduced. In any case, he did say something as his farewell to the people who took care of his conversations, correspondence and travels for twenty years.

However the Constitution is destined...for a hundred years, isn't it? It describes a society to such an extent successful and free that it is unthinkable to imagine that these differently minded people will still be thrown into prisons and asylums. These far-sighted clauses prompted by yesterday's and partially today's feelings have been introduced into the same Constitution where we can read that the Soviet Union is striving to harmonize all global problems, to achieve convergence, i.e., "mutual approaching" of the two world systems. AND..."FORMING THE WORLD GOVERNMENT IN THE FUTURE MUST BE A POLITICAL EXPRESSION OF SUCH AN APPROACHING"!

It is not hard for someone to smile at this phrase, As Mayakovsky said on another occasion: come back in a hundred years or so, and we shall speak.

The "World Government" was mentioned by A.D. Sakharov in the form of a logical conclusion from discussions of "long-term prospects" of the processes which had *already* appeared in history. This is a distant goal of which A.D. Sakharov was aware. However, it is a realistic goal as long as, without it, the chain of inevitable convergence would be broken. Convergence in its turn, Andrei Dmitriyevich was sure, is a necessary condition for *the survival of mankind.*

I would not say that in A.D. Sakharov's draft little attractive details of eliminating a secret political police, unlawful arrests and asylums and dazzling "world government match poorly in psychological, political and legal aspects.

On the contrary! This is a draft worked out by a Soviet dissent. And this is a draft belonging to a scientist meditating on the problems of the future of humanity. A.D. Sakharov's thought naturally was developing between two oppositely charged poles.

The rights of man *here and now,* legal protection of an individual under the conditions of a free economy and democratic parliamentarism which must appear at last in our country because of the compulsory force of all-humanity: scientific and technological progress.

On the other hand, there is an internal, technological necessity for convergence. In A.D. Sakharov's cherished conviction, his inevitably global character human rights *would not be secured with the future.* They would not have a future in a global sense. Without convergence - what would human rights mean?

A guarded look at the not too distant past, combined with bold theoretical ideas for the future, an attempt to balance it all, this was an attempt to invent a Constitution emanating from the present conditions but surmounting this by imagining a state not yet existing.

Generally speaking, is this task concrete?

A historian will answer: were Solon's laws in action in Athens before Solon's laws were adopted, really? Is the Constitution of the United States the child of the "founding Fathers", did it not come out of the heads of it creators as Athen Pallas had sprung out of the skull of Zeus? Does it not apply to the majority of revolutionary Constitution, Declarations, Decrees? Of course, our situation is extremely complicated with the fact that not only a new political system will have to be invented but also a new concord of nations and even a new economy.

If you want to change the order of things in a country and propose new laws with this purpose, these laws must be *devised*, precisely what they are doing in the Supreme Soviet.

Frankly speaking, it is difficult to believe that the future Basic Law will turn out to be, in its principal features, close to A.D. Sakharov's constitutional ideas, and that the day of the formation of the European-Asian Union is not distant.

It would not e easy to implement A.D. Sakharov's testament, while its very sense and essence cannot be simpler: "The goal of the people of the Union of the Soviet Republics of Europe and Asia is a happy life full of sense, material and spiritual freedom, prosperity, peace and security for the citizens of the country, for all the people on Earth irrespective of their racial belonging, nationality, sex, age and social standing".

Postscriptum. Only a few months have passed and it has already become clear that the future of the Commonwealth of the Countries (members of the present USSR) will hardly assume the contours currently outlined by A.D. Sakharov. Most probably a common Constitution will not be needed at all; only the Union Treaty and something like the declaration of Human Rights (or an appropriate preamble in the Treaty) will be common. Perhaps the contracting republics will not need a common president or a common *two*-chamber parliament. All is possible...and each month everything becomes still more problematic than when Andrei Dmitriyevich was working on his draft last fall.

However it would not be enough to admit that this text will remain a stirring moment of legal and political reflection. Though lagging behind the events, A.D. Sakharov's draft, at the same time, continues to take immeasurable lead over our reality. It will produce educational influence o the minds of fellow-countrymen for a sufficiently long time. Finally, many formulas of A.D. Sakharov, particularly what concerns civil rights and social principles. must be at hand with the authors of future republican constitutions including the Union Treaty. These formulas will still work, the more so as even the bread-up of the USSR cannot and must not mean that its place will not be taken by a different type of national-state connection. You know, not all the members of the USSR would wish to leave. Those who stay will have to join a new Union. And even those who left will evidently wish, in due time, to maintain their certain participation in this Union in those forms and to such an extent which will be beneficial for them.

PART II
RUSSIA AT CROSSROADS

IDEALISM OF ACTION

An almost mystical desire to look into the future at the same time meets the practicality of politicians attempting to connect their activities with the most probable results of the events. History seems to teach them nothing. They are pragmatists, i.e. people of purpose. If they had looked into the past closely they would have lacked the spirit to make the step into the unknown. It is one thing to analyse the consequences of deeds and quite another to accomplish them.

A routine definition of the policy as "an art of the possible" is a paradox. It has to be considered "an art" here, in the sphere of non-permanent, individualized, unique events and "the possible", by definition, is what is not existing in real life. In other words it is still exactly impossible.

Moreover, the certainly possible is also insufficiently expressive in this capacity, it makes "possibility" feeble, deprives it, so to say, of pathos and essence. The really possible has no territory of its own; this is a badly outlined transitional zone between the inevitable and the unrealisable (i.e. negatively inevitable). It is a dissolving border between two immense deserts of two absolutely incompatible inevitabilities.

It turns out that politics is an art of the theoretically possible but sufficiently inconceivable. Consequently, it demands the rare combination of caution and circumspection with large-scope goals, lofty fantasy and extraordinary personal conviction. It is this that is sometimes called "idealism" in politics.

I am now putting aside the question of a cospiritual quality of this *idealism of action*. But in times of great historic events all true leaders - from Moses to Roosevelt and from Solon to Lenin - were practicing "idealists".

A result depends on actions, actions depend on purposes, purposes depend on means, means depend on a choice, a chance, principles, or a public mood, moods may depend on a certain TV fraud or a declaration of a popular leader or on prices of meat. People become animated, grow furious or lose heart and in the unprecedented turmoil of historical incidents, we see a revolution, a reform, a war, a putsch, or an ordinary election campaign, all depending, of course on a result.

So a politician attempts - calculating, surmising and prophesying - to be both an accountant and a prophet. He must create history, i.e. create what has created himself, create with a sober mind, in other words, daydream with open eyes and think at top speed. Though it is not necessary to think in politics, it is only necessary to consider.

Thinking is too jealous, it demands that we forget about everything else an recklessly love it alone and for its sake. Thinking is unselfish; its aims are too odd, inopportune and useless not to consider them purposeless. Thinking is somewhat arrogant and at the same time playful, absorbed in its own flow, its fastidiousness and consistency.

While a politician is unpretentious and tactically inconsistent, he often changes logic and actions, obeying circumstances rather than intellectual paradoxes and refinement.

While in practical politics one should absorb a great many facts, analyze versions, estimate, persuade, make successful decisions, generally speaking, get to the evident. He must suggest it at the precisely chosen moment and by means of the most calculated words, being a little ahead of other politicians and events themselves, suprising us with assertions and suggestions which would become popular and clear to everybody the next morning.

As for history, on the contrary, it considers in no simple way.

It creates to such an extent that an ineradicable temptation of historiography is that of detecting in History a certain substantial *sense*, though inconceivable for us.

So a politician considering good or bad deals it is terrible to say with history, perhaps meddling with it. But if we speak about *an event*, a real politician is who "makes history" at the very least.

Very likely, it is exactly big politics. This occupation is called forced, important but also dirty and vulgar. Regretfully it is unusually so. However, in this political boredom and narrowly utilitarian outlook, there happens to be this strange cultural condition: politics takes pains over the most unyielding and amazing material on earth and it conceitedly processes the future.

THE TRADE OF FORECASTERS: "THE USSR IN THE YEAR OF 2000"

Natural curiosity, or maybe something incomparably more profound, the essence of any reflection born out of the temporal character of human life, is particularly aroused regarding the future, a subject more mysterious than any UFOs. "Ten years after" excites people more strongly than "light-years" For certain people death is horrible above all because they will never learn what will occur later! "They will not live till that time".

Perhaps the majority of such people are among Russian intellectuals. For us since the time of Chaadayev, the Decembrists and Slavophiles, the future has been the subject of utmost importance. With all this it was nearly impossible to be guided by the past. Regarding the past there was never national concord and quiet satisfaction in Russia. It served as a constant ground for arguments in which these or those historical landmarks and epochs were furiously erased. On the other hand, as for the present, the arguing parties fully agreed that it deserved only despair or, in any case, refection.

The future was the only hope as well as the only guide. Consequently, we remain a country of expectations and (inevitably) a country of forecasters.

With all this, appraisal of the present and the nearest future is postponed beyond the horizon. Our future holds either an apocalypse, or salvation; wither "a civil war", or "a return into the world civilized society".

In short, it is such a future which will not be an organic development or transformation of the present but will only aggravate or refute it. There is no middle course, as Russia for already 300 years has remained in tumult, on the cusp between the "Occidental" and "Oriental" ways of life, living on historical cross-roads.

I prefer not to describe the geographic and social space of what is still called the "USSR", as to think in what a degree a historical forecasting is useful for us (which I distinguish from a political one).

But as long as I, like others playing politics, are expected to demonstrate no certain philosophic or historical reflection but a more or less concrete opinion, say, on "the USSR in the year 2000" the period, of course, relatively, convenient with its unusual roundness and meaning approximately the following: "How will it all end in your opinion?" Well, I shall answer briefly, and later I shall explain what logical and historic premises I shall use as the basis and what is evidently an intellectual risk. I do not wish to enumerate possible "scenarios". Of course, we can exclude almost no outcome completely (except simple repetition of the obsolete Stalin or Breshnev-like totalitarian forms).

I belong to those who are convinced of a happy ending. It is hardly by "the year 2000", rather in some twenty years from now that a free economy and a liberal-legal state of more or less a "Western" type will settle in the USSR with certain original features and after a poignant transitional period. The USSR is sure to collapse by itself thanks, in great part, to the attempts to oppose it with threats and force. However, contrary to what is predicted more often, centrifugal processes will be replaced by centripetal ones. The countries now united in the USSR, even Baltic ones, after the downfall of the empire will reestablish close economic, currency, political and cultural ties on a radically different basis (whether as a confederation, or its partially associated members or as something resembling Europe-92).

A long-term forecast in this case is much easier than a short-term one because it is based in a bast and prolonged retrospective on the analysis of thorough and decisive lines of world development, particularly in the last decades. Even totalitarian regimes appear from such a height to be an interim result of superimposing of new "perturbing" tendencies upon stagnant, once flourishing and now inadequate zones of traditionalism, a kind of multimillenial history shedding its skin (but by no means its outcome). This historical change cannot be avoided. Now, though the USSR is somewhat better prepared than 70 years before, it remains on the threshold of such a change of world importance.

The point is that the destiny of "the USSR-2000" to a considerable degree, of course, was being decided in the deceitful March 1990 and behind the scenes in the perfidious October. This destiny would reveal itself, we must think, particularly clearly in March-April 991 when the slow putsch achieved a more open shape. This does not mean that we shall enter the third millennium still under the heels of the CPSU and KGB, far from it! However the dates of our future resurrection and what we shall live up to are in many ways predestined by the most recent events.

Meanwhile day by day short-term forecast leaves less and less room for well-argumented hesitations. It is either severe or very sever.

So, "perestroika", i.e. a forced attempt to modernize the regime essentially ended by the fall of 1989 (Many of us and people in the West in particular failed to notice it before the gunshots in Vilnius). The CPSU reformist resources were already exhausted after the 1st Congress of "people's deputies" as it was a principally inflexible system. "Perestroika" reached its thrust, by starting a series of deadly frightening events not at all planned by Gorbachev and his group; East-European revolutions and the starting of a national and state breakdown of the USSR. The matter of the complete serious demise of the party military regime now came to the foreground.

In the course of one and a half years the events of the growing total crises were running in waves rolling over Gorbachev's head while he replied by assuming grander titles by attempting to regroup his apparatus, by redistributing power functions among party and state structures. During this one and a half year period, a strange new dynamic stagnation lasted; an interval between what and what? Between an attempt of "perestroika" to bring political life back to the country, turning it upside down, and ultimately starting to go out of control. In short, between the momentum of "perestroika", on one hand, and, on the other, an outcome, whether forced-revolutionary, deep-structural, or as a right-wing dictatorship, may be headed at the beginning, by the same general secretary and president, an exreformer.

So, that is how to make political forecasts. That a return of the brutes authoritarianism is possible has always been evident, just as is the idea that our domestically cultivated new authoritarianism will not wish to and will not be able to assist in forming a free market. This is neither South Korea, nor Chile, nor even Iraq where at least a certain local bourgeoisie had existed before the dictator came to power; it remained thereafter and developed as if nothing had interfered. In our country there is simply nobody to be interfered with.

Dictatorship will not last too long, it has been doomed in the bud; it will not save the economy from a terrible collapse, it will drastically worsen even the present semi-miserable standard of living, it will be suppressed by centrifugal republican forces, it will evoke civic resistance, it will fail to find sleeping pills for people to sink into lethargy again, it will arouse fear, that is true, but people learning that this regime will not last a thousand years, that this Kaschei[1] is mortal will overcome the fear. There will be millions of renegades rather than thousands, they will start a general political strike coming out into the streets - and they will wipe out the dictatorship.

Meanwhile it is useful to lend an attentive ear to the forecasts of not only political scientists but also to the mediocrities of a military-history magazine, to listen to "Nash Sovremennik" ("Our Contemporary") magazine. After all it is a country of not only the miners of Kuzbass and Vorkuta, liberals from Moscow and St. Petersburg, and national democrats. No, it is still the country which brought up "our contemporaries" and cultivated by them, produced aggressive and wildish Soviet mutations like Alksnis, Shafarevich, Nevzorov or Prokhanov; is for the time being *their* country. In some way "from the right wing" things are more optimistic because there are enough right-wing forces to impede anything, though not enough to glue together the broken "USSR". The situation is to such a degree that we are forced to believe the most foolish forecasts for tomorrow.

However, a long-term optimistic prognosis is correct. It happens that I seem to understand what will occur in a decade or two, but I am at my wit's end as for what to expect towards the end of March. A state of emergency, the leashed press, dispersal of democrats? And after that? Perhaps the beginning of protracted fighting for a democratic break through?

I see that, alas, I am falling into a crevice between historical optimism and political hopelessness regarding what is awaiting us the next morning.

What will take a upper hand in each of us depends on or state of mind and our temperament. Personally I prefer to feel a joy that I have lived to see though not the death, at least the last convulsions of this bestial regime. No matter how nasty and dangerous things would await us at present, our present is still quite lively, intelligent, open for unexpected

---

[1] Kaschei the Immortal is an evil creature from Russian fairy tales.

happenings and acutely historical. In any case we shall not come back to mass terror, nor obscure hard times.

Now it is clear we shall LIVE to see this time. Fore example, my life corresponds to the time of six general secretaries. But, everything has its end and the name of the seventh general secretary will interest no one, and will become politically insignificant. Who will succeed Gorbachev in this post? It does not matter at all. Do you remember who was the first secretary of the Polish communist? Or the Hungarian or Czechoslovak?

However, in what way is a practical leap possible from an alarming short-term prognosis to quite a different distant one?

It is only thanks to a direct interference of those who, in quiet times, would best be called the masses and who, in special historic moments, happen to be the very people on behalf of whom ideologists and politicians speak. It is not the place for concrete calculations on precisely how extraparliamentary actions could be amalgamated with a corresponding behaviour of B. Yeltsin who, in point of fact, has nothing in store except the support of exactly such actions.

The veil separating us from the future is much denser than usual, and this means that something unprecedented is on the horizon and democrats have to consider absolutely extraordinary, bold steps. Nothing is yet known except that experience will be of little help to us.

Political scientist study the behaviour of the existing public systems, how *such* societies change, how much change already occurred. A forecast is more or less successful depending on to what extent a system is stable and the factors influencing it are recognizable. (It resembles a weather forecast). Unexpected historical factors are regarded as inevitable interference's, certain noises too weak to impede decoding of the signals from the past serving as the basis of any prognosis. If the question was, say, about the "USA in the year of 2000" then evidently it would make sense to apply to politologist. In case of the USSR it is almost senseless. We do not yet have political scientists.

Practically speaking there are no precedents for what is going on in Soviet policy. Any analogies are suffering from inaccuracy, touch only one side or a part of events, but not the situation as a whole.

Something principally different is added to the usual difficulty of forecasting resulting from too complex a society, and too many elements to be considered. Extrapolation fails as a motor when a car gets in a rive.

A *historical* prognosis is possible rather than a "political" one, the former based not only on knowledge but also on a fantasy. In other words, if it is really historical, it proceeds from the understanding that the process is determined by what has already happened and by human actions, desires, etc. For example, a talented politician or shortage of such politicians; that is not determined.

The "unexpected: at the appearance of brand new public mechanisms is not an interference noise, but the essence of information. People not only receive and process, but also create it. This is what physicians call a bifurcation point, and Ovid named :metamorphoses". Consequently, a "historical prognosis is a contradiction in terms, "a hot ice?" Perhaps, however, it has not stopped a single forecaster. People want to understand something in their future even when (and especially when) it is more mysterious than usual.

The totalitarian regime is in convulsions, the victory of democracy is inevitable, but what are the terms and price? The nearest future depends on this very prognosis: spreading certainty in the unsteadiness of a new dictatorship would make its opponents act more energetically and then it will not last long, and vice versa. In such situations like the present one, the balance is upset by "a subjective factor": political determination and imagination.

At the same time long-term foresight based on world history in the 10 -20 years of real Russian modernization must include a certain very important correction, even more so as the whole world will also become substantially different. This is what I would call a paradox of historical extrapolation (or "a werewolf of extrapolation", as it was the case with the most famous historic prognosis of XIX century, the prognosis of Karl Marx). In other words: the way it will happen most likely will be marked with amazing novelty and suddenness.

I seem to finish as I started with an almost senseless note, - I am predicting that something unpredictable will occur. Such is the trade of historical forecasters, with its disappointing and fascinating risks. Tomorrow's reality will be what we are going to do today. It is only uncertainty of the future that provides us with the ability to act.

P.S....I am sitting at a regular meeting of the democrats where one can do little more than fly into a rage because of our unpardonable ineffectiveness, our inability to come to a quick agreement and to adjust a practical organization. Trite English verses about a nail and a horse-shoe come to mind: "For want of the nail the shoe was lost", etc. It is clear even for a hedgehog[2]; what we do need now is a formation of sections of "Democratic Russia" at factories and spreading of slogans of the *halted* Kuzbass strike in the entire country, rather than predictions, the more so

---

[2] A Russian saying equivalent in meaning to the English idiom "It is as clear as day" /The translator's note/.

apocalyptic ones. It is necessary that Yeltsin will grow cool to empty compromises in the Russian parliament and appeal to the Russian population for support, openly asking the people to say "no" to the deceitful question of March 17. Is it possible that all will be lost for want of a nail?

Today it is more important to find that nail than to make political forecasts, but it must be done as soon as possible.

"THEY ARE NOT SCOUNDRELS"

Such is the assertion of Anatoly Denisov, People's Deputy of the USSR, regarding the communists settled in the Latvian "committee of public salvation". Speaking on the "Echo of Moscow" radio program on January 21 and published by the "Izvestiva" newspaper on January 25 Anatoly Denisov first of all emphasized that there was nothing unlawful in the behavior of the committee's members.

I wish to emphasize that Rubiks and his people declared on Saturday, January 19 that they were ready to assume absolute authority beginning on Monday. It sounds at least like a threat of a putsch or its instigation, doesn't it? In fact the very next day and night a group of OMON[1] people seized the building of the Republican Ministry for Home Affairs by storm. Anatoly Denisov, with good humour, called them "dashing lads" and after that, explained: "Someone is trying persistently to provoke OMON in order to justify his retaliatory actions". "Someone?" However, Denisov immediately told a story about how "a general, a member of the public salvation committee came up to him and said that according to his information a night operation to annihilate OMON was being prepared". "At first I took this information for a fable, - impartial Anatoly Denisov advised thoughtfully. But after the imaginary assault of the apartment by OMON I interpreted it quite differently". In other words, logical Anatoly Denisov came tot the conclusion that provoking fads having one and the same aim: to create the impression that OMON members were going to be killed and slander that they were the attacking party, are two purposeful

---

[1] OMON is a special militia force./Translator's note/.

lies, decided that in the first instance the general from the "committee" was not telling lies.

In the opinion of Professor, Nevzorov was right too when he had shot on film this "operation aimed at annihilation of OMON" although it never occurred. The "dashing lads" including Nevzorov protruded their chests and were ready to die about which the entire country saw a horrifying film. Nobody had fired a single shot at them but they had shot and killed five people. Oh, they were not "ours".

"Ours" are the company of Rubiks, Nevzorov, Anatoly Denisov. The former were buried. While "ours" are safe and sound having done nothing unlawful, Professor Denisov found no words of anguish or blame after the Riga murders. Instead he told a story of an officer who "stood up in a uniform at the crossing of two streets to demonstrate how it had actually been going on. He kept standing for an hour. During this time he was called a "fascist", and a "scum", 46 times and, well, I cannot even repeat the other words as they were spitting on him. The professor was watching this scene on a day of national mourning. Ah, how could one abstain from shooting at those "not ours"? They even spit as they were being killed,

It is a pity that deputy Denisov was not wearing a uniform himself. A great pity, as the experiment would have been much more convincing.

The "committee's" declaration about their intention to seize power, Denisov said, is only a declaration; mere words and nothing more. He, Anatoly Denisov, a member of the CPSU Central Committee cannot bear responsibility that there are fools in the party leadership.

Denisov is entirely right. Rubiks was not present at the seizure of the City Soviet in Jurmala, the House of the Press in Riga, or at the night storm of the Ministry of Home Affairs. There were neither Pugo, nor Yazov, nor Gorbachev there, nor in Vilnius.

Perhaps, the chairman of the Ethics commission of the USSR Supreme Soviet is right. He does not consider the first secretary of the Latvian communist party and member of the Political Bureau of the CPSU Central Committee to be a clever man. In this case, the professor could refer to precedents. In fact, not all the members of the Political Bureau of this party are intelligent. There are no exact data as a testing was never made. Nevertheless, a communist deputy, A. Denisov evidently would not like to be one of the fools. Well, he is not a member of the Political Bureau after all. He is a member of the CPSU Central Committee and he is a man of sense.

Anatoly Denisov is a curious figure, having gained fame here with his declaration that Albert Einstein's theory of relativity was erroneous. Now he has succeeded to attract still greater attention. Comrade Denisov is rather noble looking, and he resembles a member of the first intelligent Bolshevik Council of People's Commissars. There is no one else in the CPSU Central Committee with such an imposing professorial appearance and manners. He was often listened to by the Soviet Parliament, at first puzzled with and now quite accustomed to him. Denisov delivers his speeches in a prepossessing manner, that is both laid-back and academically reasonable. This Marxist theoretician seems to be an expert in systems.

In the previous case with A. Einstein our Marxist might seem to be at his wit's end. Now it is more evident that it is not so and it is clear to what particular end Anatoly Denisov's wit reaches.

It is far from being accidental that Anatoly Denisov was appointed to be responsible for ethics at the Supreme Soviet. Such people are rather few in number and are at the disposal of Gorbachev, Pugo, and Yazov. In my opinion, he must be highly valued by comrade Lukyanov and other poets and thinkers from the party and state leadership. Professor Denisov is a feather in the cap of the President's party. Although, he hardly suits its Polozkov's modification as he is too intelligent. Denisov represents a rare example of a competent Soviet professor.

Unlike perestroika-time "Ellochkas, the cannibals[2] know only a few dozen phrases such as "processes are going on", "we'll exchange" and "we'll determine ourselves" unlike Professor Denisov. Take, for instance, this: "The most interesting thing is that one part of my TV interview was cut off in Riga while in Moscow they showed on Central TV only what had been cut off in Riga. So the result is that in one case I said one thing and in another - different. Though it was one and the same press-conference". Poor Anatoly Denisov, of course! It serves him right; this is what happens when a man is ambiguous and is a clown.

I have heard how the professor remarked, on the radio, (when trying to prove that the declaration of the "committee" of Rubiks about seizure of power was nothing but a foolish thing): what would happen, say if he, Denisov had declared in public that he was - the Turkish Sultan? Well the speaker continued, no one in Turkey would even notice such a declaration.

That is true. In this imagined case Anatoly Denisov would be pure before the law as was in the case of his denial of the theory of relativity. In a similar case, the professor would seek to appear as Gogol's Poprischin but

---

[2] "Ellochka, the cannibal" is a character of the novel by I. Ilf and Ye. Petrov. /L.B./

he would not be taken to a mad house, he would not be tortured there; in no case would he become a tragic figure. The thing is that in no case is our deputy and member of the CPSU Central Committee in danger of being placed in an asylum. While Anatoly Denisov is not only far from being a fool, neither is he a madman. Professor Denisov is nothing but a demagogue.

Indeed, let us discuss his delightful assimilation. Does Anatoly Denisov actually destabilize the power of the President of Turkey Ozal and his government? Was the building of the Ministry of Home Affairs in Ankara taken by storm following his "declaration" and were the Union enterprises in Istanbul on strike? is the leader of the Turkish communists a member of the Moscow Political Bureau? And finally, did Anatoly Denisov occupy Turkey in 1940, now pretending that there is "a confrontation of two equal forces" in Turkey?

By the way, "the splitting of the people into two parts" (Marshal Akhromeyev), into allegedly "two equal forces" and a pose combining utter sympathy for the OMON, "the committee of national salvation", etc., with an accentuated readiness to ostensibly tower above the conflict, to reproach the putschists, at least, with "simple-mindedness", that "they take themselves maybe more seriously than they actually are" - all these words are splendidly needed by Gorbachev's present course." That is why I always used to say in my speeches, that *it would not be a bad thing to introduce the president governing!"*

"Generally speaking, there sit people without humour also in this committee. However, it seems to me that they are but simple minded...in fact to my mind, they are not scoundrels, no, they are honest people". Deputy Denisov undoubtedly considers himself to be the same with an advantageous sense of "humour" of which, judging by his playful remark about himself as "the Turkish Sultan" no shootings in Vilnius or Riga can deprive him.

Well, let us forget the legal aspects of a conspiracy, instigation of a coup d'etat, etc. But don't those who resort to brutal force on the people of Baltia have *political* guilt; those who send their airborne troops for provocation's sake, who rule hidden in a dense veil of hushing up, "rumours" and open lies, in short, create a political and psychological basis for violence and behave like Stalin in 1940? later however, maneuver, temporarily retreat, give orders to incited "committees" "to halt their activities" after the bloodshed has made the entire country and indeed the whole world stop and protest? So, we are asking: isn't Rubiks politically guilty? That also means the All Union Political Bureau of which he is a member? Is there no political guilt, though Rubiks was not present that night. And aren't Yazov, Pugo, and Gorbachev guilty as well as every-body behaving like Anatoly Denisov? Who and in what civilized country could behave *like this*, allowing himself the luxury of not retiring after the events in Tbilisi, Baku, Vilnius, Riga?

So, doesn't the expert of systems understand what system he shame-lessly shields? Doesn't he, an expert of parliamentary ethics understand how blasphemous it is to pose as a parliamentary Poprischin[3], such a titular counsellor from the CPSU Central Committee?

Comrade Denisov does understand, and if nearly the highest ranking professor among the members of the CPSU Central Committee is such, so much the worse it is for the CPSU. Once again we are convinced of the unlimited political hypocrisy of this party's leadership.

I am not interested now in it. Neither in Anatoly Denisov himself but a phenomenon of Denisov, denisovschina, what becomes when logic and ethics try to make an unusual alloy with the policy of the CPSU.

It is know that Soviet parliament members are different but in most cases all the same. Perhaps, someone resembles a camel, reserving an im-portant grand bearing and foolish arrogant look, as if to say: yes, I am a camel, but one belonging to the padishah himself.[4] Another member re-sembles Skalozub.[5] The third and the fourth as we.. Still another may be a friend of the steppes and is dear to Pushkin (at least he thinks so), but truth is not dear to the former.[6]

However, it is the scientific variety of professor that I am singling out. In this respect, Anatoly Denisov is beyond comparison. He is Golik[7] at his best.

The subject of denisovschina is not without political urgency today. A new dictatorship is approaching with a new wave of "educationality" rising to meet it, and sympathetically precipitating its advent. The "letter of 53" shows up, in which orthodoxy in represented by the patriarch Alexiy II, autocracy by marshals and national character and by those writhes who know their onions. If 106 writers, composer, theatre people, cinematographers, and scientists have published *their* letter expressing their unwillingness to have anything in common with the continuation of the bloodshed and lies surrounding :"perestroika"; with the political

---

[3] Poprischin is the main character of N. Gogol's "Memoirs of a Madman" /L.B/

[4] An allusion ot R. Nishanov, Chairman of the Soviet of Nationalites. /L.B./

[5] Character from A. Griboyedov's "The Misfortune of Being Clever". /L.B./

[6] An allusion ot poet David Kugultinov, deputy of the USSR Supreme Soviet. /L.B./

[7] Golik - the chairman of one of the committees of the USSR Supreme Soviet.

course of Gorbachev once and for all swinging to the right, then divide 106 by 2 and you will get a list of quite different names, a disgraceful obliging alliance of the army, church, party leaders and "cultural workers". Here is what we call "denisovschina".

Never will they achieve "consolidation", which means the intimidated or shameless surrender of the overwhelming majority of intellectuals, and even talented people. Such was the situation in our country and for half a century, but it will not happen again. There will be no second Gorbachev and it is even good if it becomes inconceivable because Sakharov means a lonely struggle, a wall of people's ignorance and lack of understanding. Anything may happen but there will be neither this deadly loneliness, nor this blind wall.

Why on earth am I writing about Anatoly Denisov? Why do I get irritated by what this man is doing and saying? Irritated to a much greater extent than the half of Rafik Nishanovich or the tar of a certain colonel Petrushenko, or commanding bellowing from the rostrum. It is precisely because of this. The professor is talkative and resembles the likes of us, the intellectuals.

Such is a beautiful landlord's daughter in N. Gogol's "Viy" flying in a coffin inside the church. "Reasoning soundly, - Khoma Brut addresses respectfully the sotnik (she is of noble birth) but not to provoke your wrath, she has accepted the Satan". In fact the sotnik's reply was not worse than that of the OMON squad.

Well, is it long ago that you have reread "Viy"? A young philosopher though a good man, perished for nothing. And right away Khalyava, a bell-ringer, gives good advice to other philosophers and intellectuals: how not to perish ourselves. "Well, I do know why he perished: because he got frightened. If he had not been afraid the witch could do him nothing. One should only cross himself and spit at its very tail then nothing can happen".

In conclusion. It is still possible to take something useful from Anatoly Denisov's discourse. If I have understood it correctly, let anyone head the democratic committee of Russia's salvation declaring that they will remove Gorbachev and the USSR Supreme Soviet (together with the Ethics commission) from power, say, on the 1st of March or next Monday. It would be impossible to find anything illegal in this (compare this to Anatoly Denisov's interview). Further, suppose that Moscow is Riga and Riga is Moscow. So, we declare on Saturday that we are taking power. These are but words, our simple-mindedness, excessive seriousness and nothing more. Besides, we were constantly provoked with decrees, peremptory shouts, orders and Kravchenko's Central TV steadily pulling the wool over our eyes. We can be easily understood. Anatoly Denisov says that "in mass media there was not a hint of pluralism. And this is very dangerous...A small group must not decide for the people what they need know and what not".

So, while minister Pugo left for Riga, here, in Moscow, the building of the Ministry for Home Affairs in the Oktyabrskaya square was taken by assault. But have we, the Committee of National Salvation ever given our blessings openly to those who stormed? And is it worth in general to discuss Gorbachev's dismissal other than aesthetically.

Especially so, if it comes from honest people - the professor explains. The thinks that Turkey will notice nothing at all.

There is something here to think about.

VOTE FOR YELTSIN
BUT WITH OPEN EYES

The TV screen presents Russian presidential hopefuls. We keep watching with fatigue and indifference, yet we nevertheless remain astonished with the inexpressible sadness of the Russian political landscape. A certain person with a familiar face is speaking in a dismal and cracked tone: Kravchenko's reporters seem to show another old film. Here is Ryzhkov again, a dashing company commander with general's stars, a square "real Patriot" growling at "cosmopolitans" and other suspicious civilians. Was it not those curt commands of a school military instructor Makashov that have accompanied us since our childhood? We must also add an energetic, evasive Bakatin, a cousin-in politics of Pavlov and nephew of Gorbachev. We remember in what an affected casual manner this heralder of "values common to all mankind" did comment on the bringing of troops into Moscow o the occasion of a democratic rally. And here is something really new, an operetta character, Zhirinovsky, producing upon the laughing, pleased "communists of Russia" almost the same strong impression as Benya Krik[1] did on Odessa bindyuzhniks[2], pouring out words and showing off provincial smart, with the hysterical manners of a candidate for a little domestic duce. They are mummers on Christmas Eve, with an empty bag, without a tree and without Christmas itself.

But still there is Yeltsin.

It is for the sake of his election that we have to withstand the usual perestroika show. Only with Yeltsin is something of political importance

---

[1] A character of I. Babel's :odessa Stories".

[2] Jewish carters and loaders, etc.

connected. Only about him can we think in serious and it is useful to criticise him and there is sense to argue.

"How" - I have already heard this indignation, - How can we criticize in public, argue, especially before the elections? Is it compatible with an election campaign? "Why not, esteemed *practical figures* of the Russian democracy. From this moment on, millions of people are directly involved in politics. It is on their minds, and governs their moods and their behavior. Consequently, it is their trust and understanding that ambitious but far-sighted politicians should fight for and value, while the population judges by real circumstances and concrete results. It is nearly impossible to hide something essential or to manipulate us, we are too great in number and the sources of information are now various. We in the present-day Russia are particularly sensible to the *authenticity* of what is offered to us as a policy. Therefore, please, don't use the words "morals" or "honesty" with regard t politics! From now on honesty and openness of aims and means will be a part of politics. To be (or to take oneselves as) "clever politicians" without honesty is too silly, perfunctory, outdated and impractical. So, gentlemen, aim to be practical rather than moral. The rules of the game have changed, with strange politicians being valued. Like A.D. Sakharov, for example, whose name you repeat in vain, having understood *nothing* in him, or like Havel or Mazowecki or Adam Michnik.

Second. It is of no use to bring the methods of Western routine election campaigns into our upside-down and tragic life. Intensive, active, continuously growing stratified citizens become less and less inclined to blindly "support" anyone. In respect of this conscious strata (miners, for example) no leader should rely on personal suggestion, absolute authority, or on "charisma". The time has come for Russia to say "yes" with open eyes. The Democratic movement will never become something deserving such a snake while it serves only as a background and a kind of a support group for a popular leader. It is much more essential to what an extent the leader himself is useful for the moment as one of those who desire to unite and represent the Russian democracy as a political partner and an ally, or if necessary, as an opponent for Yeltsin.

Formerly I used to say something like this about Gorbachev. Well, nowadays this must be said about Yeltsin, a new hero of our story, and to warn that if Russia happens to get disappointed it will not take five more years. things get worse quickly and people become wise even more quickly; as Boris Nikolayevich recently said "people will not bear it". Yeltsin has little time for maneuvering, much less than Gorbachev had.

Testing his steps could be valuable for Yeltsin in "Democratic Russia". While for the latter (I mean "Democratic Russia" as an idea rather than in reality) B.N. Yeltsin is neither a banner, nor the object of a new solidarity and loyalty but, rather, an instrument for speeding up a radical transformation. In short, support of Yeltsin is conditional for people of good sense. But what are the conditions on which "Democratic Russia" is ready to support him? And what does not suit us absolutely in Yeltsin's present moves, what do we expect or demand from our candidate for the Russian presidency? Have the appropriate talks with him taken place? Has a protocol been signed? Alas, nothing of the kind. Then, what is "Democratic Russia" worth in the person of its Coordination Council?

Third. Leaving aside for awhile the contents of the "1+9" declaration we cannot help seeing that the highly praised "compromise" was singed at the moment needed by Gorbachev and in the atmosphere dictated by him, It was hailed by the Plenum of the CPSU Central Committee, the "Soyuz" group, and Pavlov's cabinet. Yeltsin has not deemed it his duty even to consult either strike committee or. of course, "Democratic Russia", or those he leaned on and who (in February - April) demanded the dissolution of the present Union structures, not to add with it to Boris Nikolayevich in the Novo-Ogaryovo bargaining. There was no basis found for convoking the Consulting Council under the Chairman of the RSFSR Supreme Soviet: if it exists not for such really important occasions, then why does it exist at all? In short, an armistice in the top echelon was concluded without the participation of progressive public forces, behind the scenes, in a traditional apparatus manner. I was astonished that this meeting of the group of top national-communist leaders with Gorbachev was considered by B.N. Yeltsin to be "the round table" ("which has proved it effectiveness several times" - "Izvestiya", May 23)! AS if Boris Nikolayevich is not aware that "round tables" in Eastern Europe were open and strictly conditioned negotiations between representatives of the *society* and the *state* on a stage by stage and bloodless transfer of power. On the contrary, in Novo-Ogaryovo the idea of the "found table" mentioned by Yeltsin himself tow weeks earlier, was thus crossed out. Yeltsin's signing of this declaration knocked down the unprecedented rise of the workers' movement, enabled the "Center" to unleash violent attacks against Armenian peasants and Baltic customs officers, declaring that strikers would be persecuted as well. Many people were taken aback, got on the alert and protested against Yeltsin's reversal. How should one react to this in the course of the election campaign for Yeltsin? To repeat as the candidate himself does, that in fact in Novo-Ogaryovo "the President's retreat was greater than that of the representatives of the republics"? It will not convince those who have taken the trouble to get a grasp of the text.

The selection of Rutskoy for the vacant post of vice-president became the logical continuation of Yeltsin's Novo-Ogaryovo improvisation. However, it will not bring him additional votes in the country, but only at the Congress. Is he a capable of influencing a substantial number of voters? Those CPSU members who had sympathy for Yeltsin before will now support him rather than the yet unknown Rutskoy. But on the other hand other voters (particularly intellectuals) may not be content with the "Yeltsin-Rutskoy" tandem. The Rutskoy movements useful as an element of confusion but it does not mean that those communists "unable to just simply leave the party" together with those who - "it must also be understood - owe the party their position" when supporting Yeltsin "will embark upon the path of renovation" by doing so. Rehabilitation for communists *as such* is impossible without breaking off with the past. Therefore, radical voters are hardly ready to accept "the interesting version" and find hope in Yeltsin's bloc with moderate communists. However, by gaining in one place Yeltsin may lose in another.

It is permissible to suppose that Yeltsin's support in major cities and industrial areas will be somewhat more languid than it could have been prior to April 23. Nevertheless Yeltsin will undoubtedly win the election, but it is political content, durability and the quality of confidence received by Yeltsin that are important rather than the quantitative results. For the time being he will receive nothing in excess. Yeltsin's destiny will not be decided at the time of the election; the main things are yet to come.

So, it is of no use to say to those whom Yeltsin disappoints now with this unpredictable behaviour and doubtful maneuvering in the "top leadership" : "one and all we shall vote for", etc., in the best old style. It is a *conditional* support that is one of the most important elements of the new policy. This is a new understanding that when differences are not obliterated or ignored in silence in a political bloc, civilized solutions worked out among our "own people", in our own camp, in the course of open internal discussions. If we continue to demonstrate zealously our "unanimity" with Yeltsin, to teat him as a sacred cow alleging that criticism from the left can weaken his opposition to the right, then it will mean that we shall remain in the grips of quasipolitics with Yeltsin as we did with Gorbachev. Out of a new-fangled "consensus" there appear the ears of the old "unbreakable unity and solidarity". I felt ashamed to hear at the Coordinating Council of "Democratic Russia" that "morals" must be left for "speeches from the ambo" - and "this is politics" and arguments with Yeltsin now are inappropriate. As Lenin used to say, this is still an injurious "luxury": When at last do we learn anything?

Let thinking people vote for Yeltsin on an honest and healthy political and psychological basis: Boris Nikolayevich is also a transitional historic figure, after all, only a few of his concrete steps are appraised by independent democrats, but nevertheless today we shall support him.

Why? Well, at least he is better than the other hopefuls. He gives the impression of being a sincere man even when he is mistaken. He can admit his mistakes, is capable of changing quickly (sometimes too quickly), but mainly because his basic thesis is correct: "partial reforms, their gradual implementation will ruin us" (I continue to cite the "Izvestiya" newspaper of May 23). "Transition to a free market must not be delayed persuading people that the more radical changes are, the worst it will be for them, people. But is there anything worse that our making no headway and in fact our staying on the verge of disaster".

That is right! Decisive changes have turned on the historic necessity for the quickest non-violent replacement of dead structures. It is unthinkable to secure such a replacement without powerful *organized* pressure from below, i.e. without a general political strike. If it is delayed, *spontaneous* excesses and state violence will become the alternative; the party bigwigs and generals are provoked to demonstrate that civil disobedience and the insufficiency and weakness of rallies and strikes are drawbacks of the Russian democratic movement. The idea of a peaceful overthrow of the communist regime by the people is not the "left radicalism", scare tactic of the official and "liberal-centrist" propaganda. Radicalism in this sense has been invented; it does not exist at all, but means a forced and prudent thinking out of the situation to the end. And otherwise - Yeltsin is right, "people will not bear it" and something unpredictable will be started. There is nothing resembling a garish lumpen-revolutionaries here. Civil disobedience means nothing else but the idea that people thrown into a river must feverishly move their arms and legs. If that is radicalism so be it. Then, please include in "left radical" the entire Eastern Europe, then Baltia and Armenia, then all the miners and millions of Ukrainian democrats and suddenly Byelorussia, and do not forget to mention Sakharov and Yeltsin, especially as he was in March.

But Yeltsin is mistaken in saying that the CPSU has lost its chance to head the real radical structural changes. The party has never had such a chance. I do not believe that all promoted Communists and apparatus people without exception must be pushed away, but it should be done individually. Yeltsin contradicts himself convincingly demanding " a radical end of the mighty bureaucratic system" rather than a "stage by stage one" and at the same time advising to "enlist" for it..." in a more moderate way...not to frighten people with ultra-left speeches, to move closer to the center". Of course, the question is not about speeches, but about the unification of the majority around the "radical changes" of which Yeltsin himself is speaking.

Rank-and-file communists will be convinced not by duality and moderateness but, on the contrary, they will be captivated by the all-national democratic enthusiasm as has been the case from Bulgaria to Albania and in our land as well. "Centrism" can prevail in calm an steady situations but on the eve of those great changes we speak of the leftish tendency that appears in the center of society and this is precisely the "center", that is the majority of people. Yeltsin will miss the target if he fails to target the workers movement, major cities, the highly skilled and young people.

I am far from being against a compromise with Gorbachev. However, I will only support one which will advance the country with the participation and approval of the workers' and democratic movements; which is legally precise, with a control mechanism and without ambiguity, rhetoric and receipt on the very next day.

I am not overestimating the significance of the precious deal in Novo-Ogaryovo. It was a deliberate confirmation of the well-known redistribution of the political weight, and the republican authorities readiness to take the "Center" into consideration. A little later Gorbachev explained once more that they had in mind a "renovated" federation and then the USSR Constitution, so "sovereign states" are nothing but a *phrase* existing in the text of the present Constitution, "with due regard for the results of the All-Union referendum". Just what are *"the* results"(The position taken by the democrats and B.N. Yeltsin was that the referendum question was deliberately cheated and therefore it was impossible to get a reply with a clear legal and political meaning). It is difficult to imagine such a treaty which would be signed by Kravchuk, Nazarbayev and others, and Yeltsin as well. Meanwhile this splendid Supreme Soviet of the USSR adopts "The Law" on KGB the authors of which, in their simple-mindedness, are unaware of a certain allegedly forthcoming treaty of sovereign states (compare to Clause 9 of this law!), neither about the inadmissibility of violation of rights of USSR citizens" (precisely such a violation is allowed by Clause 14, Sections 3 and 9). Meanwhile Pugo and Yazov's committing acts of violence in the Transcaucasus, what lawlessness! The Novo-Ogaryovo declaration also contains a funny phrase about "further" (?!) strengthening and developing economic ties between enterprises and republics with "increased responsibility for it (for horizontal ties!) of the USSR Cabinet of Ministers". It means "mutual anticrisis measures" according to Pavlov's plan, and economic punitive sanctions against the republics who will refuse to sign the treaty, but without the immediate granting of independence to them at all.

The transfer of mines in the RSFSR (in the Ukraine it happened last year) passes to Yeltsin the necessity of further explanations with miners living a hard life with no means to help themselves. This Presidential Decree left no doubts what a gift the "extraordinary regime" is. And how could the democratic leader put his signature under the words bout "incitement of civil disobedience, strikes"? It surpasses all understanding.

In return, at that moment, Gorbachev hid the card of "autonomies" in his sleeve (but now what? Is a real problem solved with senseless word playing about entering the Union both directly and as a member of Russia...so to say, both "at home and married"). Gorbachev seemed to reconcile himself at last to the fact that in the future he will have no dealings with Yeltsin, though the exchange of biting remarks in public was going on even after that. Yeltsin felt his tactical progress in these old mutual relations, was able to breathe and tension at the regular Russian congress was lessened. To my mind Yeltsin made a bad bargain. In a few days we shall elect him President of Russia. It is even more difficult to imagine Rutskoy at his post. The Union treat will hardly be singed, as was declared "in recent times". It is more doubtful that we shall see the reactionary former Union Congress adopting the Constitution for the "new" Union. Moreover, the priceless "general compromise" in Novo-Orgaryovo may be totally forgotten in a few months. I do not know which of the participants won the game, but the course of historic events will turn out to be much more intricate than this game. But I am worried now by another thing. How will Yeltsin's tactics fare on the strategic line of the fledgling Russian democratic movement, on his relations with this movement, and with the workers?

We need Yeltsin very much. But it will be difficult for him to remain up the mark in his unusual historic mission.

YELTSIN HAS WON - SO WHAT?

The next day after the election, Sobchak said in the "Fifth Wheel" TV program something like this: July 12 would be recorded in history as an extraordinary event and a great day for Russia. I doubt it. What happened only confirmed the earlier state of affairs and aggravated the former problems.

Yeltsin's victory in the very first round with a tremendous majority of votes over his closest rival had been beyond any doubt. The "dramatism" of the election campaign was clearly feigned. The CPSU crudely bluffed and certain democrats fell for it, those who felt a new wave of fatigue and disappointment after mass civil disobedience had been knocked down in Novo-Ogaryovo. Nevertheless the inertia of Yeltsin's popularity still continues. Besides, Russians had no choice. Rivals of Boris Nikolayevich looked caricatured and terrifying, except Bakatin who guardedly showed his position to be slightly more to the left than Gorbachev ("Gorbachev tomorrow"?) and deservedly got his 3% of votes.

The lethargic departure of nomenclature people in uniforms was reconfirmed and with them went their "socialist choice" from the political scene. It was a self-evident vote *against* the social system under which we are still living. The fact that the majority of "the city on the Neva" urged on by Gorbachev's appeal, preferred the pre-Revolutionary sounded name "Saint-Petersburg" preserved in the dilapidated splendor of palaces and embankments though outrageously contradicting the "sovok"[1] reality, only not to be called Leningrad, - proves that the ideological and psy-

---

[1] A sconful Russian slang word for "soviet".

chological collapse of the regime occurred with amazing speed and fore-
stalls the structural one.

Further, we have taken another formal step forward towards turning
the "soviet power" into a normal democratic state structure. Yeltsin's political and psychological authority in the minds of the country and the
world public has been "legitimized" thanks to the *direct* mandate of the
voters. However, whether it would become one of the factors of real and
speedy change in Russian life depends on how Boris Nikolayevich will
wish and, how he will be able to use the fixed-time credit he has received.
For the time being I feel that reserved satisfaction with the July 12 results
is more suited to the real scope of what has happened than is particular
joy.

Were the elections really free and democratic? Perhaps partially. It is
not the behavior of the Central TV, nor the numerous and unpunished
violations of the electoral law and nor the fact that there remained a lot of
local "stagnation" areas and entire regions where party and military
bosses are still ruling, quite a number of people dependent and ignorant
vote as they have been told, live a back-breaking and backward life, and
elect nothing. Much deeper is that there is no real multi-party system, society is still too amorphous, its civil structures are not born yet, and there is
no collision of mature and revealed interests. Consequently, voting for
Yeltsin, Popov, Sobchak in many ways was an echo of the protracted
situation of March 1989 (negative motives, rejection of the nomenclature, I
am voting for Yeltsin because he is better than "those), an orientation on
personalities rather than on parties and programs ("Yeltsin will help",
"well, he is not lying after all", "I know Ryzhkov, he is sympathetic", and
so on), and add the familiar symptoms of adoration of a leader and sometimes demagogic vituperation.

Significantly absent are symptoms of a well-thought-over and stipulated *political bloc* of Yeltsin's supporters and allies and this, above all,
rests on one of the most dangerous circumstances: Russia has no independent, responsible and effective radical-democratic movement which
would politically represent on a nation-wide scope what found expression
in the desperate courage of a group of miners in February-April. There are
radicals but no clearly outlined radical stand or organization. We have
plenty of people inland to a "centrist" attitude but there is no expressed
centrist force.

Yes, it is for the first time that Russia was electing its leader freely
(and this is splendid!) but we ourselves are not yet free people and are not
certain what have we elected after all except the hope for something bet-

ter. Whether Russia's leader will be precisely such in the arms of the Center, in a word, with what contents the election results will be filled.

There is no use now in referring to the evaluation of the conditions on which the armistice of Yeltsin and Gorbachev was signed in Novo-Ogaryovo. But until now M.S. Gorbachev, when speaking on TV (as usual verbose and evasive) said that "the results of the referendum" will be fully taken into consideration. That there will be "the strong Center and strong republics" - yes, we have not misheard it, the same formula of the CPSU program of 1989! And that "the renewed federation" will be a return to "Lenin's treaty" of 1922. As for the "mixed" economy providing "even private property", another commission has been set up in which opponents to any "privatisations" have been included too. I trust the President and think that he has stated everything adequately. If the situation is just like this, it is easy to imagine what will come out of the next "last chance" of Gorbachev, the glorious "Novo-Ogaryovo process", maneuvers of the same communist state team.

The "scenario" which Gorbachev and his CPSU will be able to use, to follow tough, i.e. post-soviet and post-communist, if necessary, immediate and rapid reforms, would be wise to consider to be utterly speculative, simply improbable in political and psychological respect. In the economy too, we face half measure and quarter steps. These people will keep their social identity to the end. They have neither power, nor will and know how to bend over backwards.

I would wish very much to be mistaken. I case Yeltsin nevertheless signs the good-for-nothing treaty of the alleged "sovereign states" intending to go forward later and tries to gain points gradually, such ("Kadar-like")[2] tactics which would be sufficiently clever in a less dramatic situation, will make him a victim of historic time trouble.

Therefore, he will be forced nevertheless to "quarrel: again, and deeper than ever, with Gorbachev, i.e. the policy of Gorbachev, Pavlov-Scherbakov, Pugo, Kravchenko[3] and many others. There is no other way out.

Already in this year missions of people will join still more powerful movement and if this movement turns out to become spontaneous, lacking a clear political form and leadership, the more so it will develop counter to the Russian government's policy. But it is not accidental that

---

[2] Kadar was the leader of Comminsty Hungary. /L.B./

[3] Pavlov ws prime-minister, Scherbakov - deputy prime-minister Pugo - minister of home affairs, Kravchenko - chairman of the state TV committee.

we have handed the mandate over to Yeltsin precisely on the eve of the great change. We have elected Yeltsin. And what just what that means remains to be seen.

In my opinion, the end of "Democratic Russia" in its present form will be one of the most important results of June 12, Yeltsin, Popov, Sobchak have won what is next? Without its own policy, "Democratic Russia" is a symbiosis of ill-assorted "parties", their ambitious leaders ad new functionaries and bureaucratic democrats, crafty and inclined to conformism, as "democratic" careerism has begun to show distinctly, frightenly, naturally and inevitably. Such a "Democratic Russia", is hardly needed in a *political* respect, even by Yeltsin and his associates; perhaps only for the election campaign and organization of meetings with the "public" but not for consultations or the principal choice of a course and not for "feedback" with the country.

Present-day "Democratic Russia" had done its duty and gone out of use. and later it will be rather harmful, blocking up the Russian political space with its fragile clumsy body. Time is coming for the combination of, say, two or three democratic forces (parties, blocs, movements) distinctly oriented, and ready to coordinate their efforts within certain limits. The birth of the "union of independent democrats" is particularly, indeed desperately, needed as one of such political components, at least in the form of an important center of ideological and moral authority. I am speaking about the crystallization of intellectual and far-sighted radical liberalism, with its own strategy and vision of historic dynamics and prospects. Such an organization could count on the sympathy of workers, intellectuals, and farmers. And what about "Democratic Russia"? "Democratic Russia" would remain a reality, as was meant, a mechanism of *coordination*. However, the present tendency is to turn it into something like a party: with utter confusion of programs and persons accompanied by vulgar squabbles and intrigues.

It is often said that a "round table" in an Eastern European manner is still impossible here mainly because there are no serious representative public movements which could sit at a table of negotiations with authorities as equals. Therefore they say that Gorbachev's meeting with the highest officials of the republics is, you see, our "round table" or "a step forward towards it" but, we must be realistic. A "round table" is not possible yet, and extremely complicated from the viewpoint of our national-state situation but if you are real democrats, please, concentrate on the creation of more favourable conditions towards that end. Don't be in a hurry to run to the either side to make a repeated pleas for "centrism" and "compromise".

We must explain ourselves once and for all: I am also in favour of centrist tactics, in case it is constructive for the radical strategy and, of course, for compromises, but not for imaginary ones. For a compromise to b e possible between you and your political opponents, we must be real opponents; we must exist ourselves as a *special* force with *our own* principles and intentions known to society. In short, one must be someone at first and then as this definite and serious someone on may enter negotiations with partners, or authorities. A compromise? Let people see within what segment different circles have coincided, where initial positions are and where the precisely outlined zone of compromise is. What is left beyond the boundaries of this zone and what are the conditions of checking, time limits, etc.? A compromise in politics is something like a business contract but it needs a minimum of two real contractors. A compromise happens to be needed to end a dispute. Now ad then we see nice liberals and even "radicals" starting with a compromise contrary to the normal strategy demanding toughness at first.

As for centrism, it is impossible in our unstable situation as an independent party leaning on the majority of the population; however, it could, perhaps, express itself in an agreement between moderate (but consistent) reformers and radicals, with an absolute defeat of the right-wing, I. the present-day regime. But, there are no priorities to come to an agreement.

There are energetic and honest people among the "democratic leaders"; and millions of supporters, but we lack concentration and political moral substance.

HEALERS AND POLITICS

This man all of a sudden stepped out from behind the scenes as a puppet on a string abusing all his rivals except general Makashov, as "knowing nothing" about the "Memory" group and immediately finding an ally in Nevzorov - Mr. Zhirinovsky has all the reasons to consider the election results his "brilliant victory". Unknown until three weeks before the election he gained six million supporters as a result of just a few TV shows!

As many others, I spoke ironically and laughed at his vulgar and shameless devices at the IV Russian Congress, but soon after, having studied him in the course of a long interview given to the first program of the Central TV I thought it over and realized that third place was ensured for him. A bow-tie instead of a plain one convinced me that Zhirinovsky had a correct political instinct. Repeating that the "is living with two hundred rubles" in "an ordinary two-room flat, I am one of you", at the same time, in every possible way he emphasized his originality. " I speak four languages" He distinguished himself from all other candidates with their absolutely "our" appearance and familiar manners, more or less stammering speech, unusual Soviet constraint or rudeness or a combination of both. Zhirinovsky's rudeness is of an absolutely different kind, and there is no hint of constraint at all! Stupefied voters with a growing interest were examining at last a *real* demagogue of just a foreign, previously unheard of level and tone. Hysterical and sometimes losing his temper (never mind, he will learn a bit) hopeful with his commanding grimace and haughtily twitching lower lip spoke with competence and smoothness and three times quicker than all his rivals together. Oh, how important is political style!

This style was tested in the old days in Munich beer-houses and on a balcony on the Rome square in Venice where from the duce used to prophesy. Unlimited self-confidence once more! Knowledge of immediate answers to any questions! The slightest pensiveness or the problematic nature of any answers are pernicious. " I shall defend you", "I shall se-cure", I shall be the protector and father of the nation, you must just make the right choice, elect and then put everything out of your minds, think about nothing and do not care, I know myself what is to be done and how and I shall observe everything. I shall defend Russians, Russians, Russians, - do you remember?- I shall put down "southerners", shall get any required money in Iran, Turkey and Afghanistan, I shall rule the *entire Union*, abolish republics, divide this whole country into provinces from Baltia to Kushka, I shall liquidate and ban someone, I am a tough customer. I am a lawyer, everything will be done only in accordance with a law, I shall be "Western" president, I am for human rights, as a matter of fact, I am a "liberal", down with communists, I am not against communists, I stand for the army, for minor nations, for private capital, for the sale of cheap vodka in every corner, only Russia will be everywhere with no national problems, and not a word about OMON squads and KGB. Let everyone find something pleasant in this continous current of words. It is all the same, if not now then 6 months from now you will vote for me, believe it or not. I will count to ten, and you will feel better...

Such is the phenomenon of Kashpirovsky[1] - Zhirinovsky in both method and social nature. And this is serious: exactly to such an extent and until the country remains in stagnation, disintegration, apathy, social confusion and depression.

Such mushrooms grow perfectly well in moisture and darkness. And what is not neglected here, what field of our daily life and work? Where is it not damp?

You are welcome! - the fifth act of the Soviet historical play with the same characters (i.e. ourselves) and Vladimir Volfovich Kashpirovsky[2]. He looks perfectly effective side by side, for example, with Nikolai Ivanovich Ryzhkov. They complement each other almost perfectly. If we come to it with a certain historic and sociological insight it is not clear who is a healer and who is the patient. Ryzhkov treated the country for several years. The general is a parapsychologist and Tuleyev[3] is quite a folk healer.

---

[1] Kashpirovsky is a TV "healer" "curing" diseases for the entire country.

[2] Hyrid of christian name and patronymic of Zherinovsky and family name of a cheat of an ESP man.

[3] A reactionary populist Tuleyev is a hopeful for the Russian presidency.

The most serious healers always worked in the House on the Staraya square[4]. while Zhirinovsky is from our five-story houses.

As dying Mercutio remarked about the policy in Verona: "A Chu-plague on both your houses!"[5]

---

[4] The building of the CPSU Central Committee..

[5] Play on words: Chumak is the name of another healer appearing on TV screens.

VENDORS IN A TEMPLE

At the end of February, I proposed a resolution to the Coordinating Council of the "Democratic Russia" movement. It was neither rejected in its essence, nor accepted but postponed for discussion and revision. As a matter of fact, the text that I passed to the organizing group had been lost somewhere. Having prepared it once more, I read it with my report at the extraordinary Plenum of the Soviet of Representatives and succeeded, as the result of repeated urgent requests in having it discussed before the plenum's closing. This time, again, there were no objections on its substance, however the majority of the voters did not support it. It was decided to give it back to the Coordinating Council for revision and adoption as a final document. Nevertheless this decision of the plenum remained unfulfilled as well, I do not know why. The text was lost once more, then after my incessant reminders it was found and returned to the author. At the meeting of the Coordinating Council on March 7, I told my colleagues that I did not intend to keep our dirty linen in our democratic home. And I felt obliged to submit this subject for public discussion in the press.

What is the "subject"? And what is a resolution?

Approximately the following.

"Certain participants of the 'Democratic Russia' movement occupying leading posts in the Soviets and working at executive bodies are at the same time registered as heads of certain commercial ventures (investment funds, banks, cooperatives, etc.). The council of Representatives of the "Democratic Russia" considers this absolutely unacceptable. Regardless of the purity of intentions of these persons, granting their names to a commercial venture inevitably suggest the idea of possible reciprocal, albeit indirect services. Obviously this creates a breeding ground for corruption, and provides material for propaganda hostile to the arising democracy. The reputations of democratic politicians must be secured against suspicions and ambiguous situations. That is why the Council of Representatives calls upon all those leading state figures who act on behalf of "Democratic Russia", ad who consider themselves participants in and enjoy the political support of our movement to immediately renounce practical or relative "honourable") participation in commercial activities".

A declaration like this would be far from artificial and useless. It is difficult for me to judge whether the number of respective cases is great, nevertheless, they do exist. Unfortunately there have begun to appear reproaches in the press, perhaps groundless though. Moreover, even if such incidents are few, there is no need to keep silent and exchange glances. Until we reject in principle such a state of affairs, (not prohibited by our laws as in developed countries) it is the movement as a whole that is responsible for each possible incident.

This is the most elementary thing, a practical policy. The ensuing scandal is always possible even with a stable, perfectly adjusted democratic system, however compromising persons rather than the system itself, in our situation, would inflict a blow at the very idea of democracy. They say it is practiced by all state officials from the CPSU, even Pavlov. They say politicians do not receive salaries for being on commercial boards of directors. They also say that economists, cooperators, and businessmen have the right to be elected to the Soviets. But, we are speaking, on the contrary, about politicians acquiring commercial sinecures. Second, suppose, a cooperator was elected to a certain commission of a Soviet, and became a functionary in addition to being only a deputy. If he can now officially or indirectly influence registration, distribution of premises, raw materials, etc., then he must say good-bye to a commercial business and work for the benefit of *all* the companies. One must choose: either a commercial career or a state one.

Finally they say: what if it casts aspersions on may democratic politicians who never dreamt of it, and in short, on the entire movement in case we have sounded a preventive alarm. However, let us proceed from the fact that no criticism of the democratic movement following precisely its own principles, no warning or unpleasant diagnosis, if it is correct, will do any harm to the movement. To think otherwise would be dangerous, of course.

P.S. It is a sad lesson that only tow months after this review was written I have succeeded to publish it; very good people in certain publishing houses were confused whether it would be properly understood and wasn't there an excessive irritation in it. I confess there is, what can I do? And it will be understood exactly the way it was written. It was dated march 12, 1991.

P.S.S. Only a year after the publication of this review did President Yeltsin sign a decree (in April 1992) stipulating future punishment for combining appointments in the state system with direct or indirect participation in commercial activities. And it was only on the eve of this decree that the Coordinating Council of "Democratic Russia", in January 1992 still resisting furiously at the movement's plenum against the appropriate resolution that I repeatedly proposed the same opinion. But it is still early to send to the archives such a disgraceful story, hardly comprehensible in Western countries where they consider such officials to be criminals worthy of prosecution. Without it, one cannot realize what the present Russian "democrats" are: the procurator-general of Russia Stepankov recently wrote in the "Kommersant" that "corruption is everywhere...among state counsellors (i.e. in Yeltsin's immediate surrounding. L.B.) there are chairmen of joint-stock societies and funds and even an owner of a foreign-currency restaurant". Yeltsin's decree has changed nothing and has not been fulfilled as, in fact, the majority of the President's other decrees.

A LOVELY ROUTE

My acquaintance with economist G.Kh.Popov[1] who coined the expression "commanding administrative system" started after he incessantly advised in he press "not to jog Gorbachev's left arm". In my collected articles "It Cannot Be Otherwise" I tried to explain as I could why this advice was good for nothing. At the time of our meeting, Popov said that, in fact, he shard my opinion.

I am one in nine million Musovites and the municipal novelties of Gavril Kharitonovich interest me. In the Moscow situation, certain more general features of the Russian leadership in general are expressed, those problems and dangers which will inevitably reach each town and region of Russia. Upon becoming the mayor of Moscow, G.Kh.Popov assumed responsibility for all the decisions in his office and as he is, perhaps, the most prominent ideologist among the new administration, criticism addressed to him only personifies and gives concrete expression to the growing protests and doubts for which, of course, not Popov alone s responsible. This criticism refers to him, to the Russian leadership and to us all.

The last year was marked in Moscow with the issue of "visiting cards"[2] (sellers did not even intend to view them), distribution of distant "sotkas" of land ("a sotka" is 1/100 of a hectar) among townsfolk for independent substance and the return to mass construction of private cottages in the capital's environs. At that time I was confused with the simple easily understood, but emphatically contradictory populist spirit of these measures. Nothing seems to have come of either of them? Well, I am not an economist. We had better switch to the year of 1991.

---

[1] G.Kh.Popv, the Mayor of Moscow since June 12, 1991, unexpectedly resigned in May 1992.

[2] "Visiting cards" are identity cards giving the right to purchase goods in Moscow shops. This Popov venture failed quickly and was cancelled.

To begin with, G.Kh.Popov endeavored to deprive the Moscow Soviet he had headed for more than a year, of significance. Deputies are numerous to the point of absurdity; they love to make speeches, the majority of them, especially democrats, are non-professionals in communal services and amenities, finances, economy, etc. They are touchy and disobedient, they are unreasonable, well, they are like a veche. (Sobchak complained about the same in St. Petersburg). They say in general "Soviets" were fund to be unfit as soon as they turned into real representative bodies, but nobody seems to argue about it any longer.

Our newborn democracy has to undergo reforms, its present forms being transitional, at best. We did elect these people, thought they are very far from political perfection and in this respect they resemble us; they more or less reflect the structure of the population, the interests of various social strata. Their heterogeneity is a necessary counterbalance for the administration, the more so as the bulk of the apparatus is the same as before, the new nomenclature being also quite far from perfection.

We realize that power was and is everything in this country. It was solely of an administrative, executive character, and remains such, as there have been no real legislative or judicial powers. Bureaucratic power perfectly preserved the "executive" apparatus with some present-day hurried modifications: a bulky hierarchical structure and inflated "staff", unavoidable privileges of officials, finally, in the very psychology ("chiefs know best").An additional mighty temptation arises from the fact that those who like (and often know how) to command receive a unique opportunity not only to make a career out of following certain regulated rules of the game but also to work out these rules (though only outward, official) anew in order to make them more suitable for business, as honest people of great ambition sincerely believe but, also to make precisely their own administrative activities easier. It is too difficult to tell one from the other, even for people fanatically devoted to the cause as they understand it. The deplorable experience of the bolsheviks has not been forgotten though among bolsheviks of 1918 - 1922 there were more people with true firm ideological principles and selflessness than among the present administrators.

That is why both legislative and, no less importantly, judicial and executive state institutions must e brought up to the modern level in principal combination and simultaneously. A real and painful crisis of the "soviet power" called for division and strengthening of both of its functions, justifying G.Kh. Popov's criticism.

This is known only too well, but in practice Popov seems to decide otherwise: it is troublesome to deal with the city council in such a critical situation. Real power in the city must be concentrated in the hands of the Mayor; no sooner said than done. Liking Popov and seeing him on a team with Yeltsin, Muscovites elected him Mayor, with greater power than that of a governor-general. Most remarkable was the fact that the Mayor was elected first and later the President's decree determined these very authorities and it became known what "a mayor" is, properly speaking.

Well, in our capital city there appeared the Mayor, the Vice-Mayor and "the government" naturally meaning ministers, a department with its general director, prefects and subprefects, regions and many other things, it is difficult to remember them all. A good start was made for a strong executive power though one can hardly call it "executive", as whose will does it execute? District soviets will be dissolved, prefects will obey G.Kh. Popov, who has appointed the, while some people in the Moscow Soviet submit and others go on hunger-strikes.

Empowered assistants of Gavril Kharitonovich and his companions have become "ministers" or are now commanding the "national guards" and militia, even the Moscow GB. Certain people, myself being one of them, have doubts. There is no independent court in town, no firm representative power and no private property and no market economy capable of providing the townsfolk with goods and services without any "ministers". In a word, we are still on the same social ground with the accustomed habits of the apparatus and suppliants, with a shortage of honest officials, without a democratic "counterbalance", with no serious political opposition. With the best of intentions, and irreproachable decency, they cannot help doing it. Such are the traditions and logic of the Commanding System which was so well described by G.Kh. Popov. I am afraid that this system may regenerate now in Russia - though in an Absolutely New Democratic form.

We should assume that G.Kh.Popov knows what he is doing. He will suddenly answer me in his sober-minded and timed, but sympathetic manner: "You, Leonid Mikhailovich, are wrong to jog the left elbow on the unsteady new power, and so on and so forth. Or is it the right elbow? Now it is hard to make heads or tails in our situation. And I cannot unfortunately see proper legal ways to push for the next five years with our unhappy population. I am probably just exaggerating a little bit the new (ancient?) danger until it is too late.

It is still uncertain whether the Muscovites will gather enough potato from their sotkas and put it on their balconies covering it as they were advised to do, while businessmen are already indignant with the pressure put on them, with the administrative robbery. In what way is the "market-enthusiast" Popov comforting us on Central TV? It turns out that there are "good" businessmen having none of their own among the officials and "bad" ones who have obtained access to the "secretary of the city party committee or his assistant" and are exclusively inflating prices. Therefore the Mayor must have the right to cut down unrealistically high prices. First, as for corrupt officials; it is very likely that they are no longer in the CPSU Committee, but in the Mayor's office and the city government. Then, fight against corruption rather than businessmen. Second, who will separate the clean from the unclean? It is O.K. if it is G.Kh.Popov himself or, suppose, the master of Moscow's routine life Luzhkov, we shall trust their unerring volitional interference with the prices. But they will be informed. That means that a large new field is being created precisely for an arbitrary rule and corruption. Introduce anti-monopoly laws, by all means, but don't touch prices.

It is still unknown whether this hastily erected tremendous power of which Promyslov (together with Grishin[3]) never even dreamed of, will be really effective and useful for our modest everyday needs. Meanwhile in addition to the enormous bulk of the Moscow Soviet building they have also obtained for the management both the stories in the CMEA[4] and the city's duma building (i.e. the museum of V.I. Lenin).

I was astounded with the news. What are they starting with in our poverty-stricken Moscow! We recognize the style, but it's not democratic. And is it possible that sometime later, (when total administrative system is no longer needed) these crowds of apparatus officials will gladly give up their offices, resounding in the last of Peter the Great titles, apartments or offices? Or will a perestroika be needed?

When I heard G.Kh. Popov explaining on TV in his same sweet and democratic manner why, if the Ukraine decides to become independent, the question must be raised about the Crimea, Donbass, Novorossia with Odesan and something else, - I, astounded and indignant, had to state that G.Kh. Popov still does not always understand what he is doing. But he is a very wide man which means that he does understand it quite well. That is why I am seriously worried.

"The Government" of Moscow consists entirely of "democrats" and such an original and Soviet Mayor as Gavrill Kharitonovich. But in this country there exist only weak sprouts of a civil society and we must create precisely this rather than a "strong power". A democratic system must

---

[3] Highest Moscow leaders under Brezhnev's regime.

[4] The skyscraper of the "Council of Nutual Economic Assistance" of the Warsaw Pact countires.

secure the independence of as many people as possible from the power and in greater varieties of the relations which make a democratic power stable and effective. The executive power must not provide the rules of the game but only effect control over their fulfillment, and this is what makes it strong. I would hate to hear that Russians will have all the reasons to say soon: "Everything has changed but in fact nothing has been changed".

IF failures occur in winter with the bread supply and the heating of houses will be useful to walk from the former CMEA building, past the White House to the might building of the Moscow Soviet and, say, to the Old Square. A lovely route. And it will be possible to freely visit (if you receive passes) the familiar democrats. How are they looking now, in their "high offices"?[5] Oh, what an incomparable Soviet style, truly unfading.

---

[5] "High offices" is a journalist-bureacratic expression.

VODKA AND POWER IN RUSSIA

THROUGH A MISSED OVER BOTTLE

I hate politics as much as I am interested by it. On the contrary, I like vodka though I do not drink it almost at all because of poor health. But, in my opinion, a possible new combination of vodka and politics, invented by the Mayor of Moscow, will cheer up even the most indifferent citizens and will make everyone but on their thinking caps. Here a coarse material interest is combined with a strictly theoretical interest. It immediately demonstrated what we can expect from the democratic power offered to us, in the development of a free market economy, civil society and social justice. That is why I am tempted, all of a sudden, to look at certain political and psychological problems, so to say, through a missed bottle.

The present-day ration, two half-litre bottles a month for each adult, is still in force. However, vodka will be (or to express it with more caution, is supposed to be) sold freely without coupons. AS for the price it started at 30 rubles in Moscow.

And the most interesting thing is ahead. If you wish you may pay 60 rubles, drink your litre of the vodka and in addition get back the difference between the old and new state prices: you will receive 20 rubles per bottle. If you do not drink, the Mayor's office will also pay you for each unbought half-litre bottle and within your allotment, same money. You may spend as it pleases you: on cheese, stocks of dishes, and only those who drink too much will be the losers. That means with subsidies from the Mayor's office it will be easy to toss off a glass on a regular basis of knock back once a week but not to gorge oneself with vodka every day like a swine.

By so doing, the power penetrates into the innermost depths of people's lives. This way or another the Mayor's office will be seen at the bottom of each glass. The power that has embarked on the path of democratic legitimization will do in the most original and witty way precisely what it has been called for since October 1917 - *redistribution*. Sober people will become rich and drunkards with red eyes will ruin themselves. The most important will be the blow at profiteers and ordinary taxi drivers.[1]

THE HEAD IS IN A WHIRL

How many adult people live in Moscow? Let it be five million. Suppose half of them are old people, nursing mothers or very intellectual women. To add sick people like myself, sportsmen training for contests and finally people merry even without drinking, let it be 40% rather than half. Let us multiply 2,000,000 by 40 and we shall have 80 million "wooden"[2] rubles a month and about 1 billion a year. Now it would be as good to sell vodka for this amount of money *in excess* of two bottles per head as to get the money for distribution among the abstainers if it is not enough vodka for *all* the Muscovites. Let us hope that they will bring sufficient vodka and that drunkards plus visitors will save municipal budget.

However, *in any case*, as long as an additional billion rubles will be offered by the population as a demand for the goods which cannot be pt away as booze and which are impossible to find, inflation will be increased by the same amount, i.e. prices will go up for *everything*. Inflation will also be favoured by the fact that there will be no cheap vodka for which you must stand in line for five hours. In spite of the unprecedented financial circulation (you drink, pay 30 rubles to the Mayor's office, get back 20 rubles, add 10 more rubles, drink again, and so on) the amount of money in circulation will be increased at the expense of those who drink. It is nothing, they will print more. But, they *will not produce*, which is the most important thing as any political economy teaches, more vodka to fill up the market for reasons unknown to me. In short, when the official price of vodka goes up it will immediately become more costly on the "black market". Until this invaluable product is desired less, the official price will never keep up with the black market price. The more so as there is no sugar, and no eau-de-cologne. And in case vodka's price goes up,

---

[1] In Russia taxi drivers often sell vodka to night passengers.

[2] "Wooden" rubles is the name of the inflated Russian currency.

everything will rise in price, as vodka is known to be a real convertible currency in Russia.

Perhaps vodka lines will become somehow shorter during the first days. And as a matter of fact, why if, thanks to compensation, vodka will be not more expensive, but even cheaper than on the black market? But you never can tell. At the same time, with the continuing deficit and free sale at higher prices, it will become more profitable and incomparably easier for organized crime to sell it. The proposed vodka financial reform would be an excellent present for them.

Let us consider it further, as the subject is inexhaustible and captivating. Coupons or some kind of "corresponding documents" for savings banks will still be needed, G.Kh.Popov says. 40 rubles can be added for vodka to salaries, pensions and student grants, but what about citizens employed in the private sector or, housewives who do not work? Will they be required to present certified documents that a person neither works nor studies, in addition to passport registration? No, coupons will have to be issued for all. Coupons will be provided, not for vodka but as compensation; It would be real Moscow money! You might ask your friend: "Will you lend me four ten-ruble notes to two coupons till pay day?" Arkady Murashov[3] would have to fight against the coiners of false coupons as they are much easier to counterfeit than notes.

But, perhaps, instead of coupons they will open nominal compensation accounts for all the adults at savings banks? It would result in the furious growth of a number of operations, and a proportional increase in the number of bank employees and their salaries. Well, it is not my concern. The Mayor's office knows better. Let them decide and we could be better off drinking.

Generally speaking I admit that I lack the concentration to think this idea through to the end. My wife thinks that as long as the problem of vodka is, to a considerable extent, the problem of empty bottles, they should also compensate the cost of empty bottles not returned by those who do not drink, naturally at prices approaching market ones. My wife also says that the trouble is with glass factories but something new should be also invented in this respect.

G.Kh.Popov's reasoning is cool. If we are still short, he will use his power as the Mayor and order that it be sold at 35 rubles a bottle, then 40 rubles and so on. Such is a well known method of trials and errors. And if vodka is everywhere and sold without any lines then the Mayor will re-

[3] The chief of Moscow militia.

duce prices. But if, as the result of price reduction, vodka is immediately sold out and goes to the black market again, the Mayor will increase prices once more. Until, at last, Gavriil Kharitonovich personally adjusts the balance between supply and demand.

OH, TEMPORARILY?

I presume that as the Mayor has many other things to attend besides vodka, he will need a special assistant or an adviser for *white wine*[4]. This adviser will have to collect information every ten days or, say by the 25th of each month about lines, "black market" prices in day time and at night, about underdrinking and overdrinking in the entire city. And to prepare well-researched proposals, naturally with the help of his own small staff including a computer operator. The Mayor will then only have to sign a price for the next month, and we having stood in a long line at a savings bank and later at a shop, shall either kick the bottle, put away a lot of booze, or confine ourselves to the first line in order to take money from the abstainers.

Unless a famous philosopher called me on the 5th evening and told me to immediately switch on my TV set, finding G.Kh.Popov on the screen explaining "What is next?" I would have no idea about it or would understand nothing. Popov, as usual, explained everything with the utmost clarity and wisdom. He said that this proposal had to be discussed with people and warned that the same measure with sugar seemed to be ahead.

Let all those who like to drink tea with a lump of sugar in their mouths or with sugar in, as well as those baking pies or making jam pay more to the benefit of people with rotten teeth, who do not need even one and a half kilogram a month and, of course, diabetics. Why not to sell meat too in state shops at 40 - 50 rubles a kilograms of tenderloin and to give the difference to vegetarians and toothless people?

Those who luckily combine all these merits, i.e. not drinking even tea and eating almost nothing, will save by means of such a racket and will buy a shop from the Mayor's office.

For all that, will privatization and similar things take place or not? And why wasn't it started in Moscow a year or a year and a half ago? Is it

---

[4] Vodka.

possible that even after the 1992 new year and many months later we shall buy (suppose, this verb is realistic) vodka or meat as usual in state shops?

All the same G.Kh.Popov will not supply us, issue goods, bring them from a warehouse, throw them on the market, etc. In short: there will be no vodka, or anything else. Perhaps I have been lost, missed something, I had better not start these calculations, economists will calculate everything and the proposal will turn out to be brilliant. It is possible. But nevertheless I somehow feel that it is mystically mad to improve *something in buying or selling anything* (in addition, if we have in the mind the general equivalent with a pickled cucumber) through an *administrative* interference.

However, "the transitional period" - G.Kh.Popov reminds us that all this is purely temporary," for the period of privatisation".

Isn't it possible to sell businessmen licenses for manufacturing vodka and bottles for it for a round sum of money? Is it possible at last to start selling *thousands* of Moscow shops and not only small ones to private persons, stockholders, anyone, and to let them attract buyers. And vodka, as long as it is still a state monopoly, should be sold to private people at agreed upon whole-sale prices and they will resell it to us at retail-liberated prices, legally earning profits. And the word "speculation" (profiteering) would mean what it means in other countries, namely: "reflection, meditation". On the other hand, *there* it may also mean stock-jobbing, etc., demanding careful *thinking* but, at least, not selling vodka by Aund Dusya through a secret passage in a shop.

If something is nevertheless an impediment to our becoming a free market, then the Mayor must speak to us about one thing; *who* or *what* is preventing it? And how can we, the population, the voters, help the Mayor *in this respect*?

I AM TERRIBLY ANNOYED

If Popov, Yeltsin and others need support from below, we demand from them, call for rallies if necessary, but not rallies to support obscure hunger strikes against the actions of an elected Mayor considered wrong or illegal by certain of his opponents, or a disgraceful rally "of support" of G.Kh.Popov, as if someone strongly oppresses the Mayor or violates his rights. We are not always eager to support "against" rallies, but they are at least natural. People displeased with authorities are always found; they have frequent "against" manifestations near the White House in Washington, DC., but a rally "in support" organized in particular by V. Boxer, assistant to the Mayor himself, is something of a very Soviet style. Far more Moscovites will go to city square "against" the new, this time "democratic" making no headway and "in support of " radical economic reforms, beginning with an agrarian one.

Nowadays, Moscovites do not need or at least cannot find a better mayor than G.Kh.Popov. Nevertheless, not only the general political ideas of G.Kh.Popov but also such details demand the most derive opposition on the part of consistent democrats and liberals.

In the course of these days and weeks following August, something most important is being decided, perhaps, our destinies.

G.Kh.Popov himself is both deservedly popular (though his popularity has started to quickly decline) and interesting to me, for example. He deserves to be Mayor, but to our strongest regret, he is acting, I don not know why, as Schedrin's town governor - take as an example this project, remarkable in its kind. I am terribly annoyed. Both Gavriil Kharitonovich and the Muscovites do deserve a far better destiny.

MIRAGES IN THE SANDS OF NOVO-OGARYOVO·

ON IMAGINARY QUANTITIES AS THE MOST ESSENTIAL CHARACTERISTIC OF THE SOVIET INTERNAL POLICY

Having read a lot of G. Orwell, who of us does not remember what Orwell called a double consciousness, the famous phrase: peace is war, etc., that is the distinctive indication of a totalitarian regime rather than violence which we have enough and to spare or lies we have as much as we like. It is the incompatibility of words and meaning which differentiates people's existence into the real and ideologically deliberate. The imaginary and the real are saturating each other, becoming indistinguishable, and in this respect reality does not exist at all.

Presently we find ourselves in a different situation: a political reality has appeared, but it seems to exist in a dense cocoon of the imaginary, and we wonder what I means ant whether it means anything at all. Do we have the power of the CPSU? Perhaps, and perhaps not, and nobody can clearly show where its authority ends and where another power starts.

Is there a military-industrial complex all-powerful and really ruling the country? All of us know that it does exist, but where are its limits? Who speaks on its behalf? Do those characters appearing on the proscenium communicate with others like O.D. Baklanov, supposedly "responsible" for our "general machine-building industry"[1] at the CPSU

---

* Recording of the report read in the "Moskovskaya Tribuna" club on June 29, 1991

[1] "General machine-building industry" is the offical name of the military-industrial complex.

Central Committee/ Maybe it is Baklanov who is ruling the country, we do not know. Do we have a budget? Yes, but until this moment, nobody could even guess what part of this budget is intended for military expenses.

WE have the Supreme Soviet or perhaps, we do not have the Supreme Soviet? What are these people doing there? Do we have a legislative power? Nobody can say with any certainty. And, suppose, when embarking upon his duties, Pavlov utters something fantastic about Western bankers buying our notes, nobody can tell what it is: hooliganism, a well calculated provocation, foolishness or a craft scheme? Nobody can tell, but it is clear that we are facing a certain fata morgana, a mirage. And here is a new mirage, Novo-Ogaryovo.

It is symbolic that one "S: in the "USSR" means not what it meant before. This mirage, this carnival, turns out to be the most essential item of the negotiations of seemingly serious politicians. What have they agreed upon? I have studied this treaty very thoroughly and have come to the conclusion that there is no treaty at all. There are plenty of good words, and pleasant formulas, but no treaty. A compromise follows approximately the following logic: I shall not say this but in your turn you should not say that. I shall not say "socialism" but, please, do not mention "confederation". If you like to be sovereign - excellent: let it be called "the Union of Sovereign States". However, sovereign states without a race of sovereignty will be included into another state, also into the RSFSR. A matryoshka wooden doll is fitted into another and the RSFR as a :"sovereign state" consisting of sovereign states is fitted into the third matryoshka, the sovereign state called the Union of Soviet Sovereign Republics. There is also the fourth matryoshka because the new USSR happens to be fitted into the old USSR, with six republics unwilling to sing the treaty, there still exists the old USSR as if the new one had never appeared.

For all this, it is known to every school boy that if it is a federation (with all agreeing that the new USSR is a federation), that means that its components cannot be sovereign states. A federation all over the world has always been a unitarian state. You want to be called a sovereign state? Nobody is going to seriously attach legal and political meaning anyway.

It is said that all states directly entering the future USSR and at the same time remaining in corresponding federations (which is also absolute logical, legal and political nonsense possess equal rights and equal duties. (RSFSR and North Ossetia, Mordovia and the Ukraine, etc.) But then why does Clause 13 of this treaty read that they will have different numbers of representatives in the Soviet of Republics?

It is phenomenal what this draft has stipulated for the six republics considered to be "fraternal", near and dear, our own even yesterday. Let them not sign, but as Travkin said on TV, the next day we shall set our economic relations on the basis of world market prices. This is an utter absurdity from the viewpoint of those who stay in the Union. but even if it is so and if you are going to treat them as foreigners, then why do you write in the treaty that the old norms of the USSR will be in force with respect to them? Do these old norms stipulate a trade with foreign currency? And if you wish to treat them as foreign states, please, take away the army and the KGB, do not impose rubles on them, let them arrange their own custom houses, and frontier posts and trade with them like with France or Luxembourg.

Now let us discuss the problem of property. There is no word about the USSR's property. There are only properties of the republics or their joint property. However, there appears a phrase "to manage" and it becomes clear that, though the center has no property of its own, it will continue "to manage", i.e. to possess and to command everything and all. (See the chapter dealing with joint competence.) And what will become of the military-industrial complex? It is not very clear but we may guess what after a thorough analysis.

And here is the simplest practical legal question: how will this "managing" be conducted? What will be its mechanism?

But here is something astounding. The matters relating to joint competence are handled by the republics and the Union (not be republics among themselves though it is also their joint property!) "by means of concordance, special agreement, adoption of legislation principles of the Union and republics". So, how? Quite simply, they will be coordinated by means of concordance. You realize that is but a mine filled with empty candy-wrappers scattered around and everyone hoping to find candies for himself. Everyone hopes to beat another playing with this legal and political ambiguity, uncertainty and the principle of bifurcation; unsolving happens to be the main constructive principle of this document. They say, as long as we have not yet decided anything, let us sign the treaty fixing the situation when nothing has been decided yet. Is it a real, serious, responsibly policy?

The way our policy is worked out, it does not matter that everyone has some political sympathies and antipathies. I myself am not satisfied with the very modus of political thinking and political action. I do not understand how, in such a situation like ours, the most crucial historic measures can be taken in secrecy, through some reticence wand deals without legal clarity, and without an accurate account of all political interests. Is it a realistic policy or mirages and imagination seeming to be useful for the sake of interests in a certain situation, for a small lottery prize?

Yeltsin has supported Yavlinsky's plan which I can understand; at least it is clear. He says that this plan is good an that the rest do not suit us. The President says: I shall take with me neither Yavlinsky's plan nor Pavlov's, but my own. But there does not exist an economist Gorbachev; he can take with him only one of several different concrete plans. One cannot cut small pieced from them and sew them together. In case Gorbachev carries with him Yavlinsky's plan I shall welcome it, but I do not believe in this. It is not a matter of sympathy or antipathy toward Gorbachev personally, though each of us has his own opinion of him. I have not yet seen distinctive facts proving that Gorbachev, in Novo-Ogaryovo, gave up his home policy which we used to call right-center and since the fall of 1989 you may call simply right-wing.[2]. Gorbachev is far from taking another political platform, and I do not wish to listen to nonsense about his "last chance", his "left-center turning" etc.

We were all shocked with what took place in the USSR Supreme Soviet at the end of June. There are deadly dangerous extreme right-wing forces; one is the "Soyuz" group, the other is a group of supporting Andreyeva, Makashov, Zhirinovsky and others. Therefore me must support Gorbachev nevertheless. As a matter of fact I do not share the opinion that all this is a show and provocation. On the contrary, it is, perhaps, one of the few realities. With the crucial crisis in leadership there are real arguments and a struggle is going on there. There exists a real discord between the right-wing Gorbachev (it is wrong to call him so) and the ultra-right people. The ultra-right would like to use force against society, while Gorbachev is more sober-minded and realizes that one cannot use force, and that one must try to preserve the system in a modernized form, preserve the Union, but in a soft wrapping with redistribution of the power, preservation of the communist party (or something else in its place, the "socialist choice" with the face having undergone plastic surgery, and, it goes without saying, preservation of Gorbachev's own power and that of people not dear to him but nevertheless, psychologically understood and near, for example, to national communists. Certainly there is a difference between the present day right-wing policy of the center and a possible ultra-right policy.

---

[2] It is accepted in Russia to call communists and ohters - right-wingers, and liberals, etc., - left-wingers.

But what actually feeds this possibility, what does make the ultra-right (both orthodox and national-fascist) danger more of a reality? It is already a year or a year and a half that we have been going on about the threat of a military coup-d'etat, a right-wing one, i.e. extreme right because the right one already took place in 1990. First, there is no direct threat as yet, as there are no facts proving that a real danger is presently threatening Gorbachev. Just remember how he coped with the last plenum of the Central Committee, how he spent twenty minutes bridling Pavlov and managed this Supreme Soviet who, from time to time, acts as a Polish gentry Sei,. Gorbachev manages it quite easily, though he has potentially dangerous opponents. (Pavlov, Lukyanov, Pugo, Yazov, Kravchenko) and he needs a good team for this purpose.

On whom does Gorbachev actually lean? Why does he succeed in managing these people so easily? In fact, we know what he did with loyal Yakovlev, Shevarnadze, even with Bakatin, etc.

They are Lukyanov, Pavlov, Yazov, Pugo, Kravchenko. Today they constitute his team and tomorrow they will act as his adversaries. Well, Gorbachev seems to feel completely at ease and it is due to this that he is taken for almost a great politician. The previous structure has not vanished, but is vaporizing turning into a new mist and delusion and until there is so much mist that the apparatus spirit is indeed alive rushing over the abyss. Tomorrow's reality exists in omens, appeals, hints, and vain attempts with different republics and regions existing already in different historic time. Above everything stands the President ideally summarizing this situation, the President who has learned to speak in such a way that people can listen to him for an hour with rapt attention and learn nothing and understand nothing.

They say: "he is powerless, he can do nothing!" It is not true. He can do a great man things. He is the President and can appear on TV and tell the country anything he wants. He can dismiss Pavlov tomorrow and appoint another Prime-Minister, say, Yavlinsky. he can dismiss that liar Pugo and return Bakatin; he can dismiss everyone and appoint whom he likes. He has almost unlimited authority and he issues a decree everyday. Then why does he not use his power *in this way*?

The say: he is a realistic politician, it is all not so easy, then our ultras will take up arms against him, then they will eat him up. No! Perhaps he will be eaten up but just because he does not take "left" steps.

I wish to express a very simple idea: two years ago, destabilization was born by Gorbachev's policy. I am speaking about a specific present-day (post-Novo-Ogaryovo) policy of Gorbachev's. In the shadow of precisely this policy, under its protection a danger on the part of the ultras is growing and intensifying. They are uniting, getting insolent, devising new steps and snarling at Gorbachev, thanks to the President himself.

Kryuchkov speaks at the Supreme Soviet Andropov's 1977 report about a conspiracy of the CIA, who intended to infiltrate our structures (here Kryuchkov is definitely cognizant of the time and therefore surpasses Andropov). The massive Lubyanka complex in the center of Moscow is far from being a mirage. But, Kryuchkov hints that it is CIA agents who are ruling us. It turns out that it is Gorbachev who is..."tossing up"[3]? Or perhaps it is only Shevarnadze and Yakovlev? or Lansbergis and Ter-Petrosyan? Nevzorov who was supplied with this recording is listening attentively to it, and we are listening to it as well. So I am thinking: in fact, what Mr. Kryuchkov is saying means an attempted breach of the USSR state security! It is a subversive speech challenging the top persons and structures! I understand little State Security Committee's functions, but I think that this committee should immediately reconsider their chief's activities.

Well, what is next? Later, after the notable Friday meeting of the Supreme Soviet Gorbachev left accompanied by Kryuchkov, Pugo and passed a remark to journalists with a smile: "Here is the end of the coup d'etat for you".

Gorbachev means the disguising of Mutalibov's Azerbaijan fighters in OMON uniforms, the deportation of the Armenians, the violence and blood. Gorbachev means the breakdown of the talks with Baltic countries, attacks at custom houses and other places. Gorbachev is much stronger than Pugo and Krychkov and Yazov but it is of little importance whether the President is pursuing such a policy because he is strong or weak, whether he gives orders or yield to others, it is the result that matters. And as far as politics is concerned, Gorbachev means the ambiguities of the Novo-Ogaryovo compromises which, in fact, are not compromises and do not promise us peace and stabilization. Gorbachev means the continuing downfall of the economy into an abyss, talking about a "free market" and at the same time new anti-market measures. All this constitutes Gorbachev's policy. There are those far the right of Gorbachev, but at present he is doing exactly what they would do though they think that they would do it better, tougher and more consistently.

How should Democrats behave? Should they support Gorbachev's policy because of the ultras? No, they should not. They have to determine their own policy and demand it from Gorbachev and all others. It is not

---

[3] "To toss up" harmful "ideas" is the favourite expression of Gorbi.

us who should support Gorbachev, but Gorbachev who must support democratic forces in the country instead of acting in the mask of a cheerful centrist at the carnival.

How shall we take the attempts to form a new party or movement of "democratic reforms"? The split of the CPSU and its decay are both widening. Let the existing groups inside the "Democratic Russia" consolidate and let us see, at last, a more mature structuring of the fundamental positions on the political stage. Let these forces, including the new reformist party which Gorbachev's and Yeltsin's closest people are going to sit up, be ready to enter coalitions on concrete occasions and advance on their own interests and positions. The mechanism of such a coordination may be represented by the "Democratic Russia" itself. But I am against mixing everything and everybody up, against spreading mirages to the very democratic movement. Though it has not escaped ambiguity and imaginary character as well, alas, in any case of we have in mind the central Coordinative Council, the "fraction" of the "Democratic Russia" at the Congress of Deputies, etc. This is a special and long subject, also sufficiently buffoonery and sad.

As one of Yeltsin's supporters I am very worried that Yeltsin seemed to get involved with this phantom game since the end of April. I could mention several of his acts and declarations which are also of a phantom nature: his assurances that "a special regime" for miners, i.e. anti-labour legislation with the prohibition of strikes in the industry, political strikes in general - is a gift, special supplies and secures the welfare of workers. I would not wish that Yeltsin join this game. I would hope that it will not occur at all.

If responsible positions in respect of the deepest aspects of the historical process and tasks for the months to come would be formulated in the democratic movement, then serious coalitions would be possible. The only way to avoid splits is to have different and firm stands which could be placed at the basis of open compromises understood by society. The consolidation of the Russian democratic forces, which appeared in the fall in an immature form, coped with simple tasks: to support Yeltsin in the election, and to support Popov, Sobchak and others. It has fulfilled these tasks ad has outlived its usefulness. "Democratic Russia" will become a melting pot where politically amorphous behaviour will prevent it from becoming a might national force. A new form of political organization and consciousness is needed for the sake of a real major policy.

I seem to be among those considered "radicals". Radicalism in present-day Russia is neither a frame of mind nor an angry slogan detested by some and pleasant for others. It isn't a matter of the notorious "impatience". We are speaking about a simple thing: this regime must perish and as soon as possible. Delaying its demise deepens the danger of a explosion, chaos, hunger riots. We are not in a position to wait for other half a year, a year, two years. Just ask yourselves: what if another year goes by and nothing happens? One more year without real economic reform, and a new year of political mirages. What then?

It means that those who support *stabilization*, show support normalizing our lives must be ready for civil disobedience, and must be radical, nothing else is left for them.

I would call it the *radicalism of common sense*.

WHAT ACTUALLY HAPPENED IN AUGUST

Turning the August events over in our minds we have gotten used to re-peating "junta", "putsch", "coup d'etat". But at the same time we never cease to wonder: why did so many strange things happen?

We have to consider the major mystery of the "putsch" and Gor-bachev. With any version of the coup d'etat, including the official one, the events in Foros nevertheless remain its Alpha (excuse my unintentional pun)[1] and Omega. This was the place of its start (explanations of the President with the "junta" delegation on August 18) and of its denounce-ment on August 21. Gorbachev's domiciliary arrest became the first and the most decisive actions of the State Committee for a State of Emergency (gkchepists). The "illness" of the President, though not a single idiot ever believed in it, was the most important condition for legitimization of the coup d'etat. In fact, the plotters based *everything* on it. Having failed, they suprisingly rushed to Foros again, to see the man forcibly imprisoned by them, deprived of his power and desecrated by them. The August putsch is the chronicle of events between two flights of the plotters to the Crimea.

Though Ivan Silayev[2] ("Ogonyok", No. 36) wrote that their second visit meant: "the members of the SCES will stop at nothing...A deadly menace threatened Gorbachev," What a dreamer Ivan Stepanovich is! He imagined that Gorbachev was Paul I and Yazov - Prince Orlov[3], and that the gkchepists decided on their own. Instead of an enciphered order they rushed themselves to the place of the evil deed. In fact, such an order was

---

[1] Alpha - speical squads who came to support Yeltsin in the August events.

[2] I. Silayev was the RSFSR Prime-Minister.

[3] Prince Orlov was one of the murderers of the Emperor Paul I.

known to be impossible, and we know how they actually behaved in Foros: they failed to be received by the President and were sitting quietly in a room where they were ordered to sit. I. Silayev knew and understood all this, but as far as it was "blasphemous to accuse Gorbachev" it had to be portrayed as horrible and as touching as possible. "With all his merits Gorbachev has a shortcoming - he trusts people too much..." This goes a bit too far.

Some commentators of them call the coup a farce and make fun of the blunderers ruling the Soviet Union. They say that the plotters are nonentities, drunkards, executioners and lack real estate minds. Suppose it is true, in fact, and this would have brought them to an inevitable failure a few months later. But not in the course of the first hours, nor days. Yazov's primitiveness, Krychkov's insipidness and Pavlov's vulgarity cannot provide a clue to the fact that the simplest measures were not taken and no minimum arrests were made. For that moment nobody was required but thick-skinned executioners.

Suppose this machine is out of order, but nobody can convince us that it is incapable of causing two or three turns of a heavy squeaking flywheel. Is it a "farce"? What in the Soviet system could happen without a farce; what is not a face in "perestroika"? The most serious and even tragic events were to take place in the ensuing years and months. August saw something not at all trifling, and one cannot avoid an analysis of the August conspiracy.

Others right think that the plotters did not expect such resolution and energy on the part of Yeltsin and his following, thousands of intellectuals and young people rushing to the White House, confusion among certain military troops and disobedience to certain orders even in the KGB, etc. But practical and psychological circumstances detrimental to the putschists had been gradually accumulating: the growth of resistance was favoured by that fatal loss of tempo which had been noticeable from the very beginning.

As for Gorbachev, his arrest according to certain witnesses, did not capture anyone's attention. So much so that his loyal personal guards and attending staff were left with him, and the President had at his disposal duplicate means of communication. There appeared to be contradictions in some details of his living under arrest; in short, his isolation was not at all strict, and upon his return the President behaved in a curious way, shielding whom he could (Lukyanov, Dzasokhov, Scherbakov, etc.), replacing the plotters with their first deputies, and so on. The subsequent suicides of those closest to the President-General Secretary occurred in suspicious circumstances.

I do not consider the events in Foros to be simply a "show", but the stories told by the President that his assistants are not convincing. IT is not accidental that a famous thoughtless phrase slipped from Gorbachev's tongue, that he will *never tell everything*. It will be right to proceed from the fact that Gorbachev was really dismissed and detained. However, his relations with the "junta", including the very events of August 18 -21 in no way fit the classic simple scheme: perfidious conspirators who won the President's trust, but then suddenly betrayed and arrested him. These relationships allow various interpretations. They can hardly be reduced to the conclusion that Gorbachev was wither "privy" to the coup d'etat or not.

It is important to consider the psychological aspects as well as to evaluate the concrete role played those individuals. For those who are interested in the outline and, so to say, artistic design, it is better to wait for the court hearing, *in case* it is note impeded by the disgraceful participation in the investigation of the same Trubin who has recently found no corpus elicti in the shootings in Novocherkassk and Vilnius, who has expressed his sympathy to the SCES during his Cubas visit and therefore was forced at the Congress to retire, but still remains the USSR Procurator-General; *in case* the investigation can maintain complete independence also from Silayev's idyllic version or Yeltsin's pragmatic considerations that Gorbachev is useful and he must be supported; *in case* the entire trial is open, and *in case* the cross-examination of the accused and witnesses is carried on professionally. Prior the hearing, M.S. Gorbachev told a group of journalists that the plotters would be able to slander him in court.

I am going to confine myself only to the *political* contents and the development of the August coup d'etat being a logical confrontation of generally known and indisputable facts. On the morning of August 24, using the opportunity to speak at a meeting of the inter-regional Group of People's Deputies of the USSR, I allowed myself to express my conviction: all strange elements of the coup d'etat find their explanation, if one thinks it over to the end and that it was not or not so much a coup d'etat but *a state turning.*

Before passing to the essence of the matter it is necessary to specify that what is mentioned below means in no way that "high treason' was not committed, (as defined in our acting Criminal code).

What does the "Motherland" mean? This means the country where we got up on August 19; this is "the USSR". From a legal point of view "Motherland" is a substance and subject of citizenship.

With the exception of the Russian power appearing nominal, and the municipalities of several towns, which the putschists considered important but minor factors, the vast country seemed to be almost entirely at their hands. All direct lines![4] All state forms and seals! All tanks and rockets! Departments and generals! A coup d'etat was not needed, as the plotters themselves constituted the state.

They were not preparing for a "coup d'etat". It was simply necessary to drive the democrats and the press in to a corner, to put Yeltsin and others in their place, to make a sudden political change in short, *to introduce a state of emergency* and to come to an agreement with Gorbachev. The year of 1991 was in full swing and they could not and were not going to do without a constitution just because they felt themselves to be the lawful masters rather than a "junta". To detain Gorbachev, to convene the Supreme Soviet, to ignore the helpless protests of Yeltsin and others, this is what a state of emergency is for; for resorting to force, but avoiding excessive noise, starting repressions gradually, at a minimum, like Andropov did, demonstrating a combination of force and a reliable reserve, and moving towards state capitalism and 'order". Being at the top of power they did not arrive at the notion that impetuous putsch and a putsch alone was needed.

A. Volsky[5] was almost the first to propose the formula about Gorbachev's "serious personal errors". I. Silayev expressed himself in a spirit of polite, even affectionate reproach while others rudely shouted: the President had surrounded himself only with scoundrels. All this was summarized in the inimitable question of a hot-tempered Yu.Karyakin[6] : how did it happen that the President had not noticed; it had been stamped on their muzzles, had it not?

As long as it is not that Gorbachev is as credulous as Shakespeare's Moor, a poor judge of people, on the contrary, he is a good judge of them. The essence is in the policy pursued by Gorbachev already from the summer of 1989 till August 1991.

This "right-centrist" (and simply right-wing) policy-of braking while descending unwillingly - needed people of a certain kind and Gorbachev selected them from those surrounding him, consistently and unceremoniously. For blocking any deep structural economic reforms, the uncontrolled emission of money up to 150 billion rubles in 1991, for allotting a quarter of the secret budget to military works and continuation of the

---

[4] Special state telephone communication with numbers mentioned in no phone books.

[5] Formerly an important official of the CPSU Central Committee Arkady Volsky is the Chairman of the "Union of Industrialist", i.e. an association of directors of large state enterprises.

[6] Head of department yu.Karyakin is a former USSR People's deputy.

arms race, for playing with national or quasi-national conflicts with the purpose of maintaining the position of the center, for bloodshed measured out in doses, for shadowing "the so-called democrats", for including the repression apparatus for the future, for adoption of the law on the KGB openly allowing what had been done before but secretly, even under Stalin's regime, all this required exactly such ministers, officials, generals, and deputies as were promoted by Gorbachev and his people. And when, say, the President appointed a well-drilled party bigwig closely connected with the KGB, and an army general with the experience of the colonial war to handle home affairs and command the troops it was already evident what could be expected soon in the Transcaucasian of Baltic regions.

The "junta's" program, in point of fact, contained nothing which would differ from the official or behind-the-scenes policy of the center in general and Gorbachev in particular, though this policy had to move forward to become more open, consistent, unyielding and cruel. It goes without saying that we would receive something incomparably worse than what we had. Nevertheless, tanks continued to appear in the streets of Alma-Ata, Tbilisi, Yerevan, Baku, Vilnius, Riga without any "putsch", and it was not the first time: March 28[7] preceded August 19.

Now coming closer to the subject "The President and his team" ("junta") let us consider the main fact, *that the idea of the state of emergency and emergency authorities* was Gorbachev's strongest obsession for almost two years. More than that, he demanded and received exactly such authorities cheered on by certain liberal, taking it as a saving remedy against those who were more right-wing and more dangerous than Gorbachev. Meanwhile intensification of the elements of the emergency state was going on in conjunction with Gorbachev's getting closer to the same gorillas. Miners were on strike *against the regime*, in remote corners of the empire blood was being shed, the economy was plunging into an abyss, Gorbachev replaced the inert Ryzhkov with the impudent Pavlov, the streets were boiling with wrath, and the President was nursing the gkchepists.

Why didn't Gorbachev recklessly use this authorities to the end? This is not a nonchalant question as the August conflict of Gorbachev and his followers rests on it. But the President now proposed to suspend the Law on the Press, now issued decrees allowing the "security organs" to commit excesses in private enterprises, now fell asleep during bloody probings in Lithuania and Latvia, and now the headquarters of the 4th Army

---

[7] On March 28 following the Order of Gorbachev tanks were brought to Moscow on the eve of the huge meeting of "democrats".

in the Transcaucasus allegedly refused to obey the orders of the Commander-in-chief.

To what extent everything was carried out with or without the knowledge of the President is moot. Gorbachev was determining a political course, "adjusting" fundamental directives of showing others at what he would connive. Pulses were coming down the scale of ranks. But, of course, local orders of certain major-generals or lieutenant-colonels about redistribution of troops or shooting is not at all Presidential business; he could not know everything beforehand and later, perhaps he ignored the details. However: Gorbachev never denounced with full determination the actions of his officials and officers, did not dismiss Pugo or Krychkov or, at least, the horrible Polyanichko and gave no order to bring an action against murderers anywhere, neither in Sumgait, nor Tbilisi, nor Vilnius.

They used to say that events were beyond his control. Well, in certain instances it had to be inevitably so. Say, the slaughter in Medininkai was very unpleasant and inopportune. How could the USSR President know who was conducting attacks at a certain custom house? Events inevitably escape control if a special kind of policy is pursued: with double or triple accounts and with political games. One cannot control hounds set on a hare!

The August conspiracy, and its revolutionary defeat, was the result and a great outcome of the key event of 1991, as we consider the wave of civil disobedience in February - April. Immense meetings and political strikes in particular, slowly but insistently were spreading over the country. The workers of the "Uralmash" works already started to act along with Putilov works in Saint-Petersburg. Enterprises of Minsk, Vitebsk, Kiev, Donetsk arose. A general strike was approaching. There had been no precedents for 70 years. The regime started to stagger.

At this time Gorbachev went to Novo-Ogaryovo without changing his policy and having received in exchange, an anti-workers law. He decided to cede something to the republics, to come to an agreement with Yeltsin but to preserve the center, the imperial structures and his old people inside them for the time being. Gorbachev began to play a more complex game. The threat of the federation's disintegration was put forward against Russia. The text of the agreement was deliberately ambiguous and empty, and every party had its scheme on who easily noticed the most dangerous imaginary character of the "compromise", criticized and warned Yeltsin. The correctness of their words was confirmed much sooner that it might have been expected.

Now among people finding themselves "on the top" and considering themselves "realistic politicians", it is acceptable to mock at democratic *principles*, at their "abstract character", at the "idealism" and "utopianism" of those who cannot realize that Russia is not yet up to this. At hard times one must not be overscrupulous, overly fastidious but reckon with principles exactly to the extent that it is *convenient*...for the cause, moreover, for the benefit of the Motherland. As a matter of fact, they used to say "for the revolution", and it was called leninism. Nowadays we propose to renew our authoritarian mechanisms and ways of management for the sake of future democracy. They are teaching us that in politics one must be practical above all. However that is an impractical and anti-democratic policy (in fact it failed and will fail with us) as well as a policy that is both practical and democratic. Which of these policies are these people caring for, and in whose interests?

After the August events the failure of the "Novo-Ogaryovo process" became generally accepted (on the part of the Russian leadership as well). However, the extreme right-wingers were also very much dissatisfied with the "compromise", therefore, they insisted on secret protocols which would probably concretize the vagueness of the "Union treaty". Where are these riders? When are they going to be published? They were referred to by Pavlov and demanded by Lukyanov. The "people from the team" had additional cause for alarm: in Novo-Ogaryovo Gorbachev began to expect imaginary all-union elections. Other high-level state officials were forced to be content with the role of guests rather than full-right participants in the deal. The position of the mighty structures they headed as well as their own positions were not represented deservedly and directly in Novo-Ogaryovo. The President seemed to get lost in the game and began to annoy them terribly.

The spring fright of the apparatus also resulted in Yeltsin's opportunity to maneuver in Novo-Ogaryovo, trying to gain points, speed up the breakdown of the CPSU (the Russian Departization Law and Rutskoy's movement) and activate the perestroika reformist nomenclature, formerly rejected by Gorbachev. As a reply there was an introduction of the "state of emergency" on August 19.

The arguments of the future "junta" with their President were revealed in June as a very strange episode in the USSR Supreme Soviet. At that time Pavlov unexpectedly wished to demand from the deputies what was later approved by Lukyanov's "parliament". At a closed meeting, Krychkov, Yazov, Pavlov gave vent to their words. The deputies were attending with sympathy but were perplexed: where is the President? Gorbachev remained behind the scenes keeping mysteriously silent for three days. Were they acting without his knowledge? The press started a murmur of bewilderment. The world became watchful.

Then the President arrived at the Supreme Soviet. He slightly reproved Pavlov and explained that the latter was incorrectly understood. Pavlov cast down his eyes. The entire scene took thirty minutes. Then Gorbachev entered the hall accompanied by Yazov and Kryuchkov and merrily flung a remark: "The whole coup d'etat is over". An amazed Dimitry Volchek repeated the famous remark in the "Svoboda" program. Two months later these people would try their own version of the emergency state and Gorbachev would begin to listen to the broadcasts of the "Svoboda".

On August 21 Gorbachev's assistant Shakhnazarov made a speech at the RSFSR Supreme Soviet. The strange putsch was clearly exhausting itself. Shakhnazarov movingly stated that in a state of emergency and a corresponding committee were urgently needed now and even after the plotters were defeated for, perhaps, six months. If what these people had been doing was all wrong, it would have yielded quite the opposite result. Shakhnazarov flushed with his previous work with Gorbachev on some substantial text in Foros (it would be interesting to look at its original!) and said perhaps, too much. On August 21 when the coup d'etat or the changes plotted by the wrong gkchepists wee not yet even suppressed, Shakhnazarov (was it his opinion or a ventriloquy of the USSR President?) was preaching that an emergency state would be really useful, but only the right one! Something like this was said by our President himself at the airport on his return, having had no time to see what 's what he had warned these "blockheads" that they had better not act like this.

Now let us think over what Pavlov said, having signed the order of his arrest to a polite Molchanov[8] in the corridor. Pavlov alleged he could not understand what had happened in general. Gorbachev promised to convene the Supreme Soviet in August 16 and to adopt the state of emergency there. And then he suddenly changed his mind and proposed another date: August 26. That's how it was? According to Pavlov this means that the convocation of the Supreme Soviet session by Lukyanov on this date had been agreed upon with Gorbachev still before the "putsch"? It is very interesting indeed. The junta (team) solicited to implement a state of emergency before the signing of the Union treaty while the President decided to postpone it until it was properly legalized.

If it was so, when did the team learn that Gorbachev had given up the venture of August 16? Suppose, it was in the beginning of the month when the President once more calmly thought it over with Shakhanazrov

---

[8] A well-known TV journalist.

during their vacations. In this case the plotters had very few days to consider everything and to come to the final conclusion. The coup d'etat had to be postponed closer to August 20 as on the 18th the decisive (the only one or the final?) attempt to have it out with Mikhail Sergeyevich. The President insisted on his decision, but they were ready for it and started to act without him.

There is no evidence that the conspirators said to the President: "If so, we shall have to keep you here. We shall do everything ourselves and the way we consider necessary. We shall not make harm to you and shall not deprive you of the presidency for good but for the time being you will be declared ill. When everything is settled we shall be able to work with you again. So, don't be hard on us, please. You will have the same facilities, the family and attendants will stay with you. Just rest and good-bye!"

What I have written is merely speculation which I wish to permit myself to use, but it was prompted by Yanayev's declaration at the memorable press conference when he was asked about Gorbachev.

It was a special moment when Gena[9] roused himself, even his alcoholic tremor seemed to subside, while his voice got stronger. The acting president stated that Gorbachev and he were still friends, that the historic cause of perestroika would be carried on and the he, Yanayev, was sure: after the President's rest and recovery the gkchepists would continue to work with him.

That was certainly the most significant moment of the whole press-conference. Gorbachev realized it perfectly well and declared, on his return, that at that moment it had become clear to him: he was threatened with -physical extermination. In fact, how could Yanayev have bluffed so crudely and hopelessly if, at some future date, Gorbachev would appear on TV and would expose the plotters? However, supposition about his extermination contradicts the absolute impossibility of doing away with the President's entire family without traces, his assistants and guards, all the personnel, all the witnesses of the imprisoned safe and sound President bathing his granddaughter in sea. Neither Kryuchkov, nor Pavlov, even together with Gena, were smart enough for such a horrible ruse. They desperately needed legitimization rather than the crime of the century.

That is why many of us got the impression that Yanayev was not bluffing, but believed or wished to believe in what he was saying. After the gkchpists consolidate their poem, Gorbachev will not play Quixotic

---

[9] Gennady Yanayev.

games, and unmask and challenge the entire state leadership. All of them are friends and have the same policy after all. It is true that in the critical situation they strongly opposed each other, very strongly, but Gorbachev will pardon and understand them, will be convinced by their success. He will remain their President but without arrogance or stubbornness, a more obedient president.

I don't have the right to say that the plotters would not be mistaken in their plans. I only consider it more likely that they rested their hopes precisely on this.

The arrest in Foros happened to be the consequence of the stormy crisis of the ruling clique in the USSR, the inside clashes about what reliable tactics had to be used to save their power the center, and the USSR, aid the defend what the Big Officials and Generals had been even convinced in their own way.

If this political version seems to others as evident as tot myself, then what follows from it? What should we do with it? Isn't it better to leave alone the "new" Gorbachev? I am sufficiently cynical myself: I do not know yet. However, there is one thing. We must admit that consideration of the situation to the end and an honest understanding of what is going on, are necessary for a practical policy, not only for moralists and future historians.

RUSSIA AT THE CROSSROADS

After the August events immense political power - particularly, but not exclusively in the provinces, belongs to the same structures and party officials in the state and economic machine, today all of them being "democrats", The "former USSR", ignoring this slightly adjective, continues to print ruble notes without control, to criminally hide dozens of billions of them, to drive conveyers with tanks and rockets, to help Najibula and Castro, and to steal gold and platinum. As I have read somewhere, bugging by the secret police "reformed" mainly by themselves, amounts to three quarters of the previous volume even in Moscow, according to the official data. What is most important, our economy remains the same.

Nevertheless the country has passed the decisive landmark and we find ourselves setting up some new forms of the Russian life. Though our ragged and wretched existence has shamelessly bared itself, customary everyday hardships have been unbearably intensified and what is unusual, psychologically they have been merged with uncertainty in the future.

However, there is no sense in dwelling upon the obvious disintegration of the state system. But on the other hand, the cord has been cut, the newborn society is crying, and society will be returned to Russia, meaning that there will be a state system, society cannot do without it. Will the population of Russia awake and possess the power? Or as before, will the Russian Power possess the population?

Everyone can make his own small contribution toward changing the general situation as long as he is acting on his own accord. It is now, like in February and October of 1917, the Russian people are making their choice. Politically, it is a choice between a parliamentary democracy and an authoritarian regime.

As for the former, we are justly reminded for the thousandth time that we are still lacking necessary ground, i.e. a society in which everyone is a private person and the owner of either his efforts and talents, or means of production, real estate and so on. However, a civil society needs democratic freedoms. We already have at our disposal important elements which will give birth to democracy in years to come and *simultaneously*, a market economy. It is with astonishing speed that freedoms of speech and press, meetings and strikes, independent trade unions, elements of a multi-party system, possibilities of civil pressure on the power and more or less free elections took root. Soon we shall be able to add cancellation of passport registration, the freedom to leave the country and return to it, the first steps of Legislative reform. It is indisputable that Russia will arrive at democracy only through democracy.

What about an alternative? There is a real danger of a new authoritarian ruling being prompted by the extraordinary character of the impending circumstances hopes resting mainly on Yeltsin's personal popularity, a real necessity of strengthening the operative, executive power, the lack of an effective legal system, the helplessness of a few relatively democratic Soviets, and an intricate and ridiculous double-stage formula with the Congress and the Supreme Soviet of the RSFSR being inherited from the party regime. This congress underwent two tests and confirmed its reactionary nature, having refused to consider a constitution of the new federation and having crossed off land property. In return the deputies demonstrate more habitual and ambiguous concessions: they imposed a one-year moratorium and vested special powers and responsibilities to the President. Having in mind the aversion of the voters toward any new elections and growing irritation and distrust for the "democrats", this Yeltsin's turn should be accepted as forced and right, but very dangerous.

The elite corps of the executive power to which the load of reforms is being transferred can hardly be used for society's reformation. With regard to its personnel and style (particularly its lowest and middle, the most important sections) it is the old mechanism. We mean precisely the section and mechanism rather than particular persons. The section is swelling, corruption is on the rise as the ruling sphere has been expanded to unheard of limits. With great enthusiasm, officials have begun to distribute licenses, limits, privileges, real estate rentals; a "commercial" flood is rising!

This consolidates administrative thinking among those who do not take bribes. Look, how the most incredible projects are multiplying and go bankrupt everyday in Moscow. For example, it was announced that beginning on December 1, coupons worth 60 rubles per person would be distributed to all. Won't we rush to stand in lines to buy allegedly free sugar at ten times the price? A few days later they said that it would not happen after all but I am concerned with the very psychology of our progressive administrating.

Till now the novelty has been officials are merging the imaginary market with a false "privatization". A mutation of the party nomenclature has occurred, and the power in Russia is assuming unknown but savage, twisted features as in the past. This is terrible not from a moral viewpoint but mainly from a social and economic one, with the fields overgrown.

A certain form of modernized ("reformist") dictatorship could be politically attractive for such modern "democratic" masters of life. Rather than in a modern market, in this kind of comprador imitation, unions of monopolist "directors", commercialized military-industrial complex, etc., would become an economic ground here. And this would mean, at best, a relative stabilization, another turn at stagnation, an attempt at delaying inconsistent reforms.

The other day I was told a story: a nice-looking fellow was making his way in a carriage of the Moscow suburban electric train, placards on his chest and back calling for the return to Lenin's course, etc. And he was shouting something. Smiling with sympathy people attended, hardly because of their love for the CPSU but because he shouts: "Democrats have shitted on themselves!" We must assume that such a resolute ascertaining is premature. But as the Foros prisoner of conscience loves to say "processes are going on..."

Anyhow we should examine these "democrats", are they really democrats? Answers are different and in some cases, complicated and dramatic.

The power existing now in Russia, both in social and psychological aspects, is transitional and it is at the crossroads. Society has just thrown off (well, seems to have thrown off) the burden of the previous power, hateful and irremediable, and expects serious changes from the new leaders. Ordinary people in their majority keep a sober reserve, preparing themselves to count their chickens after they are hatched. While in the midst of intellectuals, quite often voices are heard about "our power" which it is even permissible to criticise but not to oppose or irritate an provoke its wrath. Usually they are the same people who staked on Gorbachev's presidency in March 1990 and later called for the total "consensus" of the democrats. They are different including sincere and non-obsequious people. They are not difficult to understand. They have been tired of dealing with hostile authorities and now wholeheartedly are doting upon saving, they are convinced, unification with them, melting of the air.

There is another group of prosperous, aloof political scientist analyzing a chess game over the shoulder of other people, posing as experts and reminding that it was they who had predicted the arrival of the Authoritarian dictatorship.

The clear young-pioneer falsetto of L. Radzikhovsky is heard ringing the loudest (in particular, "Literaturnaya Gazeta", October 3) glorifying the "inevitability" of Yeltsin's "authoritarian ruling"! Look how he is going without safeguarding". (Let us hope that it is not so, because professionals do not go without safeguarding). The author reaches Biblical pathos saying: "It is impossible to pull a camel of democracy through the needle eye of reforms". It appears reformers are "professional democrats" and "people" who can fail to bear growing prices though "today, I think, they are glad that the "master" is coming".

Seeing the threat to reforms in people with convictions, in democracy and simply in the population, hurrying up to guess a new master and at the same time daring to cite Akhmatova's poems in such a context MR. Radzikhovsky does Yeltsin an ill turn. The argument about "the iron hand" started with "Perestroika's" dying stage in October, 1989, and also in the "Literaturnaya Gazeta". It goes without saying that *at that time* they meant the enlightened hand of Gorbachev. What else could it be? And about the use of the apparatus' might of the CPSU for reforms (A. Migranyan wrote it most openly in the "Novy Mir") or the KGB and military-industrial complex (S. Kurinyan[1] - Kryuchkov's table book of dream interpretations). However the last two years have proved a simple inner connection between the attempts to toughen the regime and the policy of breaking the reforms. And these two years brought about a remarkable pressing from below rather than toughening of the master, the spring offensive of the working people in 1991 instead of authoritarism and the victory of free people near the White House and not of the gkchepists.

Nevertheless, I do not object to the possibility of an authoritarian result, and in two versions. Either Yeltsin's administration inevitably colliding with diverse resistance and inconveniences from "the right" and "the left" will fall for the temptation to use force, starting from banning strikes, pressure on the press and so on. It is hardly compatible with the main social philosophy of Yeltsin and I rely on his outstanding political instinct.

---

[1] A political scientist, the author or the book found on Krychkov's office table after his arrest.

With the preservation and strengthening of democratic freedoms, special powers of the President of Russia will remain an element of the political techniques of the year of reforms without filling itself with authoritarian contents. Or the failure of Yeltsin's reforms and an outburst of spontaneous despair will serve as a signal for national-demagogues and "has-beens". This is more likely.

A new authoritarianism would find in Russia quite many supporters and there are serious opponents (miners, liberal intellectuals, a part of the "Democratic Russia", businessmen, many young people). I still absolutely disagree that it might be "enlightened" and would fulfill a great historic mission, i.e. "creating" a modern economy and a civilized society which would ultimately become a bridge to democracy.

For us, a "pure" authoritarianism is impossible. "Our" authoritarism would inevitably become a continuation of the autocratic-soviet tradition with a replacement of the communist ideology by a nationalistic one. "Our" iron hand has not been adapted for self-restraint, acting without tyranny, servility, nonsense, obscurantism, or simple foolishness. It would be an inarticulate, archaic approach not long ago within the system of party education. This administrative apparatus and its dictatorship would be "enlightened" only in the above mentioned meaning, with the personal qualities of a dictator, even if he had been imported from the States (as the Armenians did with their foreign minister).

It makes one laugh and feel horrified to see numbers of "gentryfolk" headed by comrade Golistyn[2], their fancy-dress Soviet "balls"; "cossacks" in moth-eaten uniforms with other people's decorations, discussing the introduction of public flogging: leaders of "Christian democrats" or "people's freedom", heading in fact non-existing "parties" but originating from real organizations; or orthodox hierarchs selected in the past and agreed upon with the KGB; or the pompous reception in St. Petersburg (by the democratic mayor and thrilled journalists) of V.K. Romanov, an old good-mannered colorless man allegedly making "a private visit" but called officially (contrary to legal, political, moral reality) "Your Royal Highness", "Grand Duke", "The Successor to the Throne". A servile line of words is running across the TV screen. Our politicians and TV broadcasters are not staunch monarchists, no nor are they orthodox. These are merely sovkovy[3] deeds.

---

[2] A descender of princes, the head of the restored society of nobles.

[3] Modern scornfu slang word for "soviet".

On August 23 I viewed an exhibition spread on two floors immediately after the door of the Chairman of the RSFSR Supreme Soviet. Its very name is amazing: "Russia Holding Supreme Power".[4]This exhibition is the glory of the State, imperial might, the good Monarch, the official Church, prosperous subjects against trouble-makers and revolutionaries rather than the Russian society. Besides, the floor was given to Stolypin as it had been given before only to Lenin or Chernyshevsky.

There is not a hint of the tragic complexity of Russian history, no signs of complete historical truth, but the same official boasting lies with all the soviet exhibitions depicting "the glorious way" passed by the "Power", but with reversed, restoration ideology, and symbols rejected in February 1917. There were the usual barbaric pretensions on behalf of Russia, only with the return of the orthodox motto: "Light To Whole World" written in obsolete Russian spelling, spread above the entire exhibition, instead of "the light of communism". Well, it is very timely. It is exactly the time for us to bear light to the world.

Therefore, even today it is clear: if the shadow of authoritarian dictatorship came over Russia, it would be dully retrograde and provincial, in no way facilitating movement into the XXIst century.

It is also clearly confirmed by G.Popov's article "What Next?" ("Izvestiya", October 3). Here are the eight major ideas of this work:

1. When "creating a new society" we must proceed from the fact that we do not have its "stable cells", we cannot lean on "large groups of people"; Russia is not prepared for the market and democracy. (In October Russia was not prepared for socialism and, of course, not for democracy either, but Russia is perpetually not prepared because it is Russia).

2. Therefore, "the experience...of Western democratic countries...does not fit our conditions", namely "a democratic republic with a parliament, self-governing, freedom of the press, multi-party system, etc." (And according to Lenin it did not fit in those times). We must "look for a unique type of political set-up". (They succeeded in finding one, so, perhaps, we do not need to look for it).

3. In order to create "a new society" under such unfavourable conditions, we must use the INSTRUMENT OF POWER (this was Lenin's idea). It is precisely what will speed up "the transition to a market economy".

---

[4] Compare: Gernanb "Reich" instead of "Staat".

4. It will be borne by "the majority of society" despite the state of affairs, its "vanguard". (Popov's matters with the "vanguard" are worse than they were at that time).

5. So, let democrats set up a "strong party": an important idea which G.Popov made public AFTER the elections of June 12, i.e. Russian Democratic Movement. In any case it is exactly what was called 'the party of the authorities" by Yu.Yu.Boldyrev.

6. The instrument of the "transitional period" is a dictatorship of the proletariat, while before it was, Popov says "a strict administrative control from the above, like in "Greece, Chile, South Korea".

7. But then: just elected "heads of the executive power" to whom "the leading role" in the entire system must belong, are not accustomed to governing and do not know how to do it. They themselves are hostages of the old apparatus. Popov proposes, therefore, to turn necessity into a virtue and to exercise the authoritarian regime with " a coalition of democrats with the apparatus". Wouldn't it be more correct to put it vice versa, the apparatus with democrats, i.e. the devil with a baby? In old times they were called "specialists", but, at least, it was a competent, real bureaucracy though it failed to civilize the soviet rabble. Nowadays we have to be content with "active party and economy members", and while the specialists worked under the old party members, now we see democrats under inveterate apparatus officials.

8. Where will "the strict regime" take us? To a free market and democracy, of course "Wohin, wohin..."[5]Mignon sings again. "Temorary" anti-democratic means to a democratic aim, though a dictatorship to its death.

It is possible to develop a free economy from ground level only in a country that is politically free as well. Such a reform cannot be effected "from above" but only "from below" (with assistance from "the above"), and is beyond the power of even the most honest, most advanced officials; it can only be carried out by businessmen, hired workers, peasants-owners, shareholders, cooperators, etc. In order to do it, they must be sure of the citizens' capacity to defend their interests in both a legal and political aspect.

---

[5] "There, there..." - an allusion to Goethe.

Then there will be power in Russia, not "in general", but as a reform-ist one caused by necessity. It is especially so because of the rapid forma-tion of new property relations, which are determined by the market, the only reformist task of the power being its refusal to interfere with every-thing, to control everything, to distribute and command. Contrary to G.Popov (who by the way, reverse the economic policy of his office every tow days), in case of such a true market reform, "the power" must in no way "divide Property" but only introduce rules of sale of its shares, put-ting up for auction, allowing peasants to divide land, etc. The state re-moves, in stages but very quickly, legal bans and administrative compli-cations, introduces rules of the game already known to the world, and then steps aside. It does not interfere, limiting itself with taxes, registra-tion, guarding, investment policy, or social programs. The state sector of the mixed economy will grow narrower under the pressure of the market. The market will be developing by itself, without the state in certainly the most important aspects. Even a reserve monetary system cannot depend on the government. The less power is possessed by the government, the more "market" power there will be. Citizens-agents of such a reform think about power only then seeing a revenue inspector, a policemen around the corner, an independent judge.

So, paving the way for the market would mean a steady narrowing of the Russian government's sphere of influence. Particularly in post-totalitarian national conditions this demands corresponding changes in the political climate.

This is why authoritarianism in today's Russia will not be able to carry out a drastic reform. This is also why democracy is the compulsory arrangement of such a reform, rather than something simply desired or someone's idealistic dream.

"The restoration of the Russian monarch" in the form it existed "at its downfall" as our tomorrow, as "a quite realistic" and "not worst oppor-tunity" for the country "within the frontiers of the RSFSR" - or "an at-tempt to restore the Russian Empire as united and indivisible" is this Utopian thinking? Of course, I am citing A.Migranyan once more (the "Nezavisimaya Gazeta", November 14). And what about two other "scenarios' described by the author in the same article: an alleged estab-lishment by Yeltsin of a "national-socialist regime in the country" in case the reforms failed, a "new totalitarianism' or "Yeltsin's dictatorship plus a radical economic reform plus Western assistance and - forward to democ-racy". Aren't they a Utopian and witty parody of a "scientific prognosis?" Either Yeltsin will become a Russian Hitler, or the grandson of V.K. Romanov will ascend the throne. They say, anything you like may happen in this country, "there are no chances only for...a democratic regime".

In fact, any distant future is a Utopia. There will be that which exists "nowhere" yet. However, Russia will no longer remain archaic in its philosophy and outside of the triumphant world-wide community.

Is it possible "to effect transition from a totalitarian system to democracy or is an authoritarian stage necessary for it? Well, in Germany, Italy and Japan it happened directly after the defeat in the war and with the assistance of Americans. In Eastern Europe (including countries without any democratic traditions, as in Bulgaria) it occurred directly, immediately after the Soviet bridle was loosened. There are no other precedents, so with the USSR, it is a unique situation. It might be said that here the extreme forms of the totalitarian system were first replaced with weakened ones (neo-totalitarian regime of the 1960's - mid-80's) after which an authoritarian stage was really needed (1987 - 1991). So Migranyan is wrong to complain that "neither Gorbachev, nor his numerous friends and advisers" accepted his, Migranyan's "proposals". Now the difficult transition from the authoritarian regime to democracy has begun. As long as the Russian Eurasian society is surviving, it will have to progress the same way that mankind on all continents progresses, having experienced torments and defeats.

Our prognosis includes not only what "must be" but also "what we wish" and how essential and energetic "we" are. The effect of public hypnosis is significant. We are told: such is an objective diagnosis, and even a physician needs a diagnosis for the sake of therapy. A political scientist, of course, has no right to avoid sober though unpleasant estimations, but how can a society block the gloomy "versions"? I am only a historian, but I would think this is exactly what citizens have the right to expect from everyone to play the role of political adviser.

However, what awaits us this winter and spring? Strong disturbances in three-four months are almost inevitable, but Yeltsin and his government will stand until the first signs of a substantial change promised for next fall.

A real question is what will happen after the first year of reforms is over? We cannot help sympathizing with Yeltsin's determination to act, and being glad that economic reforms are starting at last. However, in its present form Gaidar's program will fail, not because it is radical and the population will not stand for such tough measures, but because it is still not radical enough.

A tendency towards administrative economic and monetary governmental measures is evident. The main aspect, the revolution of property relations, remains in the background and to a great extent uncertain. It is clear that after the New Year no "liberalization of prices" will take place as long as price-lists will be fixed not by competing independent owners-manufacturers, but by state monopolists. A disorderly price rise has already begun ("contractual", i.e. partially decentralized and rising out of thin air) rather than "liberalization". It seems that the "small privatization" will translate to the sale of real estate, not to private persons, but lending on enslaving terms with a provision of changing payments and the preservation of administrative control and interference in trade and services for the future. It seems that only half-measures have been worked out regarding the military-industrial complex and 'unfinished construction projects", instead of doing away with this monstrous system, which was proposed by economists long ago. The most frightening is that *there will be no radical agrarian reform!*

Steps have not been taken which could create conditions for the natural disintegration of the system of collective and state farming. (at first, a tentative determination of a plot of arable land and a share of other properties for each peasant in a collective-state farm, and later a guaranteed procedure of dropping out with a transfer of the land as private property; or, for those who do not wish it, formation of new cooperatives, now cooperatives of owners, and in various forms). If the 1992 spring sowing is not carried out under radically new conditions, it will threaten final failure and chaos.

I would like them to explain us distinctly and in details how the "liberation of prices' and explosive inflation will start consumer goods *production* and why we should expect the abundance of goods to stop the inflation. Otherwise, it is impossible to stop it.

If this gloomy or at least very skeptical estimation is correct, if Gaidar's reforms are still doomed to fail, how should the democrats behave? The answer is without an alternative: they must cooperate with Yeltsin's government. There is no possibility *now* to offer the society a different, better alternative. And if we imagine some abstract idea like this at a later time, no democratic proposals would be widely acclaimed. After their disappointment with Yeltsin and "the so called democrats", people will believe no one.

So, we should support the reforms, however, with a view of their profound and timely correction and with our civil participation. You may object that it is a modest chance, but there is no other choice. *We must join the struggle around the realistic character of the reforms.*

Then what does it mean "to support" reforms, "to support" Yeltsin's administration? How do we support it in order to make it effective?

Some people believe that the "Democratic Russia" movement could be useful for suppressing the forthcoming dissatisfaction of the population.

If we do agree with it, we shall have to be very influential among workers, employees, young people "to hold" them down. In order to be influential we should be able to express and defend their interests, and to do so we must be an independent civil movement representing the interests of rank-and-file people in a dialogue with the authorities at all levels. Such a political partnership inevitably contains an element of opposition, of "constructive criticism". Should it be only "criticism" and not the legal opposition resulting form it? These are both elements of opposition and independent (conditional) support cannot exist without opposition. While there correlation depends on the circumstances, it is impossible to set a ratio beforehand.

Without the classic "balance of three powers", the committees of the "Democratic Russia" and other public forces, especially the press, radio, and TV, would have to play the role of a sort of second fiddle, if not of a power than of an influence.

That is why I reject the article of M. Chudakova "The Lechery of Struggle" (Lliteraturnaya Gazetta", October 30). It is politically horrible to do what M. Chudakova did, having turned O.M. Freidenber's words about "ultra-shameless malevolence...denunciation, slander, shadowing...,squabbles" as a "natural state...of helplessly brutal, imprisoned" people under Stalin's regime, against the discordance of social interests and opinions against a fee press, against 'the criticism of the government", against the "lechery" of a normal civilized political struggle, and against the very "stability of the democratic rear of the President" of Russia. I do not know whether we are Yeltsin's rear or, on the contrary the state is society's "rear". But it is clear that the lechery of the new Soviet conformism is exactly what will never help Yeltsin, nor the reforms.

I share the apprehension regarding a revenge of reactionaries and chaos and I understand the thirst for social concord and admit the necessity of compromises. However, the mechanism of their achievement is based on a sound political struggle, otherwise it is not a "compromise" at all.

"The tradition of a vigilant control over the government", M. Chudakova reminds, does exist "with them", "western journalists', while for us "it is early...to adopt" this "grip". no, the time is ripe, if we have really started reforming the country, and this is also necessary for the government, if the author considers it democratic in its essence. "Love them, black as they are", the author appeals, and she declares " a moratorium" on criticism. "They are ours, our power, we are stepping on the same land, and a chilly fall rain is pouring on us from the same skies". This strange rhetoric deserves an evident reply: there were many people with whom we stepped on the same land and the rain always pours from one and the same sky, but not all people get soaked in equal measure.

Here is really "our" accursed habit: either to hate the government or to proclaim "an affinity" for it, " a love" for it, that "all of us...all democratic forces of Russia...to unite on any...platform, to unite ourselves and with our Russian power". The author makes an ironic remark: "We shall not be afraid to look the wisest or over-scrupulous, event the most opposition-minded..." Such "unafraid " minds are plentiful, but we must hope that this program curtailing democracy at the moment of its birth is a political Manilovism.

"Our power" does not exist anywhere! As in any case with democracy, the power has its own function and its own interest and it can be understood and justified in its desire to rule without obstacles. An obstacle is, in fact, ourselves, i.e. a society in which workers, trade-unions, the press, businessmen, peasantry, etc., everyone has also his own functions and his own interests. What does occur is "our democracy" coinciding with this entire field of the confrontation of interest, including a specific interest of the executive power, but not "our power".

Let us help Yeltsin's reforms, by being wise, holding to democratic principles and if necessary, by opposing him.

I do not think that we have to fear famine this winter. We have not yet agreed with the enlightened West that there is "famine in Russia". If a "real" famine is considered to be what happened to us in 1921, 1932 or recently in Ethiopia, then it goes without saying that there will be no famine. People will not starve as during the war. Food will be scarce, inaccessible in price, there will be suffering, endless queues, talks how to get food heard even now. It will be a tough and humiliating time.

We shall withstand it, survive the winter, we will not stop working and preserving hope. We should be afraid of only one thing: that Russia will turn away from the democratic road for the second time, and therefore will remain poverty-stricken and unhappy.

THIS WILL BE DECIDED
NOT ON A CITY SQUARE

The national-sovereigners of the communist and black-hundred stripes are crating more and more noise. This is because of the disastrous slump in our standard of living, miserable enough as it is. I am also worried by the fact that "ours" are becoming insolent so rapidly. But, what is more distressing, they are attracting a growing number of really unhappy, poor, bewildered, ignorant people and drumming marches with empty pots.

It is very difficult to decide which particular political measures would be most expedient to take now in opposing the national demagogues. What social contents f should fill general anti-fascist slogans? When, where and how should we act?

I consider the venture of "Democratic Russia" declared at the end of January to be detrimental. The democrats decided to carry out a mass anti-fascist demonstration on February 9 at the same time and in the same place where the communists and "patriots" had already planned their assembly. Leaflets were posted around the city stating that the "red-browns" wished "to overthrow Yeltsin" on Sunday and people had to come to defend hi,; the leaflets were singed on behalf of the "Defenders of the White House" and "Democratic Russia" societies as well as fictitious "Anti-fascist Center", i.e. a certain Zhenya Proshechkin. Wouldn't it be better to simply ring A. Murashov[1] up? A hundred OMON men and as a last reserve on water-cannon would be more than enough. Instead something more unusual was invented.

The public declaration of the leaders of the "Democratic Russia" was astonishing: "according to their information' the Moscow militia would be

---

[1] The head of the Moscow militia, a member of the "Inter-regional Group".

able to prevent a scuffle. If the militia divides the opponents with cordons, who will benefit from this? What will a TV portrayal of two opposing crowds in front of the White House favour? It seems evident to me; it will buck up the "new right-wingers" very much, will attract an additional interest in them on which they did not even reckon, and will flatteringly exaggerate their importance. Street passions, unexpectedly flared by the "moderate" high-rankers of the "Democratic Russia", would exactly fit "ours". The latter will have something to thank for.

I think that an artificial attempt to animate the August pathos of defending the White House will fail. It would be rather its parody and its demise. The historic and psychological configuration has undergone appreciable changes for the last 6 months. It would not set at rest the population compelled to hear fashionable stock-phrases about " a civil war" allegedly ready to start in Russia, about which TV and political commentators are gabbling in an indifferent and commonplace way. The street confrontation would increase social tension, instability, and fears, precisely what the right-wingers are after.

If we even agree that the time is ripe for such an action in principle, and if we can be sure that it becomes no less than two-three times more crowded than that of our compatriots, (otherwise it would turn into a far more serious defeat of democracy than any right-wing gathering!) it would be excellent, but why not fix another date for it? why attach it to this arbitrary an coarse dramatism?

It cannot be that the "constructive design" of the arrangement consisted of a simple self-affirmation. That is to prove to oneself, the public, ad the authorities, that democratic movements and groups are still influential and strong. It cannot be that it was decided to resort to almost the only point of convergence among all "democrats" both self-styled and real. So, the majority of those who called to repulse the nazi at noon of February 9 near the White House had sincere motives.

Nevertheless, no planned show can distract the overwhelming majority of Russia's population from routine, wretched care about their daily bread. The demonstration of this obvious solidarity will be no means be able to replace another solidarity far more complex and difficult to attain, though decisive for our entire future: a certain public accord regarding the course of economic reforms.

"Fascism will not pass!" However, to a considerable extent it will depend on how many hours we shall have to work the next fall to buy a litre of milk, a kilogram of meat, a shirt. It will be connected in the most prosaic way with taxes, investments, profits, rates of interest to be paid by savings banks, etc. Our fate will be no longer decided on a city square as was partially the case in March of August 1991.

Therefore, democrats, at last, would have to really concentrate on how to *combine*: 1) a support of the reforms with 2) their most essential *criticism* and urgent *corrections*. This requires no meetings (though it goes without saying that we should not exclude them) but a real civil independence, a political feeling, a free mind and persistent daily efforts.

Demands for the dismissal of Gaidar's government in the present situation are irresponsible for the simple reason that it is better than any other inevitably reactionary government that would replace it. At the same time, it is impossible to "believe" in the success reforms, it they are stopped at this conceptual level, due to the complex social and economic problems. Consequently, the plight of the *independent* (and therefore the most organized and important supporters of the reform) is sorry. It is necessary to constantly adjust the delicate balance between the support and the opposition. The term "a conditional support" always means exactly this.

But why - not an absolute one? We all see that *a social revolution has not yet started*. That is, there is no shift in the basis of a public life, in property relations (above all in the means of production). This is the gist of the criticism" from the left". (among the latest publication is a reasonable and serious, i.e. "constructive" open letter of L.Piyasheva to President Yeltsin in the "Moskovskiye Novosti") *THERE IS NO PRIVATIZATION YET* (including what seems to be the most simple and attainable: privatization of places of habituation). That means there is no demonopolization and there is no real conversion yet. Private property in land and changes in villages do not exist and are not expected. There is no free foreign trade, nor are there reasonable taxes. Stimuli for enlivening and reconstructing goods manufacturing for the visible future are not felt, nor are they reasons for stopping the inflation.

On the other hand, we see everything existing nowadays. There is a new and renovated, more competent, but at the same time more pompous nomenclature. There exist "democratic" phraseology, interviews, promises, new signboards, decrees, anarchy and a covert corruption of officials, mass commercialization of commanding offices and persons. However, the main trouble is not what is still existing but that we often feel so dependent on the military-industrial complex or agricultural-industrial bureaucracy, and their inert or incompetent policy. Under what regime are we actually living? Not under the previous pre-August one and, of course, not under a new one not under the communist regime and, of course, not with a democracy. The gap is not complete.

The criticism of the government and President Yeltsin, does not mean a desire for Gaidar's dismissal or especially a retreat of the reforms. On the contrary, it demands their better consideration, ten-fold political courage and their absolute radicalization. We, the people, are interested in the triumph of the started reforms much more than any ministers. In case of failure, the ministers and state aides will resign and nothing more. They will go to Western universities to read lectures about the "perestroika". And what will become of us?

The "new right-wingers" are still incapable of shuttering the government and Yeltsin. However, in order to avoid it next fall-winter a tangible and convincing though modest economic success is badly needed. The reform should be developed from below, having roused millions of workers, employees, peasants, military people, industrialists and traders, having made them people of property and given them hopes for the irreversibility of improvements. And for this mass, democratic organizations, parties, and trade unions enjoying authority among them which would create a partnership with the authorities on equal rights.

"The left-wingers" are either adapting themselves to the situation, or imitating political action under the respectful name of "centrism"; or they are honest but not shrewd; or they are few in number and cannot organize themselves.

UNFORTUNATELY THE GORBACHEV SITUATION IS REPEATING ITSELF, in the sense that *real* democrats seem not to be a force, while generals, directors and former party secretaries are a real one. Therefore the top statesmen are turning their heads to the right, and it seems to be of no use for them to look seriously to the left. It is impractical as who is there? A group of allegedly "extreme" radicals, "the right-wing deviation" and "the left-wing deviation" from "the general line" - in Stalin's time; the right-wing and left-wing extremists against "centrism" under Gorbachev.

But here is a leaflet "The Defenders of the White House", all democratic forces will not sit idle. Say "NO" to the return to the Stalin-fascist dictatorship! This is our style, created for those brought up on CPSU leaflets, i.e. before the March referendum on the "USSR" last year.

It will not be "ours" who will determine the future of B.N. Yeltsin and this, our strange "democratic" Supreme Soviet and nor the strange but familiar didactic Mr. Khazbulatov nor from colonel Rutskoy. Quite on the contrary: they together are destined to determine the future of "our movement". If it turns out t be brilliant, neither Prokhanov with Nevzorov, nor Alksnis and Zhirinovsky, nor the secretary of the Moscow City Committee of the CPSU Prokofyev with Kurginyan will be the cause of it.

A real cause will be democratic members of the Supreme Soviet who looking to the left, recently expressed themselves in favour of considering illegal the decree of 1954 about the transference of the Crimea. Only 16 deputies voted against it.

Well, the decree was no more legal than the formation of the RSFSR or the Ukrainian USSR. What an urgent "real' subject for debates they found! "It is not a confrontation decision", the speaker Khazbulatov said. "This does not mean a confrontation", advised Fyodor Shelov-Kovedyayev in a placid way having found a marshal baton in his haversack. Lukin's advice was to "be strong" at the negotiations with the Ukraine, and "our TV expert" A. Migranyan advised to strike the sovereign idea from the hands of the dangerous right-wingers, and to hoist it on our own democratic flagstaff, proposing the crimea as "a condominium" i.e. being mutual governed with the Ukraine. In the case of Kazakhstan - will it be a condominium for virgin land? A condominium with Estonia for the Pskov region? The expert only failed to define with how many dead soldiers we will have to pay for this remarkable idea.

Before "not sitting idle' it would be nice to sit and think and then to get up. Maybe it is more important to defend the White House not only from the outside, but to defend democracy from democrats.

P.S. *It has been just announced that the Moscow Mayor's Office prohibited processions towards the White House*, and assigned different dates for pickets, manifestations, meetings and countermeetings. Earlier communist leaders from "The Working Moscow" demonstrated their good sense, so that there will be no fighting on February 9. WE shall come to the Liberty Square some other day.

P.P.S. To my deepest regret the idea of a confrontation on the square was supported by the "Moskovskaya Tribuna" on January 26. Having avoided its meetings I am unable to do away with the feeling of my personal responsibility for what this club is doing, the club devised by me in July 1988, and formed three months later thanks to the ardent support of A.D. Sakharov. It is not only on my own behalf, but on behalf of the "Tribuna's" founders Yu.N. Afanasyev and Yu.G. Burtin, that I condemn this unintelligent and irresponsible decision.

ADOPTERS

I realize the inexpressive character of the word proposed as a new political term in the above title, but any political term in inevitably colourless and let those who like, replace it with an "apt Russian word"[1].

Recently I opened a newspaper and the headline read: "Idealism in politics is very dangerous". Below they printed the name of the author: "Alexie Kiva, a political scientist.

A. Kiva's article ("Izvestiya", No. 50, p.7) is remarkable in that it concentrates on the most characteristic features of today's frame of mind and the morals of many people who have become democrats from the CPSU. "I want, A. Kiva declares, to dispute one assertion of Marina Pavlova-Silvanskaya: "There's no sense in adopting from national-patriots their great-power ideas...they are not only dangerous but fruitless as well". There is sense and how badly it is needed!

Democrat Kiva, with a rare frankness, declared himself an adopter of a great-power ideology. So this word was invented neither by me, nor even M. Pavlova-Silvanskaya. This is *his*, a typical Russian "democrat's" self definition.

It becomes more and more difficult to be engaged in politics of late. Why does the population lose the interest in politics? Is it because one cannot be interested in it and discuss it in public with the lack of words which are both exact and sufficiently decent. For a century they scoffed at any worthy notions, violated and stained "Motherland", 'freedom", "property", "democracy" only obscenities remain untouched and pure.

All people (especially intellectuals) began to use obscenities not without reason, but for the sake of social and psychological lessening and a certain even moral relief. Outstanding Russian obscenities helped us to survive in the historic conditions which fell to our lot; at least these words

---

[1] "Dead Souls", end of Chapter 5, below at the end of the article - from Chapter 6.

sounded reliable, sincere and definite. Sometimes seeming utterly sense-less, they nevertheless (before and after 1917) wee alien to the cast-iron great-power pathos and demagogy. Unlike all others they meant precisely what they meant and sent everyone exactly where they pointed to.

From the ideological triad of Count Uvarov they are content reserv-edly only with the national character. They were valued by Pushkin and possibly Lev Tolstoy. It is on this occasion that Gogol wrote for school-children to learn: "Russian folk-like strong expressions and if they reward someone with a witty word it will be inherited by his kin and posterity, he will drag it off to his work and retirement, to Petersburg and the back of beyound". (Ibid).

Of course, one time non-high-society expressions as well as official bureaucratic ones constituted two opposite poles of multi-layer and flourishing language spreading between the formal and forbidden. On the contrary, in the totalitarian situation the formal stroke roots in any life spheres, so people have been left with an opportunity either to talk in evenings in a kitchen or to cluster near a beer-tank. Therefore, the refined-kitchen and billingsgate expressions have stopped shunning each other. A spicy word, with or without drinking happened to be a non-punishable, consequently, popular, whether instinctive or deliberate form of mass dissident movement. As for the chiefs of all levels, including the general secretary, often such a word distinguished them from zombies. And at the same time, in fact was indicative of their standing in the hierarchy favour-ing the strengthening of the latter.

This public phenomenon actually filled what was called the "solitary" and "unbreakable unity of the party of people".

And what is the case now, when the CPSU and USSR have collapsed? Has the full meaning and character of printed words been restored? If so, it is hardly the case with politics; pollution of the national political vo-cabulary has perhaps even increased. Even those two or three dozens of notions the former regime failed to pervert and for which people were recently jailed, today are prostituted.

"PLURALISM" and "GLASNOST" have entered the repertoire of co-medians. "Liberal-democratic" means yelling crazy threatenings with a haughtily protruded jaw and sputtering.[2] "Christian democrats" or "constitutional democrats" (with added "people's freedom") are certain "whites", candidates of a philosophy preoccupied with the idea of taking back the Crimea or making peace in Chechnya. Even a seemingly neutral

---

[2] An allusion to V. Zherinovsky.

expression "the parliament speaker" points to something boorish. "Human rights" give rise to buffoonery and impudent lies, and such common words as "ours" or "memory" have been taken out of our normal language, and must be hidden from children. Consider the word 'democrat". I personally can no longer call myself so. The entire country has gotten sick of this word.

All at once, we are aware that from the USSR - hundreds of thousands of pseudo-Dimiries, Otrepyevs arrived in Russia, allegedly from the West, with a new thinking: fugitive monks of the CPSU in an unprecedented Time of Troubles![3]

In order to come to know its particulars and get out of it we shall need, in addition to many other things, to clear the language and either restore the direct meaning of notions or invent some more adequate words. Therefore we should be thankful to A. Kiva for this capacious, frank word "adopters".

I am now interested in politics s it is, i.e. in what and how politicians are doing: the less ideology taken from the viewpoint of its contents, than the manner of thinking of the Russian democrats. In other words, how do they conjugate notions and use worlds? It is all this, and their following it in their lives and self-interests that embodies their professional morals. It is their convictions or their absence that are amusing.

Communists and anti-communists willingly united themselves in an "amalgamated opposition", "A strong state' written on their common banner. The state counsellor Stankevich considers it "a natural for Russia, organic tendency". He fears only the "parasitizing" politicians of a "troglodyte kind" on it. It is necessary to adopt a nationalistic idea, a slogan of "a strong state" "at the same time" to attach a more civilized character to all this without disgraceful hatred for non-Russians and foreigners. Mr. Stankevich, looking after "parties ad movements" on behalf of the President, is reproving "the democratic camp...in any case its considerable part" for "their incapability... of meeting this ripe necessity". Russia and, of course, the new ruling nomenclature among whom we must count Mr. Stankevich himself, feels a "ripe Need" to strengthen the power with a flavour of great-power ideology and use of "the national idea". Democrats "must meet" this requirement. They have to form an idea of Russia which would simultaneously combine elements of democracy, patriotism and sovereignty..." ("Literaturnaya Gazeta", No. 11).

---

[3] Allusions to A. Pushkin's tragedy "Boris Godunov".

It seems that such is now the social order of the state leadership. They pretend to know everything about the moods and sentiments of modern Russia, whose people are allegedly worried about the same things as the "patriots". This is clearly but, rather cautiously formulated by the clever Mr. Stankevich, replying to the question of how A. Sakharov would regard what is going on if he were alive. Perfectly realizing that Sakharov would regard the idea of nationally coloured authoritarianism with wrath and disgust, Mr. Stankevich slightly and gently hints that the "lack of compromises" of the late academician was quixotic, far from a real politics". He would always find something to protest against...he would not glorify or applaud...")Is it already a time to glorify?). "This was a man who in our present-day sinful and very imperfect world stayed in amoral opposition". What, of course, cannot be said about the free-lance head of the counter-propaganda group at the Cheremushki regional committee of the CPSU Mr. Stankevich.[4]

A. Sakharov would insist today on "certain further and more profound changes", while he, Mr. Stankevich, proposes "to simultaneously combine"...any "elements", with a clever dosage of respectfulness and condescension for A. Sakharov.

In the adjacent column of the same issue of the "Literaturnaya Gazeta" the same indefatigable "Alexei Kiva, political scientist adds without beating about the bush: "A strong, if you want, authoritarian power is needed". For Russia I see no other ideas but supreme power, religiousness, folk character, including populism...The ideas of democracy, sovereignty of personality, priority of human rights over the rights of the nation, economic independence of personality, humanism...are undoubtedly needed. But they can make a decisive influence in society at alter stages of the post-communist development. We must be realistic... Each fruit has its season."

State counselors can't always allow themselves to speak freely. that is why political scientists happen to be useful too. One drops the phrase that "a strong state is needed". Others are rapping out: "authoritarian'. Some of them say something inarticulate about "an organic tendency" of the Russian people. Others are firing away directly from count Uvarov's theory.[5]

---

[4] Such groups were set up not long before the "perestroika": for a "struggle against bourgeois propaganda".

[5] The famous formula of count Uvarov of the time of Nicolas I - "sovereignty, orthodoxy, folk character".

Where is such an element (or a "fruit") as democracy? Mr. state counselor includes it in "the idea of Russia" simultaneously with "sovereignty" but Mr. political scientist cynically confesses that we must wait with democracy as well s with all those human rights. It is not yet the season, writes the realistic Kiva, to pick this "strawberry".

So, *we shall not succeed in doing it simultaneously*, corrects Kiva to Consellor Stankevich with good reason. You'd better live first if you are a democrat in law[6] with a 'strong state', adopt from "patriots", get to like "the idea of Russia". And forward..."to democracy in an imperial march".

I would not like emptiness in place of the moral authority of Andrei Dmitriyevich, languor of political will and an insufficient number of real democrats among politicians, to become fatal for Russia. The only chance for Russian freedom and hence, Russian modernization and economic flourishing is the birth of a consistently democratic, independent movement of citizens which would prove loyalty to its democratic and not to the principles before Russia's very eyes. Tactical compromises can be useful only if you have strong principles BEFORE any compromises. The latter are possible for you only to limit beyond which there is a threat of a loss of the principles themselves, a LOSS OF YOURSELF (and at the same time an inevitable 'influence on the masses"). Politics is a practical sphere; yes, we do live in "a sinful world", and "we must be realistic" (all these democrats love to say in similar expressions). But not all make themselves so comfortably at home in "a sinful world' (both under communists and after them). Politics WITHOUT ideals, i.e. without selfless devotion to ideals, without a desire to bring into life what is not there yet, is neither democratic nor "big" politics in general.

The same author who writes that "idealism in politics is very dangerous" remarks a little bit below: "we need ideals, ideals". According to Kiva this is what is called "inexorable, truly inexorable is the logic Whom does one believe? A. Kiva? Or...A. Kiva?

However there is logic here. "An idealist" is a person who professes his or her own ideals. While "ideals" are needed, those adopted from the picket of someone else in order to "influence masses".

All this together they love to call "centrism" with us. Their name is legion. Our significant author is from "centrists" and, for two years has been demanding "a compromise" and "consensus" in each of his articles Prior to August 1991 this meant: "all the democrats" uniting around Gorbachev's presidency and his team. Later, it meant around 'the Novo-

---

[6] In analogy to a "thief in law", a Russian godfather, a big fish, "officially" recognized among criminals.

Ogaryovo process" and so on. Today it means support of what was recently defined by G. Burbulis as a supreme goal twinkling ahead, "a combination of democratism and patriotism".

Quite enough has been written about patriotism in Russia since the time of Chaadayev, therefore I do not need to go into abstract details. If patriotism means that I am ardently attached to my native country and wish good changes for my countrymen, then democracy does not need "to be combined with patriotism" but includes it. If, however, it is a habit to love in the "bustling, mighty and invincible" it means the "grandeur...of military might". "The Black sea navy has always been and will remain Russian", habitual boasting with the vast space; in short, the replacement of Motherland with "the native state", be it "the USSR" or "the Holy Russia", "imperial" syndrome with its eagle emblems. It is too obvious what the "combination with patriotism" has in mind for democracy".

As democratism is undoubtedly a priority of a private person, a citizen, an owner, a personality over any collective and especially state claims, OR a great power of patriots. This is the tough alternative we are forced to face not by a certain "patriotism in general" (which in itself, beyond the modus of statehood may be harmless) but exactly the real meaning of the "national idea" it assumes when turning into an official banner: with us, here, now, in the Russia of 1992.

We are being persuaded that "the tremendous part of Russians", "broad masses" are allegedly doing nothing but thinking about the "national Idea", the "grandeur of military might", etc. If it were so I would prefer to say a democrat and not to renounce myself, even for the sake of "influencing masses". In this case it would mean that I am not going the way of the masses, and democrats of principle would be left nothing but to continue to defend what the masses will arrive at after a new "patriotic" hangover. They will arrive if there remain politicians capable of telling the truth to tsars and people with a smile.

"Is it bad that people strive to see their Motherland great?" What a feigned naiveté! This striving is not the political contents of great-power ideology. And who on earth is not striving? And why not "to look for a way to consent?", according to Kiva, for "the national concord and cooperation, according to Stankevich. "Soon we all shall be merged in a single love boundless as the sea..."[7] - this Rakhmaniov's song should be turned into the hymn of "centrists". It is next to impossible to buy milk in Mos-

---

[7] Text by poet A.K. Tolstoy.

cow. We are short of petrol, and you are talking about "patriotism". It is a lie that the population strives not for milk but a military might", especially new billion-ruble aircraft carriers and "fly up, falcons, like eagles"[8] from Kyrghzstan to the command of Moscow.

Of course, there are such "masses" also among the enormous Russian people. Of much greater scope are the masses not suffering with national complexes, but simply wishing to live a normal life. Give them, (above all those who are under thirty) passports with Western visas and purses filled with foreign hard currency. Young people feel sick to live in Russia. They repeat after Pushkin: "Devil made us be born here". You will not buy the majority of the population with the chaff of any ideology.

The majority are longing not for "the USSR". I shall not speak on their behalf but only about myself. I feel miserable too. I used to take my vacations and go as a non-official holiday-maker either to Abkhazia, or the Riga Bay shore, or the Crimea. And now they seem to be foreign lands? How shall we live further? I was born in Kharkov and have relatives and friends there. I wish in a year, in ten years to take the train No. 19 at the Kursk railway station without being bothering about a visa, on my arrival to change rubles for grivnas at the Southern railway station in Kharkov. And what shall I do there?

It is purely personal. I do not care what state is there or who its president is or about what they negotiated with our president yesterday. Democratic morals, like any idea requires a certain responsibility for what is uttered. If you accept that the "notion of" the national idea "has turned out the be strongly vulgarized, burdened with archaic and openly reactionary symptoms" and:" all this must be thrown away as rubbish" then how are you going to reach an "accord" and a "compromise" with the defenders of this rubbish? The reply is "on the basis of combining the principles of democracy with the Russian national idea".

"But we are living in a world far from ideal". Until now in this world they have taken into consideration military force rather than economic might". (Well, ask Kryuchkov or Saddam Hussein or Castro). "That is why, in my opinion, we have not to contrast a great military power with a rich and prosperous country, democratic features, with patriotism and statehood". "We have not to contrast" but, at least, we'll be forced to adapt them to our present-day 'riches" and "prosperity", and this means "to contrast", As for the other things, "democratic features" imply *also democratic statehood.*

---

[8] Words from an old soldier song, an allusion to an unauthorizes flight of several militray crews.

Under democracy people treat the state like a telephone, heating, water supply, sewerage and other useful services. They are maintained in proper condition, checked, repaired, paid for, absolutely indispensable, people speak ironically or with irritation about their failure. But they are never glorified or turned into a lofty goal and the state is never proclaimed the national ideal or "power".

Nothing good will come out of attempts "to adopt" something allegedly worthy and pure in a reactionary rubbish alien to personal and democratic principles. here is proof: anyone who adopts it may refuse anything to do with less respectable figures from whom he borrows but nevertheless he appears together with the "rubbish" he was eager to hide under his bed at the same gathering.

"The national idea", "the Russian idea" under the historically established political traditions and circumstances in Russia is such a turnip that people intended to pull it out to grasp each other at once.[9] The grandma "Pamyat" is followed by the granddad Zhirinovsky. Next goes the communist granddaughter by the name Baburin or Goryacheva followed by the anti-communist (say, "Cadet" of Democratic-Christian" Zhuchka.[10]). They are gathering in a company that is not at all friendly. They are joined by Mr. Vice-President to adopt the turnip: He pulls and pulls. The State Secretary starts to cast thoughtful glances at it, and sometimes the President of Russia himself keeps a cunning eye glued to it. And further on, al democrats, even some rosy social-democrats, and Stankevich with Kiva, and a crawfish with its claw[11] they are pulling and pulling. Mr. Popov and Mr. Sobchak happen to pull also. A complete haymaking.[12] Now wait for someone else. There is no day without a democrat turning into a patriot and a patriot into a democrat.

In a word, "adopters". And what if they succeed in pulling it out? How much stewed turnip we shall then eat.

Oh if among our *politicians* we would find some who would be able to find apt words today, like the word which made Chichikov pensive and helped him to get from Sobakevich to Plyushkin.

Our present-day road is no less worthy of hard thinking.

---

[9] A popular Russian fairy tale "The Turnip".

[10] A dog of these "grandma" and "grandad".

[11] A Russian saying _ "Where goes a crawfish, he is followed by its claw".

[12] A euphemism for an obscene word meaning - that is the last straw.

We keep reading newspapers and like the aging Gogol "are approaching an unfamiliar place for the first time" and "indifferently watching the banal appearance". It does not..."make us laugh". And it is "uninviting for my cool eyes" to look at this or that "patched"...democrat.[13]

---

[13] Citations from Gogol's "Dead Souls".

SCORING THEIR
OWN GOALS

On the evening of May 2, we were shown an unprecedented political TV show. The top leaders of Russia and Moscow, having put on shorts and sports shirts, were chasing a soccer ball at a stadium. During the break and after the game they gave interview. President Yeltsin and the capital's Mayor Popov acted as "coaches". The state secretary Burbulis, if I remember correctly, chose the part of the "captain" of the Russia's state team in which ministers were rushing about the field as well as general Grachev. Deputy mayor Luzhkov, a ramming type player with amazing speed was moving his powerful body to the goal of the President's government and I would not wish to be in the place of those who stood in his way. A handsome chief of the Moscow KGB, well-known democrat Ye. Sevastyanov said that, being simultaneously deputy minister of this department, he hesitated as to which team he should play for, but nevertheless chose "Moscow". Stout and thin, old and young, high officials ran puffing, sometimes colliding and knocking each other down. Injuries added particular cogency to what was going on: the minister of justice was even carried away from the field on a stretcher (what awaits us in the future?). Politicians were bathed in sweat demonstrating to the country and the world that this is, in fact, a rather exhausting profession.

As far as I can judge, a stadium is a rather convenient place to arrange guarding. The few spectators permitted included all the bodyguards, for the first time sitting while on duty. It is interesting to know how many blocks away the passage and traffic were closed for other fans. The ruling men, with tired smiles on their faces, confessed one after another they had played the game for the last time some twenty or so years before, evidently in their student years. Only one of the statesmen does his morning exercises every day, though a few liked movements in the open air. Unlike Boris Nikolayevich, the majority of the others have no time; they work till late in the evening an in the morning they want ten more minutes to sleep.

G. Popov said that in his young years, evidently before his work at the CPSU Central Committee and his passing to science, he was fond not of soccer, but of mountain climbing. And now (with a laugh) what sport can it be. "If we win we sahll not see allocations", he jokes. And only a person susceptible to bureaucratic humour who knows that G.Kh. Popov gets anything he wishes from the President, is capable of appraising this scene.

B. Yeltsin said that if "Moscow" (i.e. Mayor's office) won, nevertheless it would be the victory of "Russia" (i.e. President's cabinet) as "Moscow is Russia". Thus Pushkin's lines ("How much within that sound is blended for a Russian heart") suddenly became filled with modern political and administrative contents.

Of course, the show missed Khazbulatov who for sure would be able to bring into the game his specific personal coloring. However, quite recently we did see him in a marathon race of the imaginary parliament in an apt (sports) underwear making fast feints before the eyes of the entire nation resorting to force but, being compelled to end a draw game with mutual understanding. Oh, it was a real fun even without Ruslan Imranovich, but definitely to his liking.

I must confess that this vulgar political show just finished me. This cannot be called even "populism" of the cheapest sort. Populism is a policy speculating in any utterly justified or dark public moods and trying to please the man in the street, to win him around. But did they guess the moods right, did they succeed in attracting people? I realize and suppose that all TV viewers *did understand*, and that we saw on the TV screen, an attempt to crudely flatter the people with accessibility; ordinary characters and democratism.

It all started with Gorbachev's leaving his car in a street without ceremonies and quite accidentally met some workers, dropped in, say, the first food store looking around at the very frugal and neat abundance unable yet to meet our needs. Well. all right, it will get better, processes will start, etc. Now Yeltsin sometimes does things like that; but promises less, tells tough things. However, it is difficult to resist the temptation to sugar the pill, so they "change the political style" (as it is interpreted by certain persons closest to the President and he himself), and in such a radical way that Gorbachev and Raisa Maximovna have not even dreamt of. They rush into the field, play the popular game, chase a soccer ball, *like all others*. They pretend to be carefree sturdy fellows, in their own way understanding the gospel saying "be like children", romping and posing as our boys.

Well, for the sake of it, Popov in his old age went into an ice-hole without a shiver, *pretending* to be "a winter-swimmer". Such are (in his understanding) the loft demands of politicos! And now they, one and all, *pretended* to be sportive, eager to run, reckless soccer players. (It should be said in all fairness that Yeltsin sitting under an awning seemed to support quite earnestly, with all his heart and soul).

While they decided, that on seeing the leaders without pants, people will be touched, will respond with festive feelings, and they will come to believe in the reforms. They think the people are still fond of soccer, though stadiums are almost empty during real matches. I would propose for the next time that we arrange a top level of dominoes game. The Minister would play with replacements of the losers. Tables might be placed in St. George Hall of the Kremlin. It is more natural to play dominoes both for the unhealthy and big-bellies, and besides, dominoes is much more popular among the population than soccer. Knocking of domino dice and mild obscenities wee heard over Russia also in these days of the entire May festivities granted to us for no reason at all. here the imperial knocking would merge with that of people in a single rumbling of thunder. And as ambassador Lukin advises, the cossacks in Zaporozhskaya Sech would become thoughtful and the neighbouring nations would shudder form the rattling of Gogol's troika.

It would be interesting to know who proposed this splendid soccer idea, having seen enough fragments of American newsreels depicting Reagan or Bush playing golf or jogging in mornings. However, the thing is that their politicians (all lean) practice it not only for invited journalists. Though, of course, they are interested in the voters not doubting their endurance, their excellent physical shape. Put the TV report from Moscow demonstrated a falsification of these "sporting abilities" for the majority of the participants. This is the first falsehood.

Americans of any age are known to run, swim, train their muscles, watch over their health and shape, they have a swimming pool, a gymnasium and so on, within two blocks from their home. While or people, having paid tribute to sports in their young years, later as a rule have neither strength nor desire, nor elementary facilities for it. In other words, the American politicians demonstrate that they have the same habits as the majority of vote. While our Saturday match of high officials was a privileged whim about which people do not care. These mature and aging soccer players "rested" not as "all others". This is the second falsehood.

There one can photograph Bush training, but it is impossible to imagine that he is followed by a jogging Baker and all the people from his administration, including representatives of the army, CIA and the Washington's Mayor's office. In the Land of the Soviets a tradition is, or course, different. It is easy to suppose that someone would be glad to wriggle out of it. Wasn't Gaidar down in the dumps, didn't he keep to himself his irritation at having to play this unnatural, stupid and physically exhausting role in this charade? But he was told: "It must be done. Otherwise, according to our information, ordinary people are not warmed with too intellectual an appearance and sophisticated figures of speech. You should be closer to the population".

The soviet tradition of the top leaders appearing before the people at full strength in a hierarchic team, "jointly" in a well disciplined way is a tradition which was expressed a dozen years ago investing each other with orders or standing on the mausoleum. This is still manifested now in crowd departure or meeting ceremonies at the airport, with TV news reporting: this tradition of official (court by origin) ceremony has been transfigured beyond recognition. It has been democratized, right up to chasing a soccer ball, though still en mass. Before the game the leaders formed their usual rank still in original uniforms. The expressions "Yeltsin's team ", "Popov's" team they decided to interpret literally; they became mummers while the podium was transformed in a soccer field. This is the third falsehood.

The falsehoods continue as the loneliness of the persons who have become inaccessible, even for their own counselors, is feigned. A popular game looks ambiguous when performed by the people preserving the old system of private privileges, i.e. the huge car fleet of the CPSU Central Committee, corresponding service personnel, etc., and as the "openness" of officials still conceptualizing politics as a closed top-leaders' matter is nonexistent.

While the main lesson we learn during the game's analysis is the following: we are not only still living in the same social and economic system as before August 1991 with the same Gorbachev-Vorotnikov composition of "the congress of people's deputies" and the same apparatus of the executive power. Personnel are renewed only in "the center" but with the old administrative mechanism, routine, and inclination to "reorganizations" only with the ten-fold embezzlement of state funds. The *very style and psychology of the administration* in its relations with people has undergone few changes.

The new top administration, and also its best representative, on whom we are still rest in our hopes with our unconditional support of them against their right-wing enemies, is suffering from a democratic deficiency. Like post-August society, they remained the same in their basis except for the dissolution of party committees and replacement of the "socialist" ideology with the "imperial" one.

Numerous phenomena in all the spheres of state and public life at first sight having nothing in common, are today amazingly focused at one point. This social and psychological focus, *turncoats* and *disguises*, is preserving the essence of the old "soviet" structure.

That is why an insignificant but remarkably expressive event, the May soccer game, may be seen as an emblematic image of the present-day state of both the administration and society in Russia. And this is despite the fact that Yeltsin's Russia is undoubtedly ahead of all the CIS members (except Armenia) in reforms, departizaton, etc.

Trying to analyze the nature of my rejection of the very style of the political behavior of the new administration, I have come to the following self-observation. I consider it necessary to dismiss certain "top" characters, protest against the way policy is carried out inside the CIS, feel fear and disgust for the flirting with national patriotism and monarchial myths with imaginary and uncontrollable armed "cossacks", indignant at the fact that the hopes of the Russian Germans have been interred as well as at blood-smelling incitements in the Crimea and the Dniester region. Finally I am waiting to see when and how the government of Yeltsin-Gaidar, having decided to star, will pass to really drastic reforms, as the trouble is not with what the government is doing but what is not doing. But on the whole I nevertheless do not feel this administration is a hostile one. It has healthy elements. I also see certain efficient, educated unselfish people captivated with a great mission. I see the merits of their steps, and we can deal with this administration. This is the hidden motive of our disappointment.

The new power is sometimes a vast improvement from Gorbachev and his "perestroika". Like Gorbachev himself, especially prior to his right turn in the fall of 1989, was incomparably better than Brezhnev's political bureau., the authorities have radically improved over the last decade. It is this transitional state of the country, this approach to something vaguely resembling something almost democratic that saves us from a spiteful indifference, increased social ethical and, if you wish, artistic) impressionability ad exactingness.

"Am I sinning with "maximalism"? Oh, not. The country has not time to sit and wait till real politics arrive. There are no more forces, not only due to the breaking of all and any vital ties, but because of the lack of shelter for those who have lost all their possessions in fires of the camping zone, and particularly because the hour of a real freedom and openness, we should think, is around the corner.

Let the patriotic majority fly in a rage at the "congress", let communists arrange their gatherings: we shall not return there. That was a disposable regime. But let us not fall into something wrong, in a customary Russian romance with the past.

On May 2, I went across Moscow to visit my mother. A woman sitting near me on a bus was telling her neighbor that she was carrying a rotten potato she had bought today for six and a half rubles back to the store. She hoped to exchange it for a Polish one; they are supposed to be excellent, without waste. She explained that she had spent her last 50 rubles and therefore was very nervous thinking aloud whether she had to go to see a manager first and what to say to succeed. Later in a metro passage between Turgenevskaya and Chistye Prudy stations I was shocked by the great number of beggars. They always stand there nowadays, but I have never seen so many of them standing shoulder to shoulder along the walls. I gave a ruble to a young swarthy ex-soldier of the Afghan war with an Oriental face sitting on the floor, his crutch at this side. He silently bent his head. Then I visited all the bakeries in Preobrazhenka district; they were either closed or had no bread all the same. Later at twilight, I managed somehow to get through a horribly littered city to my house. I arrived just in time to watch "Vesti", a news program. I saw the top leaders of Russia and Moscow chasing a soccer ball in order to improve people's moods.

PART III

STAGNATION-
TIME ARGUMENTS

A FEW PRELIMINARY
EXPLANATIONS

In April of 1980, I received a letter from a friend from Petersburg sympathizing with academician D.S. Likhachev's just published "Notes About the Russian". I had a different opinion.

In the heat of the moment I took my typewriter, opened an issue of the "Novy Mir" magazine, and soon realized that what I was writing was not at all a private letter. Even the form of address to my real correspondent appeared to resemble an old literary device. However, it was not an article. I typed the whole thing in two days without retyping or correcting, and without preliminary plan.

Having made a dozen copies for certain of my friends and acquaintances, I mailed this improvisation to my friend in St. Petersburg. I remember mailing a copy to the late Boris Shragin working then at the "Liberty" in New York. I have never attempted to publish it. It was, of course, impossible to do so in this country.) I preferred to leave the text unsigned, as it was not worth giving explanations to KGB officials. I had enough troubles without it. There was not "politics" as it has not been present in the "Metropol" in which I had participated a year before. Nevertheless after the ":Metropol", I was interrogated at the Lubyanka. Everything was considered politics in this country.

Writer Mark Kharitonov asked my permission to send my polemic consideration to David Samoilov in Parnu What I wrote about suited their own arguments about Kharitonov's story "Two Ivans". I was not acquainted with D. Samoilov and he did not know I was the author of the letter for the above reasons. The poet gave a wrathful reply but, he nevertheless answered me. I started wiring again, and mailed another text to Parnu.

Many years have passed since then. Whatever I think about these articles now, they are undoubtedly characteristic of our Russian arguments and emotions of that time: they are "comments of the epoch". They are, to my regret, hardly obsolete, as the epoch in a certain respect is the same.

I argued with people esteemed by me as well as by all in Russia. But only with such people is it worth arguing. If there exists an outlook seeming to you false and even dangerous, it is the outlook of such people that is expressed not only most sincerely but in the most convincing way and to the best advantage. If you argue with the psychological and intellectual basis of such a position, take it in it cultural aspect, its best samples. If I had written not as a private correspondence, not in a rush but had intended it for publication, it would have been, somewhat more profound and delicate, at the expense of certain vehemence, banalities and reiteration. But as "a document" these drawbacks of too hasty writings may be more interesting that absent advantages. Now preparing the text for publication, I have changed nothing except minimal editing in certain places.

I have changed, as we all do, but not principal stand remains the same. Today it has become clear than at that time: it is best for the national feelings and national principles if they remain a private matter.

Perhaps. nobody can do without a certain ideology but I hope that ideology would not substitute for culture and would not encroach upon my way of thinking. I still consider and even keenly see that a "simple" ideology lacking a noble appearance is much better than "cultural" ideology. It has less temptation.

But any well-intended reasoning based on the cult of anitonal principles as super-personal and super-historical is a dangerous one, compromises and hopeless at the end of the XXth century.

National ideology, like any other, cannot be "cultural" as it is always an attempt to avoid a paradox, difficulty for oneself, tragedy of any *principles* for thinking.

In conclusion I must confess that even now that censorship restrictions have been removed, I for a long time have thought the publication of these papers from my archives inappropriate, and hesitated until the last moment. First of all there David Samoilov is nor more and I would wish so much to hear his voice in reply. And won't Dmitry Sergeyevich Likhachev be pained; what he is saying is not always profound or right, but on cannot help listening attentively to and admiring this handsome and sad man on the TV screen.

The 1980 letters cannot be separated from the circumstances of their writing. My views of Russian history and culture, of the problem of "the

Russian" are by no means restricted to what I intended to emphasize precisely in the polemics against Likhachev and Samoilov. The problem of the correlation of Russian and Europe will evidently remain, but will lose pain in time. We shall be inevitably changed. Dozens of years will pass and it will cross nobody's mind to write about "the Russian" as it has been written by D. Likhachev ad my objections will also become unnecessary.

A LETTER FROM 1980

One would suppose that both the "right-wingers" and "left-wingers" would be displeased with the notes of D.S. Oh, no! The latter will please almost all: our Slavophiles, internationalists, "moralists", authorities, everyone will find something pleasant in them. Dmitry Sergeyevich is wrong to think that he is going against the stream and he expresses the hope that at last 'two or three persons will agree": not two or three, but thousands and thousands. Only a few will be against and, among those few I consider myself with full conviction.

"The Notes About the Russian" are written in such a lively and fresh style, their tone is so winningly intelligent and it is clear from the first sentences that they are written by a very outstanding man full of the best sentiments and intentions who writes them sincerely, well, ALMOST. Quite often he means desirable and proper things. For example: "One may but rejoice, living in a country where quite different people meet and come together..." (Instead of : "One would but rejoice if not...,etc.). Or "Russians, though not always but in the majority of cases, lived in peace with the neighbouring peoples". Was it so? Where did the Russian Empire come from? Spread form the Pacific to Kushka? Was it on empty lands that it was firmly established? And has not all this, form the seizure of Kazan and subjugation of all sorts of Cheremises and Mordovians, until more recent events had influence? "We are all citizens of our nation, citizens of our great Union and citizens of the globe". To say that we are "citizens" of our nation; how nice it would be to be CITIZENS.

Our most prominent historian of culture remarks that "there was a certain freedom of the ancient Russian ideal from any kind of implementations". As long as "reality" was sometimes too wanton an cruel. Aren't we "children", "sons" and "daughters" of our ancient history? According to D.S. "the tremendous gap between the ideal of culture and reality" also results from the fact that the ideal consequently is really lofty.

Of course, ideals are ideals in order not to coincide with reality. Each historical reality has its own particular character of such a lack of coincidence and the very ideals are its own flesh and blood, so that two opposite realities, cultures and non-cultures, sufficiently explain each other, wile ideals, embracing with their structure what is rejected by them, can never avoid internal discrepancy.

And the big History is a history of reality together with an ideal arguing with it from inside The national character, we must think, is forged between a hammer and an anvil, in tragic arguing of different circumstances and different ideals, and therefore any national character in its essence is arguable (we say: "mysterious", difficult to define). In a character the history of people is summarized, assumes certain forms which may seem even eternal, but what is summarized are different, changing and transitional features; summarized is what cannot be summarized while it remains alive. Therefore the "formula" of any national peculiarities must contain the possibility of paradoxical reformulations, and self-denial. We shall refer to this later.

For the time being, let us read thoroughly this passage about "the ancient Russian ideal" and ask a question whether, as Dmitry Sergeyevich says, it resulted in "the ideas of seclusion, self-denial and abandoning cares and troubles, helping the Russian people to endure their hardships"; to look with a kind and all-forgiving grin at their tormentors whom he is ready even to pity having distracted themselves for hateful vies and actions..." and so on. Well, it precisely this that Belinsky wrote in his dying letters to Gogol.

It turns out, for example, that archpriest Avvakum was not "a dismal fatalist" as he could "watch vain efforts of his torturers with a smile". O.K. let him be not a dismal fatalist but a patient one. But were the efforts of the tormentors so vain? Aren't Avvakum and his torturers from the same history, the same reality, and are their mentalities so alien? Not more than right and left, heat and cold, nor more than the Russian "all forgiveness", pity for their tormentors, and "the Russian riot, senseless and merciless". Admiring Russian "God's fools" is it worth to condemn the bloody deeds of the God's fool Ivan The Terrible, as if any such deeds in Russia did not stem from the same root? Shouldn't we look for the Russian big-way enterprise, Russian vastness and so on, a hybrid of the Russian riot with the Russian despotism in Rasputin's playing the God's fool beside the degenerated dynasty, and how to separate in this really national powerful character certain heart-winning features from their horrible development?

Or shall we ignore this in analyzing 'the Russian"? Shall we forget what was so clearly understood by the best Russian people beginning from Radishev, that is with selfless, obedient and sacred folk ideas that the vile monarch lasted so long. And wasn't it the same social and psychological ground as pity for tormentors that gave expression to the lust to kill, to rob, to set everything of fire, to foul in landlords' gardens and libraries following forbearing irresponsibility? Shall we forget the long-known truth that it was serfdom and monarchy rather than our admired vast distances and flowing rivers that to a great extent brought up "the Russian" for five hundred years and during this period "the Russian" served as a pedestal for serfdom, boorishness and violence. And everything that opposed *this* "Russian" was also characteristic and absolutely Russian.

If D.S. admits that in "reality given birth to certain ideals is itself at the same time an attempt of their realization" (with an inevitable striking dissonance"). In no case can we agree with an appeal "to appraise both", i.e. reality and ideals "separately"; not separately but together, in the full volume of their often unexpected interaction, without breaking up their opposition and alliance, their tragic dialectics. It does not mean, of course, that we should limit ourselves with putting black paint side by side with pink. "The Russian" is not a sum of attractively beautiful and disgusting manifestations but a certain *problem* a certain living contradiction.

This work by D.S., filled with starry-eyed idealism, is out of season. The author wishes to love our people, our history. We haven't been given another life or another history and it is quite impossible to "simply" love, only to love.

The distinction of patriotism from nationalism give by D.S. is not useful, as this distinction is not that a patriot loving his native things does not blame foreign. (As a matter of fact, one excellent Russian writer recently wrote that the need for love of the foreign is no less necessary in people than the need for love of their native and it is not yet known which is more important for self determination). A person attached to his native things and valuing the foreign as well, is not yet a patriot and, of course, not a nationalist; a serious talk and serious concepts cannot yet start at such a level.

But a grown-up man is going from St. Petersburg to Moscow: "My coachman stroke up a song, as usual plaintive. Who knows the melodies of Russian folk songs, can agree that there is something meaning a grief of the soul. Almost all the melodies of such songs are soft. *Be able to establish the reigns of government basing on this musical mood of people's minds.* In this mood you will find education of the souls of our people. Look at a Russian, you will find him pensive. If he wishes to dispel boredom, or as he himself calls it to have a jolly time, he goes to a saloon. *A barge hauler walking to a saloon, his head hung, and coming back stained with blood from boxes on his ears, can decide many things guessed before in the history of Russia"* Radischev's words are underlined not by me but my Herzen (v.VII, p. 4542). And they do not fit D.S.'s interpretation of "the Russian" not because the author does not find bad things in the Russian history or even in Russian character. Of course, he does, but he does not wish to accept, unlike Radischev and Herzen, the internal fusion of these bad things with what he wants only to admire.

Such is the trouble with our "village-life writers: they wish to notice only good and enlightening, "eternal" moral values of the people, etc., in the survivals of patriarchal morals and conceptions, and do not wish to take these occurrences of patriarchal life (though utterly decayed) in their *full* volume and meaning, with entire social, civil)and by all means *moral*) backwardness, savagery and stagnation.

What is D.S. doing? He takes "separately" not only "ideal" and "reality" but also affirms that "we must distinguish a national ideal an a national character". Thus, a national character seems to relate to reality and to be deprived of the right of idealization? But one of the chapters is called "Russian Nature and Russian Character", why not an "ideal"? *An ideal* of the character? Here and there the author speaks about "national features", :national peculiarities" and with all this apparently as something totally and on a mass scale in a Russian character without reservation that it is but an ideal. However, when the author suddenly recollects, fearing onesidedness and insincerity, as D.S. would never agree to be insincere - then new reservations appear, that we must judge by "summits", by the most beautiful, and then he seems to continue to write about "national peculiarities" which exist not only on summits? The result is that the "Notes" demonstrate vagueness and confusion, surprising for such an outstanding scientific mind.

I repeat that D.S.'s conception contains, despite *the phrases* against nationalism in accordance with the *logics* of the author's thought, neither love for the Russian of Radischev and Herzen, a bitter love, a love-hatred, not "as strange love" for Motherland of Lermontov. Likewise, it contains neither the real, unrestricted by "harmony" Pushkin whom the "Devil made be born in Russia with an intellect and a talent", nor Gogol glorifying "the Russia-troika" driving a britzka with a swindler Chichikov in it, nor, of course Schedrin, "The Village" by Bunin, Tchekhov's "Peasants" and "in the Ravine", Gleb Uspensky (disputes about village morals and values are far from being new). Regardless of D.S.'s intentions, his "Notes" do not support the *democratic* tradition for the Russian patriotism.

From the very beginning he sets his goal in interpreting "the Russian" in this way: to speak about "the most valuable" in it. No, by no means; I would prefer Lenin' s article "on the National Pride of Great Russians", an article roughly ideological, straightforward, strongly simplifying the gist of the matter by means of only two colours, but nevertheless *containing a position*, and not losing its way in broad daylight. Culture cannot be mechanically separated from political point of view after Lenin into "tow cultures, culture is a single whole contradictory in various and many respects and not only in respect of the "tops" and "lower strata". But, *a position* is preferable to non-scientific and non-political sentimental impressions.

To speak about "the most valuable"? This determines the level of the discussion. A woman addressed a French woman with a word "little daughter" D.S. makes Francoise understand that this address expressed a particular Russian warmth and wholeheartedness. "oh!" - a French interpreter was moved by the village patriarchal word. "Little daughter", "sonny", "daddy", "mummy": here are deep Russian feelings. And did anyone say a foul word in addressing Franciouse once, at least those good-humoured senseless obscenities which follow every word with us? And did not she see animosity, rudeness and boorishness in millions of queues and buses?

Does boorishness come from town and not from the countryside? No, it was born in the villages where any forms of respect were based on kinfolk relations, communal ties, neighborhood, but not on individual relations and where it was quite enough of brutality, scuffle, etc., especially regarding wives and inhabitants of *another* village, strangers in general or traditionally humiliated people.

So, village folk who only yesterday migrated to town and are not familiar with respect for any chance met personality in a town crowd, not civilized like in Western Europe with hundreds of years of the development of town freedoms, personal principles, democratic struggle, etc. - IN a Russian crowd, nobody is safe from a sudden and bitter insult on a trifling occasion. It was not in town that a truly Russian saying: "Swearword sticks no color" (harsh words break no bones) was born. Isn't this ignorance of personal dignity, historically connected with an ancient form of an affable address: "little daughter"?

The subjectively honest author refutes nothing in the national morals and character, but he has a ready, comforting simple answer: if there has been anything nasty, these are not "truly Russians". Suffice it to call all unpleasant things for the eye ad noses, "not truly Russian," and to exclude from the very essence of the Russian, things if not *the character*, then the essence of *the ideal*. For example, *"real Russians* have never been sick with praising themselves". Have "real Americans, Chinese, British, Jews, Germans ever been? It turns out to be simple to speak about "national peculiarities" if they are seen in their "ideal form" taken "separately" from "reality", the more so without excessive socio-historical refection. Thus, Russian chauvinism seems to disappear, i.e. it seems to be not "Russian" as it cannot be related to "the precious". What "Russian" is, *truly* Russian, is if we have a distaste for it.

Please, note that this *method* is such that were it another man in place of D.S. *not* highly honest, a certain nationalist condemned by hi, *nothing would have to be changed in the method*. Immediately D.S. himself, or you, or myself will be considered "not truly Russian". If already "these regions where...backwardness is noticed are simply less characteristic of culture of ancient Russia and they should not be judged by", then leaving aside ancient Russia, this method, so objective and so scientific seem to me more priceless in reference to Russia of modern and recent times. What can be simpler: "There are many Karamozovs in Russian life but nevertheless it is not who are directing the ship". They, Karamozovs, are sleeping in cabins, they are also the crew, they are sailors, but for the captain, - writes D.S. "a tiller and a star" are much more important than sailors.

What "a captain" is laying the course for Russian history, determining "the national character" and "national peculiarities"? We must assume that "the captain" is same as "the ideal" of all-forgiving, etc., by which we must judge "the Russian". But we have just learned that reality does not attain the level of the ideal, in short, "The captain" is simple rhetoric, while "the star" happens to be Pushkin. Looking at Pushkin alone, one can learn everything "true".

Pushkin himself did not look in the mirror and meditate on the Russian Shall we really take from Pushkin "separately" his thoughts about the Russian so dissimilar and complex; separately Boris, Grishka Otrepyev, the God's fool, Pimen, silent people: separately the truth of Pugachev and the horrors of his movement ; separately "The Prophet" and "Gavriliade", his friendship with Decembrists and "Stanzas" his girlfriend of censorship, Russian principles, Europeism, "Chetyi Minei" hastedly opened at the appearance of the prior of the Svyatogory Monastery", "Will the hour of my freedom ever come"; separately his attitude to Peter, Radischev, his disagreement- agreement with Chaasdayev? (remember the tone, meaning, method of Pushkin's judgment about the Russian) where are Pushkin's lessons in D.S.'s "Notes"?

And where are the lessons of F. Dostoyevsky? Dostoyevsky as a creator is not taken into account on the strange grounds that it is impossible to judge Dostoyevky's world outlook by the words of his characters. Why has D.S. stooped to use his argument on such a level? Is it possible to judge the world outlook of Fyodor Mikhailovich by the novel's style and structure, by the exchange of messages and disputes of *all* the voices including that of the author, by everything we learn from Dossstoyevsky about the Russian, Russian life, the Russian way of thinking, suffering, rebelling, loving? We shall not ignore his publication and his evolution from Petrashevsky to "The Devils". We shall miss nothing, neither the most strained search for the truth, nor his spite for Poles and Jews, nor his intercession for the innocent, nor his staggering novelty of world perception, nor his obscurantist dicta but what is most important, we shall appraise all this together, i.e. the Russian in Dostoyevlsky, a tragic writer!

And here D.S. is limiting himself with a single remark about Dostoyevsky's love for Pushkin. Dostoyevsky, who was a full antipode of Pushkin almost in everything, esteemed him highly. Dostoyevsky like nobody else repealing the Pushkin period of the Russian culture, loved Pushkin who, in fact, was loved by *all*. Without hesitation the author of the "Notes" comes to the conclusion from Dostoyevsky's love for Pushkin that "a Russian for Dostoyeevsky is a man...accepting all European cultures, the entire history of Europe and *not at all innerly contradictory*" (underlined by me - L.B.). that is, Dostoyevsky is the spitting image of Pushkin/ It would be evidently false to deny a discrepancy even in

Pushkin. As for Dostoyevlsky, shall we also separate him into "real Dostoyevsky" and "ideal Dostoyevsky" (i.e. Pushkin)?

No, Pushkin is Russian, Dostoyevsky is Russian and Herzen is Russian as well, but "Russian " are all of them arguing an utterly disagreeing, *together*. Not only they, but also the Karamozovs, and the Karamazovs opposing Dostoyevsky and together with hi,, in kinship with their great creator (as was Dostoyevsky's on father with him). Father Karamazov, Mitya, Alyosh and Ivan and footman Smerdyakov with them cannot be understood separately, out of socio-historical context. No one can be excluded form this cohesion and collision, neither Smerdyakov, nor the elder Zosima, nor even the staff-captain who says "You, sir, don't despise me: drunk people are kindest in Russia? The kindest and most drunk people are with us".

Well, if the four Karamazovs are not related to the very essence of the Russian, and Dostoyevsky, as a Russian ought to be, is "not at all innerly contradictory", let us judge the Russian by "the summits", simultaneously trimming them. What can we oppose in the nationals way of thinking except heated verbal censure? What does not fit the starry-eyes scheme is not truly Russian, and there is no sense in looking in this direction. "The Russian people had not only good but a lot of bad and this bad was great, as great is the people, however, it was not always that people themselves were to blame but Smerdyakovs assuming the image of statesmen..."So, Smerdyakovs are not Russian, they constitute "the antipode of the Russian", statesman are not Russian and the people, they are not all the people but the best among our nature.

The "Notes" are attractive because of their love for the Russian combined with love for the Scottish, Georgia, with the affection for country life and for Europe, etc. In a human way all this is very good and very kind. But won't you a free to analyse the intellectual quality, the *system of thought*, orientation of arguments? As long as the RUSSIAN is taken out of the *socio-historical reality*, tracked down among eternal geographic, climatological and other constants, constructed as an "ideal", traditionally derived for the 'spaciousness", "daring", plain landscapes, etc., the nation is mystified for the sake of convenience of the love for it and tender emotions, for the sake of our emotional comfort. Therefor good words about other peoples will not help.

The author's way of thinking is a way that objectively favors the support of an uncritical, super-historic, *non*-sociological and *non*-culturological approach to "the Russian". It is the most natural road to nationalism and though most honest, D.S. Likhachev himself adjures and warns against such conclusions from his "notes'. Such last, decisive conclusions will be made by our retrograde people without the author and they will be perfectly right. It is simply impossible to draw different conclusions from Likhachev's way of reasoning. It is wrong, D.S. says that " we indulge chauvinist instincts emphasizing national peculiarities, trying to determine the national character' (or an ideal - I am still confused.. If there is no "peculiarity" then we do not indulge. But if we have "precious" peculiarities, if we reason tactlessly - alas, we do indulge.

Well, suppose I am arader not meditating over the system of D.S.'s reasoning, religiously following his thoughts as a whole but still wondering whether this whole is wellgrounded by this example or another. Suppose, I agree that the national bias (whether Russian or any other) can be judged by comparing and analyzing the meanings of these or those Russian words, proceeding form linguistic ethnography or ethnographic linguistics. D.S. cites N. Roerich's transports in respect of an untranslatable Russian word "podvig" (feat, with Roerich pointing to the shades of something intransient, immortal and so on, distinguishing "podvig" form "geroistvo" (heroic deed). D.S. connects the root of this word with this favorite idea of a specifically Russian movement on vast lands. What do we call a man who accomplished a "podvig" (feat)? A "hero"? Why then do we need a foreign, non-Russian word? Let us call him in the right way: "podvizhnik". D.S. knows far better than I and almost all his readers that the word "podbvig" in ancient Russia had a sacred meaning, was originally a sacred devotion and even a "battle podbig" meant service to God with the force of weapons. It is from this, "ascetic, martyr-like", "soul-saving Podvig" (or "Podvizhnichestvo" - asceticism) that the shade of something eternal is derived, that Roerich was so much touched with. When this word was secularized, evidently in XVIII century, meanings of the ancient word "podvizhnik" and a lone-word "hero" diverged. As a matter of fact, if "podvig" is translated into Occidental languages as "a heroic deed", then "podvizhnik" - as "an acetic, an anchorite, a hermit", etc. The question arise whether we can seriously derive a certain Russian national peculiarity fro the word "podvig"? Weren't feats in a monastic and secular sense accomplished by other peoples?

Moreover, D.S. finds true Russian features in the word "uda;" (daring). Indeed! D.S. defines it as "bravery in wide movement", "multiplied by vastness". "The Dictionary of Eptithets of the Russian Literar Languae " defines "udal" as "something reckless, unrestrained, useless, obunless, dare-devil athletic, pert, violent unruly, fervent, devil-may-care, insolent, intrepid, valiant, furious, unbridled, irresponsible, indomitable, desperate, drunk, Russian, dashing, perky, crazy, carried away, tough" Such is the experience of usage and interpretation of this notion in Russian literature, The difficulty in translating the ambiguity and discrepancy of this national word is striking, in which "bogatyr" and "valiant" are inseparable not simply from the "wide movement" and "vastness" but from meanings of "desperate" bravery, caused by despair, as a senseless, crazy, dashing violence. There is but one step from the "bogatyr udal" to a wild outburst and it is this bravery without purpose and responsibility - "the devil take it!", "devil take my head", "enjoy yourselves without wine" - that constitutes the semantic quality of the "wide movement" for the dissolute, merry-making, "loudness" but at the same time "crazy" Russian daring.

Once cannot help admiring its sweep and pictureaue character but what and whom one can lay hands on depends on circumstances. In many ways this brazen results from indifference for others' and one's own lives ad such a national bravery, very likely was born not only by the "vastness", but also from social realignment as well. Therefore if "courage" and "bravery" are undoubtedly positive notions, then "uda;" is no less frightening than attractive. It is "dashing" and what a "likhoi" (Dashing) man is?' a valiant person or simply evil, "an evil-doer?"

Foling D.S.'s spirity we could think about the untranslatability of this no less characteristic Russian work "likhoi" in which "bravery in wide movement" is insepartaly combined with evil doing and misfortune" A mighty dashing tribe" was said about the Borodino heroes, and same "udal" and "dash" about Russia highwaymen. It is not a simple interlacing, and but gives cause for meditations on the tragic character of the historic tradition and not for trivial delights with the broadness of the Russian soul.

D.S. is also delighted with untranslatable character of the word "volya" (free will) finding in it "the open space". Yes, open! And nothing else? Pushkin contrasted "volya" (together with "peace of mind") to happiness. what is the difference between "volya" and freedom? Freedom is a positive notion and is translatable, while "volya" means an absence of restraint. Serfs were emancipated, and "volya" is when I have no yoke, no authorities, when I am my own master, but there is neither duty, nor responsibilities In life. They *run* into the open, following their noses, wherever they choose. Two other words "proizvol" (tyrany, arbitrary rule) and "svoyevoliye" (self-will, willfulness) are also derived from "loly".

In Russian songs about "volya", it is the *"yearning for the open space"* that is heard, i.e. constraint and suppression and in the yearning, one can hear the open space itself. If there was no place to run to, the open space was bustituted by yearning and the yearning became an open space. The tremendous broadness of Russian songs in directly proportional to a crush, it was stemmed for social tightness. D.S. reminds that "volya" is the subject of highwaymen's songs, but affirms that these songs were created, not by robbers, but by Russian peasants dreaming of revenge. Well, a dream of revenge is a natural addition to patience and weakness. "Volya" is a substitution (in fact, more desirable than feasible) for Western freedom.

There is another example of absurdity overtaking the highly talented author of the "Poetics of Ancient Russian Literature" in revenge for the substation of intellectual responsibility in the "Notes of the Russian" with good intentions and delights (remember "Oh" of sensitive Francoise). he starts to speak about gardens and parks. At first D.S. insists that in the pre-Ptrine Russia there were gardens delighting the eye, monastery gardens, and he makes a casual remark that these "paradise" gardens were filled with the same cultural semantics as in the East. Further, he writes about *Dutch* gardens in Russia in XVII century, about adoptions from the West in later gardening. What follows are reasons one must not oppose notions of nature and culture; that nature is "cultural" and "social" in itself, as it does not come to chaos because it has inner measure and order, etc. the author promises that the lines will coincide an d we shall come to understand how all this is related to the elucidation of the Russian national peculiarities. This is followed by an affirmation that for Russians all of the most important, pure occurrences are possible only in a park, a garden, or in close contact with nature, etc., giving as examples talks of the Empress with Masha Mironova in Catherine's park, meeting of prince Myshkin with Aglaya in Pavlosvsk park, even Oblomov's love declaration.

This is still better than an affection to wood and wooden construction or bell ringing as *Russian* features. Let us believe, as D.S. remarks, that all the peoples can have the same features but in different turns. Perhaps the spacing of the Russian bell ringing is other than Spanish, maybe the warmth of Russian wooden benches and tables and hose frameworks in Russia is somewhat different than with dozens of other peoples and love declarations of Russians in gardens might be not the same as practiced by Britians or Persians. But as the result of all these curios pages form the history of gardening, D.S. writes that in order to come to a "revelation of the Russian nature", Pushkin had to pass from "the regular lyceum garden" into "its park section and then to a Russian village", to "a purely Russian landscape of Mikhailovskoye and Trigorskoye" cultivated by Pakovian people "since the time of Princess Olga or maybe later, that is an entire millennium back".

So what has the "Laurrain" part of the Catherine park to do with this? It turns out that "the Russian" is not parks but a countryside nature will baroque, rococo gardens and other Western inventions are Russian only the extent that there is in them an inclination of "the unification of a man and nature".

Is such an inclination an utterly Russian feature? IF the author finds in Claude Monet sensitivity for changes in nature, "atmospheric conditions", etc., a conclusion is made that Russian "national peculiarities" are qualities present with "certain accents" and "to a certain other degree" in other countries and with other peoples. In brief, Monet's style is called his "Russian" Features! And Russian features "within reasonable limits...all-human".

But if Athenian to atmospheric conditions" was found with British, French and other painters *before* paining in general appeared in Russia, wouldn't it be better to call a Russian landscape painting of XIX century "English"? And the lands arranged by people of Pskov a "Lombardian feature of the Russian valley? And why did not Russian painters prior to

XIX century value atmospheric changes? And even AFTER did anything change"?...It is impossible to judge about nature by landscape painting". But it is still less possible to derive the history of a country's art from its nature, unchangeable climatic and other features.

It is far fro being accidental that D.S. is tracing the Russian nature of Mikhailovskoye, Russian nature as a foot of *Pushkin's cultural consciousness* from the times of Princess Olga "and perhaps, even earlier", i.e. from those times when no Russian *nationality* yet existed; Or, at vest, from the Russia of Middle Ages when there was no Russian *nation* yet. D.S. even tries to derive the "World of Art" and Russian painting of early XX century, in general, as well as Akhmatova from that "playing moment", "fable, fiction", "masquerade-like and theatrical- which he sees in ancient embroidery, clay toys, skomorokh festive gathering,etc, A reader can satisfy himself that the author's benevolent perception of the poignancy of the Russian avant-garde painting of "A Poem Without A hero" is based on detecting in these national creations not a drastic change common for the entire European culture of XX century, but a certain continuation of Medieval folkloric "mischievous" Russian tradition.

If the "Bubnovy Valet" ("The Knave of Diamonds") can be by no means derived for great-granddad's "playing moment", and if the entire Russian culture of not only XX and XIX centuries, not only Akhmatova, Mayokovsky, Pasternak and Mandelshtam, but also Pushkin, then it is impossible to explain Puskin with "The Izmaragd" to any degree. D.S. makes an amazing admission: "As a scientist I deal with ancient Russian literature, *that is exactly with what period in which its Russian national character was expressed with particular vividness*". (Underlined by me - L.B.) What this means that the literature of XI - XVII centuries was more "Russian" than the literature of Pushkin, Tolstoy and Dostoyevsky, It also means that the Russian medieval and even pre-Russian culture is more original (in comparison, for example, to the medieval Western culture) than the Russian culture of the period when it was included in an association of mature national modern European cultures. That means that the "Russian character" is more distinct the deeper we look at the pre-Petrine times and, consequently, becomes the vaguer the closer it approaches our time.

Meanwhile D.S. justly points out that the culture of ancient Russia is foreign to us, as it cannot be "measured without a European yardstick". In of the words, the difference between the yardsticks of the modern and recent Times (and not simply European,as we should accept that for a *Medieval* European, the *Medieval* Russian way of thinking and relations were much less "foreign") and the ancient Russian yardsticks, i.e.. difference in historical verticals is more essential than a national succession, than closeness instationary geographic, climatic, etc. horizontal. Doesn't it appear from this, according to D.S., that the more Russian culture becomes modern European, the more distant is from "The Izmaragd" -the less RUSSIAN it is?

The author loves "the Russian" but also loves (and even considers it necessary and natural for every Russian to love) "the European", correctly feeling himself to be both a Russian and European intellectual. The author even seems to feel the incomparable importance of exactly this classic correlation for the theme of the "notes', but there is nothing more than declarations of love for both. If "the Russian nature" is expressed in the best way" in our ancient are, in "The Izmaragd", in old-believers and Nikon, etc., what becomes of "the Russian" when "the all-European" Pushkin comes to the stage? And finally, what can be said about "The Russian" of the late XX century? Despite all these references to the past, down to Princess Olga, whom would D.S.'s "notes" interest if it had not been necessary to understand *today's problems* and prospects"

But D.S.'s pathos is not of a perspective but of *retrospection*. He is looking for "the Russian" in the Russian nature and Russian ancient art. The Modern Times culture is Russian as it Though less "distinctively", *continues*, reproduces the same primordial bases. "The all-European character" of Pushkin is but a readiness to learn from others, affability to the foreign, a sort of *an addition* of something European to the Russian. This is exactly the pint, that Pushkin and all true Russians would be patriots and not nationalists, as these terms are interpreted by D.S. I have already spoken about whether such an idyllic, complacent scheme combining a *retrograde* approach (in the literal meaning of the word) with a *personal* openness, decency and refinement of the author can seriously oppose such nationalism.

I do agree with the rejection of the logic of "despite-ism": if, as you write, indecent people are interested in the authenticity o the "Lay of Prince Igor", it does not mean at all that decent people must immediately reject the authenticity of the "lay" or that D. S. defending the "Lay" might and main deserves a reproach as a scientist. In the dispute between D.S. Likhachev and late AA Simian[1] the truth did not depend on this or that ideological use. However, D.S. thoroughly and in public argued with AA Simian's work which has remained unknown to readers. Decent people agreeing with D.S. in theory were thinking about the problem more, than

---

[1] A.A. Zimin, prominent historian of the Russian Medieval time who wrote a book sustantiationg spuriousness of the "Lay of Prince Igor", most ancient work of the Russian literature (XIII century).

the problem of the "Lay"; namely how long one opinion about authenticity of the ancient Russian will be permitted, and the other prohibited. The more so, as for modern Russian culture *this* (with all love for ancient literature) is much more essential than all the rest.

In his dispute, D.S. defended a historic fact. Today we are faced with a world describing the attitude of the author to "the Russian"; we are presented not with proof of a well-known fact, but a personal opinion. In this case support of such people as M. Alexeyev[2] is not an accident for those who highly esteem D.S.

The "Notes" would be neither publicly approved by the "Literaturnaya Gazeta" nor published by the "Novy Mir" magazine if they were not imbued with the moods, a way of thinking sufficiently close to present-day trends and formulated with an elegance of which the alexeyevs could not even dream. The sheep (of cultural openness, well-wishing for all actions, etc.) remain alive but our wolves have had their fill as well, as simply people wishing to lean against such "undying' values which would relieve them from the necessity of working out their own new values, a risky and painful process.

The following things are particularly unpleasant for the authorities and for many among intellectuals: first, "intellectual honesty" (it has just been mocked at by philosopher Yyu. Davydu in the "Voprosy Litaratury" magazine No. 4, by opposing "conscience" to it, as if for people of culture, people of thought conscience" could be told from intellectual responsibility). further, a social and historic approach which begins each time anew and acknowledges nothing abstractly universal is unacceptable. "Eternal": today people of various trends are united in their lust for something existing *before*, ready, unchangeable, guaranteeing for them truth from outside, be it God or Morals.

Out of fashion are now "scientific character", "rationalism' intellect in general, while 'soul", "spirituality", "kindness", any moral admonition on these subjects, moralizing rhetoric, and for many people, mysticism including rotation of tables which has become in our capital, the newest fruit of allegedly anti-official but in reality quite tolerant education.

Any thinking *tension* is also unwelcome, i.e. when the truth is neither open nor propagated when it is unknown, when it requires suffering, when it has acute angles (that is paradoxes), when it demand tension of the readers as well, when it Keenly listens to and thinks over all other voices, when it promises neither a final answer nor lucidity.

---

[2] An untalented writer, editor-in-chief of the "Moskva" magazine.

In *the sphere of thought* an idea cannot be substituted by "spirituality" and "kindness'. A thought needs well-grounded arguments. keenness, toughness and compactness. This is a tragic responsibility; it constitutes the IDEA's spirituality and this makes it a gift to the heart, bitter as it may be. You know, if D.S.'s "Notes" contained inner, thinking *difficulty*, problematic character, inconclusiveness of the truth, then Mikchail Alexeyev, such an emblematic figure, would not have risen to them.

The contents of socio-historic and cultural notions become clear only in connection with those periods and conditions when they are revealed with the utmost maturity and problematical character. The Middle Ages are only the pre-history of the European national peculiarities including Russian ones. The RUSSIAN is above all a phenomenon of Modern times and the key to it must be searched, particularly in XIX century, in the Pushkin and post-Pushkin situations. It is not only a well known fact that only then the all-Russian shows through regional, local distinctions. But all-Russian is born only in a correlation with the European.

The Russian is a special correlation of the Russian and the European. This correlation was unusual and dramatic at first. Faustus appears in Russia at the first in the person of Tsar Peter. The first forced a letter contradictory character of the Russian Enlightenment was developed. This marks the beginning of D.S.'s aptly called ":double life" of our culture. The Russian exists on its internal border of the Russian "the Asian" and Russian "the European". As soon as *the problem* of the Russian was realized it turned out be tragic.

Hence, appeared the disputes of the :Slaavophiles: and the "Westerns" in which absolute truth as not on any one side at that time; this gave birth to the problem of the "origin", i.e. the gap between cultural strata and peasant masses. This explains the tremendous tension, a passionate character of the Russian culture *in search of it own basis*, in conjugation of its different poles for the fairy tales of Arina Rodinovna[3] to the newest fruits of the French free-thinking and German philosophy. The searches of its own basis constitute exactly the most important contstructive sign of the European culture of the modern Times. To be a cultural Russian meant to be a doubled European, a "European", i.e. a man capable (forced, inspired) to look at himself form outside, to apprehend the "European" both as his own and foreign at one.

When speaking of the good-neighbourliness of the Russians and Karelians, and similar examples. D.S. himself makes a remark that here

---

[3] Pushkin's nanny.

we deal with *"pre-national* openness". Such an "openness", therefore, contained nothing Russian nor Karelian yet and it is easily matched with closeness for all that is foreign. Another matter is with the specifically Russian openness of Pushkin in which newly European openness reaches its extreme.

To be a *cultural* Russian meant to be a doubled *Russian*. Russian features were stored, crystallized, became problematic and ere provoked on he border of the spiritual worlds of Europe and Russia.

Whether the Russian culture of the previous century really lacked "The ground" or itself was deposing it gradually and with difficulties, through universities, Zemstvo[4] etc. is a topic worth discussing and so on. It seems that neither the despotic and bureaucratic monarchy, nor peasant "Asiatic way of life" were most *specific*, I do not say "spread and dominating", for Russia is but *a combination* with economic, political, cultural elements. If this is true, is it remissible to identify the national character with he common-people, the peasants, and to look for the "Russian" exclusively among patriarchal traditionalism? What about its dislike of non-Russians, with its non-Russian and, relatively speaking, "Oriental", i.e. traditionalist principal closedness.

D.S. takes certain common places of a Christian sermon and places them on the same footing with "the principles of Bulgarians". He ascribes them to Cyrila and Mehodius and through them derives the Russian "openness", tracing it in Pushkin and others. Though there is nothing more dissimilar than the Orthodox medieval "openness", if we believe D.S. that it did indeed exit at all (in he "Izmaragd"? with old-believers?), then the open of Pushkin. "Asiatic" and "Oriental" (including in the very hear of Europe) is the source of the main deformities and threats of the future. Here the most striate national trends have been assimilated.

Even now, Russia is a country more urban than rural and it appears that, in due time, we shall have, like in the USA, 5 - 7 percent of rural, peasant population, or even less, like in Great Britain. This is a vector of modern development. What will remind them, say in the early XXI century, form the "Russian" as it is understood and interpreted by "village writers"? The British nation almost without "peasants" is possible and the Russian? On the other hand, what is a Russian man already now if not a "Soviet man"? IT would be advisable to judge the Russian in XX century without lapsing into naive-restorational illusions. If D.S. and the "village writers" are correct in their definition of the RUSSIAN, let us talk: has *this*

---

[4] Elective district council pre-Revolutionary Russia.

"Russian" withstood the trials of the XX century and *what* has grown on this earth fertilized with decomposition? It is a rhetorical question.

Generally speaking, are reasonings about the "national character" and "national ideal" so interesting today? Will they do much good for the benefit of what awaits us in the nearest decades? As for *national peculiarities* social, historical, cultural: there is now nothing more dangerous than a substation of a realistic studying of the peasantry's life in its dynamics - tender emotions for patriarchal relics and *an anguish for Matyora.*[5] It is Matyora that gave birth to all the zigzags of Russian history; all its deformities and tragedies of three-century old decay, dying of rural "Asiatic features" and its revival I quasi-modern, semi-educated and semi-literate, bureaucratic forms. There is not return to ancient Russia with its Avvakumian ideals, nor that the "Izmaragd", nor to the beautiful Matyora. By the way, their regrettable results are stable. The flat country landscape has undergone few changes, the continental climate remains changeable but the problem of the "udal's" double character has become the problem of hard drinking and hooliganism amidst the same people who overwhelmed hitlerism. Akaky Akakiyevich[6] bought an overcoat, though not imported, or, perhaps managed to obtain several sticks of boiled sausage and some vermicelli during his mission of the the country's capital. "If only no war happens"[7] - "an ideal of all-forgiveness" helps me to live and feel that it is no business of mine and the matters with Europeism do no bring much comfort

Unlike M. Alexeyev I have no force to rise to D.S.'s position. Excuse me once more for the length of this letter ad for the repetitions for failing to think over even half of what I intended to say. It is a subject of an entire

---

[5] An allusion to V. Rasputin's novel "Farewell to Matyora". Matyora is the name of a illage on an island in a Siberian river which is to be flooded after the constructionof a hydro power station.

[6] The main character of Gogol's "The Overcoat".

[7] "IF only no war happens" - the most popular platitude in talks of Soviet common people of 1960's - 1980's justifying low life standards.

book demanding not only the heart's sorrowful remarks but, above all, the intellect's cold observations.

I wish *such* a book about the Russian would be written; it would become itself a sing of good hope.

"What Russian Can and Must be Loved For"*

Of course I feel sorry of D.S. against whom your historian has heaped up so many accusations. It turns out that the only citizen is your historian and, perhaps, Radishev, Pushkin, Dostovsky in addition. Only a few men in the entire history among a savage crowd of Russians using dirty words, drunk and obscene.

I certainly pity D.S. to whom your historian has pinned M.A. Alexeyev, evidently having failed to realize that M.Alexeyev is absolutely alien to D.S. Likhachev,a and that the former "was correcting an supplementing" the latter. He has also pinned "village writers" which is also quite another story. That is if you do believe in "The Russian", formulate an ideal of the past and at the same time call yourself a citizen of a modern state, you are exactly Mickhail Alexeyev.

I as sorry for D.S., a poor Russian intellectual and liberal who, with his best intentions, is doing a bad job of falsifying the national character and national history. But the greatest pity I do fell for your historian. A poor devil, he is trying all the time to substitute the heart with the intellect, sorrowful remarks with cold observations

Therefore, his ad D.S.'s tasks are different, even opposite. Your historian is attempting to prove that he loves Russia with his intellect, ruthlessness, all his mental truth. And in fact he does prove that Russia I s not worthy of love, that it is terrible and indecent, that its history is much from ancient times.

---

*
(*An extract from David Samoilov's letter regarding the objections of the "historian" against D.S. Likhachev's "Notes About the Russian"*)

D. S. shows that Russia can and must be loved and why he himself loves it as a citizen. He loves it for its culture, not a specific "rural", "uyezd" one but for its culture in a lofty and gernal meaning of the world. Therefore he uses the notion of cosmopolitan and without any abusive shade of meaning.

Your historian again mixes up the history of power with the history of the nation and culture, the history of the society giving birth to the same Radishcev, Herzen, Pushkin, Dostoyevsky and, finally, himself, the historian. How unoriginal your historian is in his conceit for Russia, his sensual and olfactory hostility towards a crowd. There is something non-Russian,[1] foreign in it.

Likhachev does love, and one can love in a simple way, following the dictates of one's heart, sometimes contrary to one' sintellect. And that is why the history of Russia for him is not "a history in general" but also his parents' legend, a landscape and a building, his surroundings, as well as a word and an appeal.

Your historian inserts Russia in the process of world history and want to judge it with these laws. He is proving that Russia is the worst link of history and that at the point of intersection of an ideal and reality; it is there that the ugliest forms of life appeared. Liberal Likhachev is not judging as he hates to do it. He loves, and love has its own laws, and side by side with these laws all the arguments of your historian seem trivial.

---

[1] An official term used in the Emperial Russia for minorities and Non-Orthodox believers.

TO LOVE AND
...NOT TO THINK?*

1. Can one love himself? Please, refer with this to Bakhtin.[1] Who says "how handsome, kind, well-formed" I am? OR "how...we are", etc. A distance is needed, a glance embracing an object from outside, as Bakhtin puts it "outerexistence", while we are intertwined with Russia. We re in it and it is in ourselves; simply this is our country, history language, culture, life. This acute feeling and non-indifference to what we are, in fact, as Russian born and bred, is that what is understood as love? blood relationship? or love as a charm, love as indispensable delight and admiration? A national narcissism?

Probably only in emigration it is possible to love Motherland *in such a way* - "is ply", contrary to one's intellect" - only from a distance both physical and social, having lost it. And "to love" from inside is not an adequate verb. AT the moment of danger of death for the national (like personal mortal danger) "love" for *oneself* arises. And generally speaking under non-extreme conditions, people do not love themselves and are not proud of themselves; they appraise themselves desirably from a critical viewpoint. "A national pride"? And what bout a national shame? One must equal the other. Why don't we speak about "personal pride" in a positive sense but rather about *dignity*? While national dignity, (except in cases of its humiliation causing an understandable reaction) consists exactly in comprehension of what you (your country) are worthy without belittling but also without tender emotions.

---

*
Another remark about "The Russian" under the impression of D. Samoilov's letter.

[1] M.M. Bakhtin is the greatest Russian philopher of culture of XX century. He died in 1975 in Moscow.

The "national spirit" is, as always, and indicator of historical break-ups, trouble and immaturity Rejection of a reasonable and objective analysis of historical social realities for the sake of "love" can lead to the most impressive logically suggested argument: and if you, my interlocutor, cannot "love in a simple way", it is because your blood is silent and it is to the right blood.

It was painful to hear from the poet dear to me that as he does not want to "love in a simple way" splits hair, loves with his mind, is hostile to the crowd then he is not ours, "a stranger", a "non-Russian". For me, in my turn, a fervor of, so to say, a "vykrest",[2] complex is unsympathetic, Don't make Slavs from Slavs. Don't use "non-Russian" in the meaning of "foreign", "suspicious, negative, anti-popular, incapable of loving "parents' legends",. of loving Russia - Please, don't do it! Don't call "strangers" the majority of the population of the country. "Non-Russian" is a word taken from the black-hundred vocabulary, words have memory, poets must have memory, consideration of words.

So, Samoilov is not a cavalier De Grie and Russia is non Manon Lescaut.[3].

"A love despite the intellect" does not adorn a patriot. It is incompatible with good wishes for his country, with a desire of changes for the better. It is better to love "the power" in such a way but no "the nation and culture". As a nation, the more so, a great nation does not need blind and unreasoning love. While it does suit the power, it is exactly such an "inner" love that was cultivated by the power. Let it be a general love, a love not at all for the power, but *any* blindness, idealization and weakness for Capital Letters is for the benefit of the power.

Contrary to Samoilov -, a poet after all, must not make such slips of the tongue, love has no "laws". A love is unlawful, it seeks no grounds and is malicious, while a law determines a measure and a ground. It determines itself despite elemental forces.

Of course, *a creator* can "*love*" the Russian (Ukrainian, English, Japanese, etc.) by substituting an analysis with sensitiveness. "But still I love, don't know why..."[4] A creator knows, however, that such a love is "strange" and opposes ideology, rejecting the whole set of "patriotic" rea-

---

[2] "Vykrest" is a Jew joining the Orthodox christianity (thus receiving civil rights in Russia prior to 1917.)
[3] Famous French novel of XVIII century "Mamon Lescaut" by Abbe Prevost, the names of the main characters.
[4] Lines form Lermontov's poem "Motherland".

sons including "sacred love of the dark antiquity".[5] However, this aversion bring a tense reflection into "love", makes it sad, sober, tragic, aching. It has nothing in common with an adoration trying to escape a critical distance.

In I. Bunin's remarks in "The Life of Arsenyev", he loves his dear Russia lost forever. He turns over and over in his mind dear recollections of his childhood in France. But an artist's honesty does not permit him "to simply love" and Russia appears also extremely painfully, not at all brightly in these recollections directed to love. There are interactive pages about heveral uyezd "pride" for Russia, its vastness and might, its great-power character moving petty bourgeois Rostovtsev to tender tears when listening to nikitin's verses: "Oh, Thou, Russia mine": how big and strong we are, how many tribes and languages are under the Russian Crown:

2. As Samoilov thinks it necessary to express distrust of the intellect, then all his jugglings in respect of the "intellectual truth" of the criticized "historian", attribution of quite the opposite to what is aid in the text, must be explained by 'the laws of the heart".

It is not Likhachev to whom the author denies the full-value meaning of the word 'citizen", the right to be called so, but Radischev and Pushkin. And, of course, himself and all others; including you, the reader. Properly speaking, it is not the author who denies, the author is only stating something known to all.

Well, the substitution of "people" with "a crowd" was already mentioned. Must a crowd be also loved? While Pushkin did not like a crowd., pushing to be loved by people and a crowd, You see, they spat at the altar where a fire was burning and tried to throw down on the ground his, Pushkin's tipod in their childish playfulness. There he also declared that it is worthless to value people's love;[6] that is if a nation is represented by a crowd.

It is not obligatory that only a *high-life* crowd sometimes behaves improperly. Not all feel a sentimental pleasure in every crowd of common people, not at any moment and in all its movements, into every queue and every rally.

It does not mean that such individual are incapable of loving closely or remotely, or that they are not grieving for the country they were born in. Even if they try to comprehend this vast country with a millennial his-

---

[5] Lines from Lermontov's poem "Motherland".

[6] A paraphrase of A. Pushkin's poem "The Poet".

tory without limiting themselves, they are excited (they do not know why) by the twinkling lights of sad villages and dances of peasants who had a drop too much.

It is not true that the poor devil historian is proving that there has been nothing good in Russia, that it is "the worst link" in world history. The text reminds about the contradictory, difficult and finally tragic character of "the Russian" (as any national "character" which is frequently emphasized), and an appeal to consider the Russian in the "connection-struggle" of various ideals and features in their entire historic and social completeness and specific nature.

Why is the history of a nation one and the history of power another? An educated person, of course, will never mix them up, yet it is impossible to divide them, as if "the history of power" is not an essential aspect of "the history of a nation and culture". It is true that society gave birth to Radischev, Pushkin, etc., but the power has come from somewhere as well. "Farewell, unwashed Russia, the land of slaves, the land of lords, and you, blue uniforms, and you, obedient folk".[7]What would D. Samoilov write to M. Lermonotov instead of "the historian"? That he must not confuse "the land of slaves" with :"the land of lords", :the blue uniforms" with home-spun coats? That Lermontov is so unoriginal in his "sensual and olfactory hostility" for Russia ("unwashed")? That is of no use to judge about Russia but one must love? And that there is something non-Russian, foreign, in it?

That author himself let the cat out of the bag in his adolescent years: ":To the West, to the West I would run where my ancestors' fields are in flourish..."[8] However, he was not permitted to do so. They have started to exile Russian writers only recently. God knows whether this fact must be referred to the "history of power" or the "history of a nation". I let Samoilov decide it. As for the Russian culture, it s tradition was one of extreme inner tension and problems and not starry-eyed idealism.

3. There are other jugglings in Samoilov's letter of response. But the main thing is this: don't proceed form the intellect. The intellect is under suspicion: You'd better listen to your heart. Where are its "recors of a heart in pain"[9] if it "simply" loves admires, if it does not care about "the reason's truth"?)

---

[7] From M. Lermontov's poem "Farewell, unwashed Russia".

[8] M. Lermontov's ancestor was a Scottish Lermont.

[9] An allusion to Pushkin's verses: "Of person's icy observations, and records of a heart in pain".

Only this can explain Samoilov's fantastic phrase against the "inclusion of Russia in the course of world history", a phrase, in fact, traditionally hinting to a certain exceptional destiny of Russia. In this they began to believe one and a half centuries ago in Russia, when specific difficulties of "inclusion" of a backward peasant country in "the course of world history" were first realized and they sought consolation in the Messiah Russian idea. It goes without saying that Samoilov does not write it and, perhaps, this is not the essence of his remark. But if it is not, then it lacks sense in general.

It is possible that Samoilov simply wants to say that it does not matter how Russia is correlated with the course of world history. It is of no use to judge it from a historical viewpoint, because in gernal we should not *judge*, having in mind two meanings of the corresponding Russian word (i.e. to try and to think). Again and again the poet advises not to think but *to love*, not with the intellect, but with the heart.

We call ourselves "intellectuals", "thinking people". Where did such an aversion of thinking among Russian intellectual s come from? Renunciation of their intellect is in fashion. Is it accidental that such a thing found its development precisely in the second half of the 1970's? (Though Samoilov, of course, is so unoriginal with his aversion for the "intellectual truth" as it was started long before us and, I am afraid, will not end with us).

Is it difficult to think? Difficult to prove? Does and emotional rhetoric come easier? No, today any wise and profound people refuse to think, for example, Samoilov or Likhachev. However this is not apparent in the former's poems and the latter's scientific works, but exactly in their reasoning about problems of world outlook of general interest.

Is it fearful to think? As magnificent Russian poet Samoilov wrote, whose poems I am going to cite (I do not remember exact verses) when an intellect starts to work and tries to think something to the end, it starts to smell trouble.

Or is it useless to think?
Or really:

"We have now come to bucolics,
As our path was far from folic.
And a horrible dispute with time".

In this historic context "have come to bucolics" means "have come to the last limit".

> "I have learnt freedom at last,
> No matter what kind of weather
> From the window the night forecasts".

And if it does matter? That would be exactly the moment to sit down and think.

An aversion for analysis, for reasoning; a desire, I do not know why to exclude Russia from the "general course of history" and not "to judge" about it with social, economic, political, socio-psychological, cultural or any other rational categories; irrationalism, mysticism, mystification of everything on earth; general passion for Absolute points of count, Capital Letters, Morality, National of something else, if only it would neither allow checking, nor reveal historical relativity, nor demand personal choice and responsibility but would demand only Love and Faith. All this is highly symptomatic of arguments in Moscow kitchens (as well as man Soviet publications) today.

That means things are in a bad way with us. Instinctively people expect nothing comforting and reconciling with reality. It is so humanly clear that one wishes to reconcile and to live in peace with oneself. To love and believe.

Perhaps it is snowing or buds are opening.

> "There is health of days and gardens
> Thereof I, with love and ardour
> Meditating on things that exist".

Meditating after all? Oh, it does not promise you calm of heart, my dear poet.

> Can it be that return to courses
> Would fill up hearts ad minds to blossom
> In this age full of cruel deeds?
>
> May be vain that we raise so high
> Force of songs and the wisdom of skill
> Old day feasts' liquor and fill?
> *I am ignorant what we'll do still.*

Yes...A fruit of knowledge is bitter.

But the Fall has already occurred. History and culture did occur as well as all the problems over which people have been racking their brains. nobody will relieve intellectuals of their duty to think. They may think about the RUSSIAN too. It does not contradict with the fusion with Russia.

"The arguments of the historian" cannot happen to be "flat" side by side with "the laws of love". Generally speaking, arguments are defeated, not by love boasting of its blood narrow-mindedness beyound the comprehension of non-Russians (like Radishcev or Herzen?), but by its "anti-intellect", its lack of brains as a patent for patriotic nobleness. Arguments are defeated only by better-thought and stronger arguments. So, let us argue, with reasons, and analysis, sticking to intellectual honesty and mercilessness.

"No", replies the poet, - "We shall live with the vain hopes, rejoicing a mouthful of love and kindness, and listen to a jeer of the malicious truth about ourselves which is much more horrible than slander". Or the poet is saying "yes" in fact?

A poetic intellect does not allow an interruption of the semantic tension of the clashing words and prevents literal monosemantic interpretation. When Samoilov, a poet and not a publicist, starts to speak, endless tragedy of "a vain hope" and "malicious truth" is revealed. Tragedy would immediately disappear if it becomes clear that we "simply" wish "to live with a hope", refusing t acknowledge that it is "vain". If we rejoice a mouthful of love and kinds "we refuse to listen to the truth about ourselves, malicious as it is. Truth will cease to be truth without "malice". It is "malicious", not because it is glad to be unflattering for us, it is "simply" a turret... and it is our fault or trouble that it sounds more horrible than slander. Otherwise it would not be a truth but pleasant slander. To live with a *vain* hope seems to mean, alas, not to refuse thinking.

Prior to Samoilov, Pushkin took stereotype word combinations "unpleasant falsehood" and "elevating truth", broke them up and put the fragments together in a paradoxical and painful way: "We prefer an elevating falsehood to dozens of u pleasant truths!" A subject for another "Little Tragedy" is contained in these two lines. There is a literally, monosemantically and finally undecided, unavoidable collision. This, however, gives rise to creative energy in every person each time he faces a decision. Pushkin knew well that falsehood cannot elevate and that a truth cannot suppers that which is useful to learn a truth? "Leave a heart to a hero".

"I am ignorant what we shall do still", Samoilov writes with defenseless openness, but that is not required form a poet. Poetry is a deceit elevating us toward becoming a real culture under the condition that a poet is not afraid of any truths about himself, his country, the human heart. He must fear only low truths, malicious truth, a vain hope to scoop a mouthful of love and kindness. A word is not a balm on the heart, it must sear, that is why a hearty simplicity is not enough if we are speaking, in any case, not about a love for another person but a love for a country and people.

Let believers believe: Let lovers love. And let those, who by thinking - only by this alone! at least be thinking and creating people, intelligent people - wish to be free "in chlorea, in Boldino, in quarantine"[10]

One can also "simply love" a truth, and believe in a critical intellect. This is the only ontological privilege of man.

---

[10] Also a fragment from D. Samoilov's poem.

INDEX

Popov, 19, 90, 92, 103, 104, 105, 106,
111, 112, 113, 114, 121, 139, 140,
158, 161, 162, 163
Populism, 162
Private property, 54, 55, 147
property, 5, 12, 23, 24, 28, 29, 30, 37,
41, 48, 54, 55, 91, 105, 117, 134,
140, 141, 142, 147, 148, 151
public opinion, 34, 37
Pugo, 2, 74, 75, 77, 79, 86, 91, 119,
120, 128
Pushkin, 77, 152, 157, 176, 178, 179,
182, 183, 184, 185, 187, 188, 191,
192, 195, 196, 199
putsch, 4, 5, 64, 67, 73, 123, 126, 127,
130

—R—

Radicalism, 85, 121
reality, 13, 17, 22, 29, 42, 53, 60, 70,
83, 89, 92, 115, 119, 137, 173, 174,
175, 176, 178, 180, 186, 192, 198
reforms, 2, 3, 5, 7, 27, 85, 91, 104, 114,
121, 126, 134, 135, 136, 137, 140,
141, 142, 143, 144, 146, 147, 148,
163, 165
Russophiles, 15
Rutskoy, 84, 87, 148
Ryzhkov, 96

—S—

Sakharov, 11, 39, 40, 42, 43, 44, 45, 46,
47, 48, 49, 50, 55, 56, 57, 58, 59, 60,
78, 82, 85, 149, 154
Samoilov, 169, 170, 171, 194, 195, 196,
197, 199, 200
secret political police, 48, 59
Shakhnazarov, 130
Sobchak, 89, 90, 92, 104, 121, 158
Solzhenitsin, 11, 12, 13, 14, 15, 16, 17,
18, 19, 21, 22, 23, 26, 27, 28, 29, 30,
31, 32, 33, 34, 35, 36, 37
South Ossetia, 53
stabilization, 7, 30, 120, 122, 135
state power, 48

strikes, 19, 20, 85, 87, 105, 113, 121,
128, 134, 136

—T—

Tatars, 35, 42, 52
Tolstoy
L., 36, 152, 156
totalitarian regime, 70, 115, 141
transitional period, 53, 66, 113, 139
Trotsky, 20
TV
Television, 18, 55, 63, 75, 78, 81, 89,
90, 91, 95, 96, 97, 105, 106, 112,
117, 119, 130, 131, 137, 143, 146,
149, 161, 162, 163, 164, 170

—U—

Ukraine, 6, 16, 18, 23, 35, 52, 87, 106,
116, 149
Union treaty, 24, 50, 129, 130
universal suffrage, 25
Utopia, 28, 141

—V—

violence, 53, 76, 85, 86, 115, 120, 175,
181
vodka, 96, 109, 110, 111, 112, 113

—Y—

Yanayev, 131
Yazov, 74, 75, 77, 119, 120, 123, 129,
130
Yeltsin, 3, 20, 69, 71, 81, 82, 83, 84,
85, 86, 87, 89, 90, 91, 92, 101, 105,
113, 118, 121, 123, 124, 126, 128,
136, 140, 141, 142, 143, 145, 147,
148, 161, 162, 163, 165

—Z—

Zemstvo, 19, 24, 25, 27, 33, 35, 188
Zhirinivsky, 95
Zhirinovsky, 81, 118